Music and
in Lowland
in the
Eighteenth Century

David Johnson was born in Edinburgh in 1942. His career in music has included teaching, journalism and management, and from 1980 to 1996 he was the cellist of The McGibbon Ensemble, giving frequent concerts of historical Scottish music.

His other published writings include *Scottish Fiddle Music in the 18th Century* (1984), *Chamber Music of 18th-century Scotland* (2000), and contributions to the *New Grove Dictionary*. Johnson is also the composer of about 50 works, notably *12 Preludes & Fugues for Piano* (1995) and the operas *Thomas the Rhymer* (1976) and *Sorry, False Alarm* (2001). He is at present writing a further opera, based on R. L. Stevenson's novel *Kidnapped*.

Thomas Alexander Erskine, sixth Earl of Kelly
Engraving after the portrait by Home

Music and Society in Lowland Scotland in the Eighteenth Century

DAVID JOHNSON

mercatpress
www.mercatpress.com

First published in 1972 by Oxford University Press
This second edition published in 2003 by
Mercat Press, 10 Coates Crescent, Edinburgh EH3 7AL

ISBN: 184183 0496

Printed and bound in Great Britain by
Athenaeum Press Ltd., Gateshead, Tyne and Wear

Contents

Abbreviations of names of libraries

APL   Aberdeen Public Library
AUL   Aberdeen University Library
CUL   Cambridge University Library
EPL   Edinburgh Public Library
EUL   Edinburgh University Library
GML   Mitchell Library, Glasgow
GUL   Glasgow University Library
NLS   National Library of Scotland, Edinburgh
SSS   Library of the School of Scottish Studies, Edinburgh

Acknowledgements

Among the many people who read portions of this book in draft and made constructive comments, I should like particularly to thank Mrs. Helena Shire, Dr. Alan Bruford and Mr. Warwick Edwards. I must also thank Mrs. Muriel Brown, with whom I collaborated over details of David Foulis's biography; Mrs. Anne Macaulay, who made many thoughtful suggestions about citterns and lent me 'Thomas Shiels' music-book' for several months; Dr. Francis Collinson, who allowed me access to 'George Bowie's music-book'; Mr. Alexander R. C. Scott, who generously made available to me his large private collection of Earl of Kelly material; Miss Phyllis Hamilton, who drew my attention to various rare books, some at present uncatalogued, in Edinburgh Public Library; and the staff of the National Library of Scotland.

Finally I should like to thank Mr. Charles Cudworth for his unfailing patience and kindness towards me during four years of research.

Since this book deals at length with the economic conditions in which music subsists, it seems appropriate also to mention here the Scottish Education Department, the University of Cambridge, St. John's College, Cambridge, and my father, without whose financial support the research for this book could not have been undertaken.

The book originally formed part of a dissertation awarded the degree of Ph.D. in the University of Cambridge.

D. J.

Edinburgh, Christmas Eve 1970

*This book is
affectionately dedicated
to my father*

Preface to the Second Edition

THE writing of this book was begun in a large notepad, on the Backs of St. John's College, Cambridge, one afternoon in the autumn of 1968. This was around the time of my 26th birthday. It progressed slowly. Nothing I had written previously had prepared me for the task of constructing thousands of words on a complex, unknown subject. But I was determined to do the job properly, to explain eighteenth-century Scottish music in a way that no reader could ever ignore the subject again.

When the book was published in 1972, I reckoned it had a shelf life of twenty years; that it would take that long for other scholars to find all the holes in it, and assemble enough new data to put it out of date. In fact, it has done much better than that. Thirty-one years on, it is regarded as the definitive work on the subject (despite having been out of print since 1989), and I am told that library copies are wearing out and that it is almost unobtainable from second-hand booksellers. So this paperback reprint from the Mercat Press is most welcome.

In particular, the map of eighteenth-century Scottish music which the book proposes—insisting that 'folk' and 'classical' music cannot be separated from each other too far, but must be studied together to give a true picture of the subject—has been universally accepted. Indeed, later research by James Ross, John Purser and Neil Mackay shows that Scottish music had similar 'crossover' characteristics in the sixteenth and twentieth centuries.[1] Perhaps treating music in this way is a permanent feature of the Scottish psyche.

So it has turned out, rather to my surprise, that the most severe critic of the book has been myself. In my *Scottish Fiddle Music in the Eighteenth Century* (1984) I brought the material of Chapter 6 into closer focus, and discovered weird and wonderful violin

---

[1] D. James Ross, *Musick Fyne* (Edinburgh, 1993); John Purser, *Scotland's Music* (Edinburgh, 1992); Neil Mackay, 'MacCunn, Hamish' and 'Scott, Francis George' in *The New Grove Dictionary* (London, 1980).

genres—for instance, eighteenth-century fiddle pibrochs—that I had missed earlier. Writing various articles for *Grove's Dictionary* in 1980 and 2001 made me explore composers' biographies more thoroughly than I had previously done. And in the course of editing *Chamber Music of Eighteenth-century Scotland* for the *Musica Scotica* series in 2000, I realised I had been horribly unfair to William McGibbon (1696-1756); once his music was re-assembled from scattered prints and manuscripts and presented in good modern editions, McGibbon emerged as a composer of considerable stature.

For this reprint it was decided to keep the text of the book intact, mainly so as not to disturb the beautiful and accurate typesetting done by Oxford University Press in 1971-2. To play fair with the reader, however, a short list of updates is given below. These show that musicology is on the move, and that research into this fascinating subject is by no means complete.

CHAPTERS 2-3

Page 26. Miss Grisie Baillie's tutors at Mellerstain were a distinguished set of people. 'Crumbin', as noted on page 30, was Henry Crumbden, master of the Edinburgh town music school. 'Krenberg' was Jakob Kremberg, a much-travelled German composer and violinist. 'St Culume' was Monsieur de Sainte-Colombe, the illustrious Parisian bass-viol player (or his son, if Sainte-Colombe died, as is believed, in 1701).[1]

Page 28. Much more is now known about the musical life of Kilravock Castle; the National Library of Scotland (NLS) has acquired many items from its library since 1970. For details, see Helen Goodwill's doctoral dissertation[2] and my *Chamber Music of Eighteenth-century Scotland (CM)*.[3]

Page 49. It is actually very unlikely that Daniel Dow wrote his minuets for orchestra; though a wonderful melodist, Dow had

[1] I am grateful to Peter Davidson and Peter Holman for the new identifications.
[2] H. Goodwill, 'The musical involvement of the landed classes in eastern Scotland, 1685-1760', unpubl. PhD. thesis, University of Edinburgh, 2000.
[3] *Musica Scotica*, vol. 3 (Glasgow, 2000), nos. **18-20**.

difficulty composing even simple bass lines. He was probably just imitating the Earl of Kelly, in composing his minuets in flat keys.

Page 54. Barsanti's 1742 publication contains not twelve concerti grossi but ten, divided into two sets of five.

Page 57. Schetky was born in 1737 (not 1739, as I had previously thought), so was thirty-four when he arrived in Scotland, and eighty-seven when he died. His wife Mary (née Anna Maria Theresa Reinagle) was born in 1747, and so aged twenty-six when they married.[1]

Page 60. I have recanted of the view that General Reid had assistance with his compositions; see my *Scottish Fiddle Music in the Eighteenth Century* (*SFM*).[2]

Page 61. It now seems unlikely that Charles McLean was born as early as the 1690s, or that he was born in Edinburgh. He taught music in Montrose in 1736 (where the town council gave him a grant as an encouragement), became Master of the Aberdeen town music school in 1737, moved to Edinburgh in 1738, and from 1740 onwards seems to have worked in London. This is the profile of an ambitious person in his twenties, climbing a ladder step by step. It would be logical for him to have been born in the north-east of Scotland, around 1712.

Page 62. Robert McIntosh probably did not habitually give offence to people, though Farmer paints a gloomy picture of his dealings with the Aberdeen Musical Society from 1785 to 1791.[3] Part of McIntosh's trouble at the time was that he desperately needed money to support his large family;[4] mercifully his collection

---

[1] Good biographical material on the Schetky and Reinagle families can be found in Anne McClenny Krauss, 'Alexander Reinagle, his family background and early professional career', *American Music*, vol. 4 no. 4 (University of Illinois, 1986); L.O. Schetky, *The Schetky Family, a Compilation of Letters* (Portland, Oregon, 1942); and a MS. Reinagle family memoir which has recently come to light in the Library of Congress, Washington.

[2] John Donald, Edinburgh, 1984 (2nd ed. Mercat Press, Edinburgh, 1997), pp.198-9.

[3] H. G. Farmer, *Music Making in the Olden Days* (London, 1950), pp.68-71.

[4] See John Glen, *The Glen Collection of Scottish Dance Music*, vol.1 (Edinburgh, 1891), preface.

Sixty-eight new reels, strathspeys and quicksteps (1792) was a great success, and financially lucrative.

McIntosh is an intriguing figure, a composer who missed greatness by a small margin. Perhaps the time will yet come for a successful revival of his big G minor violin sonata.

CHAPTERS 5-7

Page 95. Note 2, on town pipers being players of the fife, is probably wrong; evidence is accumulating that the official instrument was indeed the Border bagpipe, at any rate in the eighteenth century, in towns in the south of Scotland. A drawing survives from Haddington, dating from around 1770, showing the town piper on his rounds accompanied by the town drummer and the town idiot.[1] Here the instrument being played is clearly the Border pipes.

Gordon Mooney has written a series of articles on pipers in Peebles and other towns,[2] and Heather Melvill has found evidence that Crail had a drummer (though apparently no piper) in the 1710s and 1720s.[3] A comprehensive study of Scottish town musicians is overdue.

Page 99. The Border pipes are no longer extinct, having been successfully revived during the last thirty years.

Page 113. The 'Reel of Tulloch' variations are in fact printed in Bremner's *Curious Collection of Scots Tunes* (Edinburgh, [1759]), a book I had not examined in 1972. The five manuscript texts referred to were probably all copied from this source, either directly or indirectly.

Bremner's collection also includes the variations on 'John come kiss me now', but in this case two of the four manuscript texts are too early to have been copied from it, as NLS MS. 1667 was made in 1723, and NLS MS. 2085 in 1740.

---

[1] Reproduced in F. M. Collinson, *The Bagpipe* (London, 1975), plate 21.

[2] G. Mooney, 'The Pipers of Peebles', *Common Stock*, vol. 1 no. 1 (Edinburgh, 1983), and subsequent issues.

[3] He was named John Oswald, and was the father of the composer James Oswald; see below.

The subject of manuscript *versus* printed transmission of fiddle music is discussed further in *SFM*.[1]

Page 117. The identification of 'Disblair' as James Dyce was a reasonable theory; it turns out, however, that Dyce only acquired the Disblair estate in 1743. The variations in the McFarlane manuscript (1740) must, therefore, have been composed by the estate's previous owner, William Forbes. Curiously, Forbes was the maternal grandfather of the ballad-singer Anna Gordon, mentioned on pages 17-18.[2] Two of his variation sets are now printed in modern editions.[3]

Alexander Munro's sonata on 'Fy gar rub her o'er wi' strae' is also available in a modern edition.[4]

Page 118. The Italianate variations on 'The Lee Rig' are not by James Clark, but anonymous; Clark contributed other pieces to Riddell's collection. For further discussion of the variations, see *SFM*.[5]

Page 137. My survey of songs about Lowland girls eloping with Highlander lovers has been vastly expanded by William Donaldson, who shows, amusingly, that the archetypal Highland Laddie became confused with Bonnie Prince Charlie in the later part of the eighteenth century.[6]

Page 148. Stephen Clarke's settings for *The Scots Musical Museum* need not be as dull as they look, if they are handled by a harpsichordist who can realise the bass lines imaginatively, and improvise instrumental leads between the verses of the songs. Clarke, who was organist of the Edinburgh Musical Society, the New Episcopal Chapel, and the Canongate Kilwinning Masonic Lodge, would have done the job excellently himself.

---

[1] Pp. 6-13.
[2] See David Buchan, *The Ballad and the Folk* (London, 1972), pp. 62-64, and my 'Musical traditions in the Forbes family of Disblair, Aberdeenshire', *Scottish Studies*, vol. 22 (Edinburgh, 1978).
[3] In *SFM*, nos. **26-27**.
[4] In *CM*, no. **8**.
[5] Pp. 167-8 and no. **67**.
[6] W. Donaldson, 'Bonny Highland Laddie: the making of a myth', *Scottish Literary Journal*, vol. 3 no. 2 (Aberdeen, 1976).

CHAPTER 9

Page 164. This is a somewhat simplified account of music in the early years of the Reformed Church (1560-1635). The more one looks into the period, the more muddled it appears, with none of the opposed religious factions seeming to act rationally or consistently.

Gordon Munro's new research[1] will hopefully clarify this difficult subject. Meanwhile, I must again regret that the Church did not continue to take its lead in musical matters from Martin Luther (see page 9), as the early Scottish reformers had done.

Two examples will underline this point, Luther's Christmas hymn, *Vom Himmel hoch*:

> *Ach, mein herzliebstes Jesulein,*
> *mach' dir ein rein' sanft' Bettelein,*
> *zu ruh'n in meines Herzens Schrein,*
> *daß ich nimmer vergesse dein.*[2]

and its excellent translation into Scots by the Wedderburn brothers, c.1545:

> O my deir hart, zoung Jesus sweit,
> prepair thy creddill in my spreit,
> and I sall rocke the in my hart
> and never mair fra the depart.

Luther's writings became a corner-stone of German culture: the German quotation above was set by Bach as part of his *Christmas Oratorio*. But the Scots version was lost: it was rediscovered and set to music by the English composer Peter Warlock only in 1925. Warlock's setting was widely circulated and, at last, the Wedderburns' translation became well known. Other settings of it followed from Benjamin Britten in 1942, Francis George Scott in 1947, and Isobel Dunlop in 1967. But this could have happened three centuries earlier.

[1] G. J. Munro, 'Scottish church music and musicians', unpubl. Ph.D. thesis, University of Glasgow, 1999; 'The Scottish Reformation and its consequences' in Isobel W. Preece, *Music in the Scottish Church up to 1603 [Studies in the Music of Scotland]* (Glasgow, 2000), pp. 273-303.

[2] The section quoted is verse 13 of the hymn.

The damage which the Reformed Church did to Scottish music is incalculable. We are probably still suffering from its after-effects.

CHAPTER 10

Page 199. My description of classical music's liaisons with Scottish folk music as 'unnatural' was an overstatement; if one looks carefully, one can find excellent classical works that have absorbed elements of folk music, and fused them convincingly with the mainstream European style. My favourite ones (all pieces I had not discovered in 1972) are: General Reid's sonata in G major;[1] Munro's sonata on 'Bonny Jean of Aberdeen';[2] Bremner's variations on 'Hit her on the bum',[3] and the arrangements in his *Thirty Scots Songs*; and Oswald's 'Hawthorn' sonata in his *Airs for the Seasons*.[4]

All these pieces, however, belong to the period 1730-65. My assessment of the keyboard works incorporating Scots tunes of 1780-1800 was, unfortunately, accurate. Several performers have tried to revive them recently, and they sound just as vapid, pretentious and insincere as I imagined.

WILLIAM McGIBBON

McGibbon is owed an apology. Since this book was published, many of his lost works have turned up—the 1740 sonatas, the 1729 trio sonatas, and some earlier trio sonatas dating from about 1727. His Scots-tune collections and the pieces that he contributed to the McFarlane manuscript have also been re-examined thoroughly. From these, there is no doubt that he is a major-sized composer, whose music has not only variety and range, but a distinct and compelling personality. Some of his work is now available in modern editions.[5]

His orchestral music is still lost. The Edinburgh Musical Society

[1] Edited in *SFM*, no. **69**.
[2] *SFM*, no. **65**.
[3] *CM*, no. **17**.
[4] *CM*, no. **14**.
[5] *CM*, nos. **1-7**; *SFM*, nos. **17-20**, **59**.

possessed manuscripts of three of his concertos and one of his overtures,[1] but no copies are extant. However, those wishing to hear McGibbon's orchestral music should note that the Society also owned ten copies of his 1734 trio sonatas, which they bought as soon as they were published;[2] they probably played those at their concerts, too, with a full band.

How did they go about this? Some years ago, Kenneth Elliott made an orchestral version of McGibbon's Trio Sonata in G, no.5 of the 1734 set, by composing a new viola part and inserting it into the score. The edition was not a complete success.[3] The viola part certainly added to the 'contrapuntal interest' of the piece, but contrapuntal interest is not really what McGibbon's music is about.[4]

My own strategy for filling out the piece would be quite different. It would involve adding flutes and oboes to both violin parts, supplementing the cellos with double basses—and gambas and bassoons, if available—and using both harpsichord and chamber organ as continuo instruments. The violas would join the cellos, transposing the part up an octave where necessary. As a contrast to the full band, the third movement (Largo) could be played by soloists, in the original trio-sonata format.

I have had no opportunity to try out this scheme, but it is worth saying that the time is ripe for such experiments, and that much good music of McGibbon's is still waiting to be performed.

Regarding McGibbon's biography, there has been an important discovery: that he was almost certainly born in Glasgow (not in Edinburgh, as stated by Tytler), and that his father was the violinist Duncan McGibbon (not the oboist Malcolm McGibbon).[5] There is no reason to doubt Tytler's other statement about

[1] They are listed in the EMS's library catalogue, 1765.

[2] The purchase is recorded both in the subscription list of the 1734 publication, and in the EMS's accounts for 1735.

[3] Dr. Elliott's orchestral edition is not published. It was recorded on the LP *Scottish Baroque Ensemble at Hopetoun* (CRD 1028) in 1976.

[4] Unlike, for instance, the contrapuntal concertos and overtures of Francesco Barsanti, written in Edinburgh at the same period.

[5] See *CM*, p. ix, and the entry on McGibbon in *Grove's Dictionary* (2001).

McGibbon, that he 'was sent early to London by his father, and studied many years under Corbet, then reckoned a great master and composer'. As McGibbon's family were not well off, however,[1] he would have had to be *apprenticed* to William Corbett (instead of studying privately, as Tytler implies), and so would probably have accompanied Corbett on his travels to Italy in 1711 and 1716. By 1726 McGibbon was definitely back in Scotland and living in Edinburgh. His projected Scottish-London-Italian education makes sense, though, and would explain the distinctive style of his later compositions.

JAMES OSWALD

James Oswald is one of musicology's success stories in recent years. Many scholars have written about him sympathetically and convincingly,[2] and some excellent recordings have appeared. His music is becoming popular with audiences, and is even finding its way into educational syllabuses.

There is no room here to set out everything new that has been discovered about him, but, in brief:

He was born in 1710 in Crail, in north-east Fife, the son of John Oswald, the town drummer.[3] He probably received his musical

---

[1]   This is indicated by Scottish Record Office Register of Deeds RD 3/85, p.198, which records a bond investment by 'Duncan McGibbon Violer in Glasgow' of £49 16s 8d Scots. The entry is dated 9 March 1696, a few weeks before William McGibbon was born. The sum of money is tiny for such a purpose (£2,000 at most, in present-day terms), and the lop-sided amount (= 74½ merks) has an air of desperation about it. By 1707 Duncan McGibbon and his wife Sarah Muir had had seven children. They can never have become rich.

[2]   Mary Anne Alburger, *Scottish Fiddlers and their Music* (London, 1983); Roger Fiske, *Scotland and Music* (Cambridge, 1983); John Purser, *Scotland's Music*, op. cit.; Jeremy Barlow, inlay note to the CD *Airs for the Seasons* (Dorian DIS 80164), 1998; and my article 'A galant Scot', *Early Music Today*, vol.7 no.5 (London, 1999).

Readers should also see the article on Oswald in *Grove's Dictionary* (2001), written jointly by myself and Heather Melvill. Ms Melvill is a descendant of the family of Oswald's wife Marion Melvill, and has been the prime mover in uncovering Oswald's biography over the last 20 years.

[3]   He was baptised in Crail on 21 March 1710.

education at home; he played the cello beautifully, and took to composition—especially in Scottish folk styles—like a duck to water. Early on, he acquired a knack of getting on with patrons, which stood him in good stead for the rest of his life.

Oswald was ambitious. He made the best of what Fife had to offer until he was 25 and then, in 1735, moved to Edinburgh, and in 1741 to London. His time in London was eventful and stressful, but a success; his triumphs included gaining the patronage of Frederick, Prince of Wales and the young King George III. Around 1763 he was able to retire to a mansion in Hertfordshire, where he died in 1769.

The rest of the story can be read elsewhere. However, a misunderstanding in the present book needs to be corrected.

On page 61 I described Oswald as a *singer*, on the basis of Allan Ramsay's poem *An Epistle to James Oswald*, written in 1741 to lament Oswald's departure from Edinburgh:[1]

> O JAMIE! when may we expect again
> To hear from thee, the soft, the melting strain?...
> Our concert now nae mair the Ladies mind;
> They've a' forgot the gait to Niddery's wynd...
> No more thy solemn bass's awful sound
> Shall from the chapel's vaulted roof rebound.

With hindsight, however, it has become clear that *bass* refers here, not to a voice, but to a cello: Ramsay is talking about Oswald's awe-inspiring *cello playing*. This is confirmed by Charles Burney's autobiography, where Burney writes about his life in London in 1748:

> During my connexion with Drury Lane Theatre, I became intimately acquainted with Oswald, the Scotish Orpheus, the celebrated performer of old Scots tunes on the Violoncello, and maker of many more.[2]

---

[1] Published in the *Scots Magazine*, October 1741.
[2] S. Klima, G. Bowers and K. Grant, eds., *Memoirs of Dr. Charles Burney 1726-1769* (University of Nebraska, 1988), p.86.

and by a letter from Benjamin Franklin in London to Lord Kames in Edinburgh, arguing that Scots tunes sound better without harmony:

> Whoever has heard James Oswald play them on his violoncello, will be less inclined to dispute this with me. I have more than once seen tears of pleasure in the eyes of his auditors, and, yes, I think, even his playing those tunes would please me more, if he gave them less modern ornamentation.[1]

That the cello was an important part of Oswald's life can also be seen from the continuo parts of his compositions, which are always beautifully conceived for the instrument, and a joy to play. It seems sad that he did not write cello sonatas.

THE EARL OF KELLY

Kelly is the most fascinating and complex of eighteenth-century Scotland's composers. Chapter 4 remains the best general account of his life and work, though interesting new things have been discovered about his composition methods and relationships with publishers. I have written about these elsewhere.[2]

The most exciting and unexpected development, however, is that a large amount of his lost music has turned up; his *oeuvre* has almost doubled in size since 1972. The new pieces are full of surprises, and show Kelly working hard at the problems of gesture, language and form in the emerging Classical style, in exact parallel to Haydn's pioneer work at the same period. They also confirm a contemporary statement that his music 'was not limited to a single style.'[3]

The Bibliography of Sources on page 212 is now, obviously, far out of date. A supplement to it is given below.

[1] Alburger, op. cit., p.45. Franklin's letter dates from about 1760.
[2] In the preface to my edition of Kelly's *Trio Sonata in F* (Edinburgh, privately printed, 1991); 'The Kilravock Manuscript', unpubl. consultation paper, 1991, available at the NLS; *CM*, pp.xi, xiv, and notes to nos. **19-24**; 'Scotland's greatest classical composer?', *Early Music Today*, vol.9 no.5 (London, 2001).
[3] By Thomas Robertson in 1784; see p.75.

I. PRINTED

c.1760-78 A Collection of the Newest and Best Minuets (Neil Stewart, Edinburgh) includes: *9 minuets*.

c.1765 A Collection of the Best Minuets (Robert Bremner, London) includes: *6 minuets*.

II. MANUSCRIPT

National Library of Scotland

c.1760-1800 MS. Acc. 11420(2) ('Kilravock Commonplace Book') includes: a portion of an *Overture in E flat*, previously unknown (ff.17v, 3v); *The Capillaire Minuet* (f.8v).

c.1770 MS. Acc. 10303 ('Kilravock Manuscript') contains: *Duo for two violins*, previously unknown; *9 trio sonatas*, previously unknown; *9 string quartets*, nos.1-3 and 7-9 previously unknown.[1]

c.1790 Ing. 153 ('Sharpe Manuscript') includes: *A Minuet by the Honble The Earl of Kelly* (p.42). This appears to be a fragment of an *Overture in B flat*, previously unknown.

Boughton House, Northamptonshire[2]

c.1775 *Overture in D, op.1 no.1*. This varies from the printed edition since it includes a timpani part, previously unknown, and parts for 'Traversa' (i.e. flutes) instead of oboes.

c.1780 Violin 1 and cello parts of a *Quartet in C minor*.[3]

c.1780 Partial bass part of an *Overture in C minor*, previously unknown.

c.1830 Partial violin 1 part of a *Trio Sonata in A*.[4]

[1] Quartets nos.4-6 are the same pieces as nos. 3, 2 and 6 of the printed *Six Simphonies in four parts* (see below). Quartet no.5 is by G. B. Sammartini and no.6 by J. Stamitz, and are misattributed to Kelly here.

[2] Items from this private collection are cited by kind permission of His Grace the Duke of Buccleuch and Queensberry.

[3] The same piece as Quartet no.8 in NLS MS. Acc. 10303, above.

[4] The same piece as Trio no.7 in NLS MS. Acc. 10303, above.

III. RE-ATTRIBUTIONS

Page 77. No.4 of the *Six Simphonies in four parts by J. Stamitz, his pupil the Earl of Kelly, and others* is by J. A. Filtz, so the ascription to Kelly is incorrect; Kelly probably wrote no.3 of the set.

Page 79. 'Miss McLeod's Minuet' is not by Kelly, but part of a symphony by J. A. Filtz.

Page 214. The 'Largo for violin and continuo' is now positively identified as Kelly's work.

There seems an excellent chance that more of Kelly's music will turn up. Peter Holman has recently discovered this fragment of his handwriting:[1]

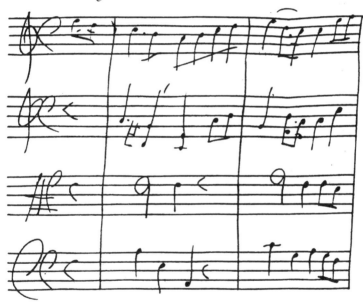

It is clearly part of a string quartet. Points of interest are the experimental double-stopping for the second violin, the likelihood that the viola part was the last to be composed, and the

---

[1] In facsimile in Thomas Busby's *Concert Room and Orchestra Anecdotes* (London, 1825), appendix to vol. 3, reproduced by kind permission of Jeremy Barlow.

style: unusually, Kelly is writing in a 'Scottish' idiom, with the first violin ghosting the eighteenth-century tune 'Gilderoy'. These two bars whet the appetite... where is the rest of it?

*   *   *   *   *   *   *

The gloomy tone of the last page of the book seemed justified when I wrote it, and those with power over art music in Scotland certainly made some terrible mistakes, between 1970 and 2000.

But one sentence is happily, gloriously, no longer true: that 'eighteenth-century Scottish music is forgotten as far as the general public is concerned'. Earlier this month I was talking to a cello teacher in Midlothian who was not only aware of the music of James Oswald, but brought up the subject of whether Oswald had written the folk-tune 'Roslin Castle'. Such knowledge, among non-specialists, would have been unthinkable 30 years ago. Perhaps this book was not written in vain.

D.J.

Edinburgh, March 2003

Introduction

I

TWO SPECIES OF MUSIC: FOLK AND CLASSICAL

THIS book is a study of the musical culture of eighteenth-century Lowland Scotland. It is a rich subject, hitherto little known, and one which remains remarkable even after it has been thoroughly understood. For eighteenth-century Scotland possessed two distinct types of music: 'folk' and 'classical'.[1] These coexisted within the same cultural framework and even, to some extent, interacted, while retaining their individualities and behaving, in a sociological sense, quite differently from each other. In this book I first investigate the separate forms which folk and classical music took during the period, and then attempt to chart the more important cross-currents between them.

This is only one of several possible approaches to the history of eighteenth-century Scottish music, but it seems to me by far the most interesting one. It opens up areas of thought outside the scope of such earlier studies as Farmer's (1947), which is concerned purely with classical music, or Collinson's (1966), which is concerned solely with folk music. It affords new insights into the Scots fiddle-music tradition, into the church music, the national songs, and even into the already much discussed poetry of Robert Burns.

My study is restricted to Lowland Scotland between 1700 and 1800: the Lowlands being defined as the part of Scotland east and south of the 'Highland line', which runs from Helensburgh in the south to Nairn in the north, and marks the boundary between

---

[1] I offer no apology for the use of the term *classical music* in its popular sense of 'composed art music'. One must call it something; and the alternatives *art music* and *serious music* imply slurs in other directions. Admittedly 'classical music' is not generally so called by its own devotees; but nor is 'folk music'. Both are equally labels attached from outside.

Gaelic- and English-speaking parts of Scotland as it stood in 1800. In the interests of comprehensiveness I have tried to say something about all the forms of music current in the Lowlands at the time, but here and there, unavoidably, gaps have been left. I have largely ignored music in the army; music in Aberdeen has possibly been overstressed at the expense of music in Glasgow. I have also underplayed Jacobite songs. It has been stated that Jacobite songs arose spontaneously out of the Scottish people's deep emotional involvement with the rebellions of 1715 and 1745. I can only say that I have seen no evidence supporting this; most of the recorded Jacobite songs were actually written as an act of self-conscious nationalism, between 1790 and 1820, by such people as James Hogg and Lady Nairne.

Music in the Scottish Highlands I have not attempted to deal with here. It seems to have differed considerably from music in the Lowlands: the medieval harp-playing continued longer, the bagpipe-playing achieved greater sophistication, and the folk-songs had Gaelic words and so were partly isolated from folk-songs in the Lowlands. But this is material for a separate study.

In discussing classical music I have come back again and again to *composition* as an index of whether the music is surviving well or not. I do not regard a country as having a 'flourishing' classical music culture unless it regularly supports original composition, of worth-while quality, in a contemporary idiom, within its own boundaries. I use the word 'flourishing' of classical music, in this sense, throughout the book.

On 9 August 1763 Dr. John Gregory read a paper to the Edinburgh Philosophical Society in which he attempted to describe the state of music as it was currently being practised by his contemporaries. 'There are two different species of Music with us,' he said, 'one for the learned in the Science, and another for the vulgar.' Of 'vulgar', or folk, music he had this to say:

In Scotland there is a species of music perfectly well fitted to inspire that joyous mirth suited to dancing, and a plaintive Music peculiarly expressive of that tenderness and pleasing melancholy attendant on distress in love; both original in their kind, and different from every other in Europe.—It is of no consequence . . . whether [this music] be simple or complex, according to the rules of regular composition, or against them; whilst it produces its intended effect in a superior degree to any other, it is the preferable Music.[1]

Folk music, therefore, was able not only to break the rules of classical music and get away with it, but even, in some situations, to do the job in hand better. Gregory speaks as though there were some contradiction, some inherent paradox, in this statement, as indeed from an eighteenth-century point of view there was. The eighteenth century was proud of being civilized; and upper-class Scots were particularly proud, for in Scotland the Middle Ages had continued in many ways until about 1720, and modern civilization —in such manifestations as town social life, the growth of religious tolerance, newspapers, modern methods of agriculture—was a very recent achievement. No educated person had any doubts that learning was to be preferred to ignorance, reason to instinct, culture to nature. Gregory himself was one of the most cultured persons in Scotland at the time—professor at both Edinburgh and Old Aberdeen universities, and founder-member of the Aberdeen Musical Society. So 'learned' music should have won hands down over 'vulgar' music. Why did it not?

In 1847, nearly a century later, Robert Chambers noticed the same phenomenon:

It is quite remarkable, when we consider the high character of the popular melodies, how late and slow has been the introduction of a taste for the higher class of musical compositions into Scotland. . . . It is to be feared that the beauty of the melodies is itself partly to be blamed for the indifference to higher music. There is too great a disposition to rest with the distinction thus conferred upon the nation; too many are content to go no further for the enjoyments which music has to give.[2]

Chambers thus blames the lack of success of classical music in Scotland upon the very success of folk music. But surely this is a

---

[1] Gregory, *Discourse* III. Many references in these footnotes are given in an abbreviated form: for full details see the General Bibliography. Books referred to are printed if not otherwise stated.

[2] *Traditions*, 'St. Cecilia's Hall'.

symptom and not a cause, and other, deeper reasons must be sought. Folk music has always, so far as is known, flourished in Scotland; classical music has flourished only sporadically, at certain periods. During the seventeenth and nineteenth centuries Scotland had practically no classical music at all: in the eighteenth century there was a brief renaissance which lasted from 1760 to 1780: and in the twentieth century there has been, since 1960, another renaissance, whose duration is anybody's guess. This is a strange state of affairs, but one which becomes more intelligible if we attempt to define the natures of folk and classical music, and consider the kinds of society in which each seems to belong most naturally.

The definition of folk music is easy: the work has already been done for us by the International Folk Music Council:

Folk music is the product of a musical tradition that has been evolved through the process of oral transmission. The factors that shape the tradition are: (1) continuity which links the present with the past; (2) variation which springs from the creative individual or the group; and (3) selection by the community, which determines the form or forms in which the music survives.

The term can be applied to music that has been evolved from rudimentary beginnings by a community uninfluenced by popular and art music, and it can likewise be applied to music which has originated with an individual composer and has subsequently been absorbed into the unwritten living tradition of a community.

The term does not cover composed popular music that has been taken over ready-made by a community and remains unchanged, for it is the re-fashioning and re-creation of the music by the community that gives it its folk character.[1]

A comparable definition for classical music has, however, so far as I know, never been attempted. Let us therefore stand back from classical music, take a deep breath, and try to view it from outside. Once we have done this, the reason why classical music is so scarce in most periods of Scottish history becomes only too plain.

[1] Drawn up by the International Folk Council in 1954. Quoted from Sharp pp. xvi f.

'Music for the learned in the Science.' Learning is an international commodity, and classical music, in the form we have had it since the Renaissance, has always been an art common to the whole European continent. It is an art which has thrown in its lot with formal education. It is composed on to, and transmitted by means of, pieces of paper. This process allows composers to calculate extremely complex effects, such as polyphonic counterpoint, which they could not have worked out in their heads. (Polyphony does occur in some folk musics, but only randomly, by some sort of group improvisation: it is not calculated by one person.) Performers of classical music, in order to realize the composer's complex instructions adequately, need to be both educated and in constant training. Neither performers nor composers can do their jobs properly if they are obliged to spend the best hours of each day doing something else to earn their livings. This means that, in its most successful and characteristic form, classical music will be a *professional* art. Poor agricultural communities, for example, where every able-bodied adult has to work twelve hours a day to make ends meet, will clearly not be able to support professional musicians in large numbers. Classical music, then, will flourish best in affluent communities, especially in affluent communities where there is great enthusiasm for music, and where patronage for it can be guaranteed over long periods of time.

European classical music flourishes in *centres*. These may be courtly (in feudal countries), religious (in Catholic countries), or civic (in mercantile countries). At any given time one or two of these centres will be regarded as dominant over all the others. At such centres the best composers and performers assemble from all over Europe, and stimulate each other to technical innovations, which in turn produce new fashions and standards of taste. The new standards then spread to the lesser centres, which do their best to catch up with the dominant centres as fast as possible. Meanwhile the next generation of aspiring musicians make their way to the dominant centres, and so, for a time, their dominance continues.

Professional musicians in flourishing centres have continually to compete with each other for individual survival, and this produces a self-consciousness about the art as a whole. All concerned with it—patrons, composers, performers, audience—perpetually discuss and criticize each other. There tends to arise a hot-house atmosphere of jealousy and suspicion, which to an outsider seems paradoxical, in view of music-making's inherently co-operative nature.

When a classical music work is copied from one piece of paper to another, the name of the composer is normally copied also, and perpetuated along with the music. This, added to the general self-consciousness just described, makes composers extremely aware of their individual talents, and has opened the classical tradition to the Romantic concepts of 'self-expression' and 'originality', particularly of course since the early nineteenth century. (In contrast, the social conventions surrounding folk music are unself-conscious; performances are not in most circumstances appraised critically; composers' names are soon forgotten; and folk music has not been directly influenced by the Romantic Movement.)

Classical music centres which are not flourishing too well, and are therefore of peripheral importance to the tradition, have a somewhat different atmosphere from main centres. First-rate professionals tend not to stay in them for any length of time: and often the second-rate professionals who do reside permanently are inferior in enterprise and enthusiasm to the resident amateurs. In such cases it is the amateur musicians who keep the place alive. However, amateurs are not usually good composers, and even if amateur composition takes place at all, it is generally of poor quality and not worth adding to the mainstream. Peripheral centres are socially less intense, but they are dependent for their supply of music on what is produced in the main centres. Peripheral centres are always liable to slip irremediably behind the fashion, if constant effort is not made to keep in touch. In very peripheral centres there is a danger that the classical music may die out altogether.

Scotland has never scored many points for suitability for classical music. Poor; geographically remote from the rest of Europe; lacking classical-music traditions; everything has told against her. General poverty in a country does not prevent classical music flourishing if the country is feudal and the aristocracy are prepared to bleed the lower classes to death—as in some eighteenth-century German states where the royal opera company consumed an eighth of the national income; but in Scotland the aristocracy were not interested in spending their taxes on music.

This was so because Scotland had no suitable centres for classical music to concentrate in. Her court life came to an end in 1603, when James VI went to London, and was only briefly resuscitated for Charles I's Scottish coronation in 1633, and in 1680, when the Duke and Duchess of York spent the winter season at Holyrood. Prince Charles Edward Stuart also held court at Holyrood, temporarily, towards the end of 1745, and some royal French refugees stayed there in 1790. After that the next royal visitor was George IV, in 1822. Clearly, not much patronage can be expected here.

There were no religious centres in Scotland after the Reformation of 1560.

Civic patronage, however, was more hopeful, and looked, at the beginning of the seventeenth century, as though it might achieve great things. Music schools, run by the town councils, were provided in the main towns of Scotland, for example in Aberdeen, Ayr, Cupar, Dumbarton, Dundee, Edinburgh, Elgin, Glasgow, Inverness, Irving, Lanark, and St. Andrews.[1] These schools taught rudiments of music, part-singing, and instrumental playing to boys up to the age of about fifteen, in addition to giving an elementary general education. They were always attached to the main church in the town—the master of the music school was also precentor at the church, and the school was expected to provide the church choir. A similar system was used in Protestant Germany with great artistic success. Unfortunately the Church of Scotland followed the lead of John Knox rather than Martin Luther, and disapproved of music too complex for the ordinary person to participate in, at any rate for use in church. As a result, Scottish choirs rarely sang anything in church more advanced than harmonized metrical-psalm tunes.[2] Organs, also, were banned from Scottish churches soon after the Reformation; there were no post-Reformation church organs until 1722.

---

[1] Dauncy, pp. 362 f.
[2] Terry, *Music-school of Old Machar*; Ian J. Simpson, pp. 31 f.

The north-east of Scotland had more conservative religious traditions than the rest of the country (after 1690 it became the stronghold of Episcopacy), and music seems to have survived there better during the seventeenth century. The Aberdeen music school was the most distinguished one in Scotland, and had an associated printed song book, notable as the country's first secular music publication. This song book was John Forbes's *Cantus, Songs and Fancies. To Thre, Foure, or Five Parts, both apt for Voices and Viols. With a briefe Introduction of Musick, As is taught in the Musicke-Schole of Aberdene by T[homas] D[avidson] M[aste]r of Musick.* It was published in 1662. But its contents are rather old-fashioned, and by its third edition in 1682 most of the songs in it were about a hundred years old. The Aberdeen music school may well have had connections with the aristocratic great houses of Aberdeenshire, many of which preserved their sixteenth-century court culture intact throughout the seventeenth century.[1]

During the eighteenth century the Aberdeen music school fell on hard times, and suffered from absentee masters; it finally closed in about 1755.[2] In general it may be said that the music schools failed to realize their potential, at an immediate level, because they lacked the stimulus of big public performances, and, at a more fundamental level, because they served little social purpose: they were preparing their pupils for professional careers which did not exist. A continental musician in the seventeenth and early eighteenth centuries had a choice of several stimulating careers open to him: at court, in civic opera, in the big cathedrals. This can be illustrated from the biographies of J. S. Bach and Handel, both of whom changed from one career to another several times. On the Continent this period was marked by the maturity of instrumental music, by the development of tonality as a means of large-scale construction, by the rise of schools of virtuoso playing and the emergence of the concerto principle, by the cross-fertilization of vocal and instrumental idioms. This tremendous, burgeoning growth was a result of there being a multiplicity of musical establishments, all experimenting with new techniques, all watching each other's progress, all prepared to learn from each other.

[1] Shire, 'Court song'.   [2] Walker, *Commonplace-book of Andrew Melville*, pp. xl f.

Scotland had no means of contributing to these developments, and few means of profiting from them. Sir John Clerk of Penicuik, in Midlothian, visited Vienna at the age of twenty-one, and compared the musical life there with what he was used to at home. He heard the emperor playing the harpsichord, and at first found this ungentlemanly behaviour 'so shoking' (for the emperor's performance was up to professional standard)

that it had like to have spoiled all my inclination to performing my self, if it had not been that I forsaw I was not to be rich enough to purchase Musick any other way than what I made by my self, especially in my oune Country, where at this time there is no such thing.[2]

This was in 1697. Yet half a century later Edinburgh had emerged as a civic classical music centre with claims to European stature.

The reasons for the change were manifold. The Church of Scotland's hold on public behaviour weakened, and Edinburgh began to enjoy its social life in a relaxed and relatively uncensored fashion. The first regular Scottish newspaper, the *Edinburgh Gazette*, started in 1699. Dances began in 1705, and after religious opposition had done its worst they began again in 1710 . . . and again in 1723.[2] The first Scottish collection of fashionable verse, *The Edinburgh Miscellany*, came out in 1720. Dramatic performances began—with some trepidation, for the church hated drama even more than it hated dancing. Coffee-houses opened and gentlemen's clubs were founded. And to this urban bustle was added a new, sociable form of music-making, which was to save classical music in Scotland from extinction: the concert.

The first Scottish concert was probably held in Edinburgh in November 1693, but the earliest we have a detailed record of took place on St. Cecilia's Day, 22 November 1695. It was an ambitious affair, and probably the most important concert in the country in the whole year. Professional performers included Henry Crumbden, master of the Edinburgh music school, with a choir of his pupils, and Daniel Thomson, the state trumpeter. There were also two professional oboists, a few professional violinists, and one viola

---

[1] Clerk, p. 23 n.   [2] Jamieson.

player. The rest of an orchestra was made up by amateur players—recorders, violins, cellos, and gambas. One gets the impression that all available forces had been scraped together for the occasion. The programme was long, and included '[Jeremiah] Clerk's Overture', 'Torrelli's Sonata for 4 violins', 'Barrett's Trumpet Sonata', 'Finger for 2 flutes and 2 haut[boys]', 'Songs and Mottetti of Bassani', 'Finger's Trumpet Sonata', and a 'Grand Chorus'.[1]

There are no locally composed pieces here,[2] but the preponderance of trumpet music, and the fact of the concert's being held on St. Cecilia's Day, show strong London influence, while the trumpet music again, and the fact that Torelli is represented, show the influence, via London, of Bologna.[3] Edinburgh had more up-to-date taste than one might have expected in the circumstances.

For a variety of reasons Edinburgh was the only town in Scotland capable of attaining European stature as a musical centre. The aristocracy tended to live there in the winter, in preference to staying at their country estates, and this tendency increased as the century progressed and the social life of the capital became more attractive. The aristocracy had money to spend on theatre and concert tickets, on printed music, and on harpsichord lessons for its daughters. Edinburgh was also the country's legal and medical centre, so the town was full of intelligent, educated, professional people. Furthermore, it was usual for law and medical students to do part of their training on the Continent, especially at the universities of Leyden and Utrecht in Holland;[4] once there, they found

that there was no keeping of good or verteous company in either Holand, France, or Italy, and far less in Germany, without as much of the practise of musick as to enable one to bear a part in a Concert.... I bestowed a great deal of pains on the Harpsecord, and in a year after was as well qualified to perform my part on that instrument as any Gentleman in Holand. I found that this piece of skill was indeed

[1] Tytler.
[2] Henry Farmer suggested that 'Clerk' was Hugh Clerk, a director of the Edinburgh Assembly in 1746, and composer of a few mid-eighteenth-century marches. See *History of music*, p. 330. This theory seems to me very unlikely.
[3] Smithers. Smithers suggests that the Bologna influence on London music was partly due to Mary of Modena's coming to London in 1673 as the wife of the Duke of York. The duke and duchess came to Edinburgh in 1680. Perhaps some of the Bologna influence on Edinburgh was direct.   [4] Innes-Smith.

of very great use to me afterwards in the course of my Travels through Germany, Italy, and France.[1]

Young Edinburgh lawyers and doctors who had just returned from the Continent were therefore likely to have up-to-date musical taste and to be in practice on their instruments.

Regular music publishing started in Edinburgh in 1725 and had developed to a major business by 1750. After a little while a steady stream of distinguished foreigners came to stay, attracted by professional employment in the Musical Society's concerts, and by the prospect of aristocratic pupils. Francesco Barsanti stayed from 1735 till about 1743, and married a Scots wife; Johann Friedrich Lampe came in 1750; Nicolo Pasquali came in 1752 and died there in 1757. The great castrato Tenducci made several visits to Edinburgh from 1768 on. During the 1770s Edinburgh managed to support three resident composers and to stimulate them to first-class work: they were a German, Johann Georg Christoff Schetky, an Italian, Domenico Corri, and a native Scot, the Earl of Kelly. The 1770s were Edinburgh's greatest period for music, and the amount of interest taken in it by polite society at the time is shown by a letter from a visitor, written in 1775:

The degree of attachment which is shewn to Music in general in this country[2] exceeds belief. It is not only the principal entertainment, but the constant topic of every conversation; and it is necessary not only to be a lover of it, but to be possessed of a knowledge of the science, to make yourself agreeable to society.

In vain may a man of letters, whose want of natural faculties has prevented him from understanding an art, from which he could derive no pleasure, endeavour to introduce other matters of discourse, however entertaining in their nature: every thing must give place to music. Music alone engrosses every idea. In religion a Scotchman is grave and abstracted; in politics serious and deliberate: it is in the power of harmony alone to make him an enthusiast.[3]

As far as the distinguished foreign visitors were concerned, Edinburgh was *ultima thule*; none of them was prepared to go any

---

[1] Clerk, p. 15.
[2] This is an inaccurate generalization: the writer means 'in Edinburgh'.
[3] Topham, p. 378.

further north. For this reason Aberdeen, which would have been the next town in Scotland to become Europeanized had the process continued, remained a city of amateur musicians, as Edinburgh had been in 1700. Concerts in Aberdeen had a much more relaxed, homely atmosphere than those in Edinburgh, and indeed the difference in character between the musical lives of the two towns may be noticed to this day.

After 1780 there was a general lowering of standards all over Britain. The reasons for this are still obscure, and appear to be complicated. Technically and stylistically classical music had developed very fast over the preceding sixty years, so that the latest masterpieces (e.g. Mozart's) were difficult both to play and to understand. At the same time, new mass-production techniques enabled pianos to be made cheaply. Vast floods of second-rate easy piano music were soon being mass-produced to match, and at this, the aristocracy gave up. Music had become, on the one hand, too difficult, on the other hand, not socially exclusive enough for them, and by 1792 William Tytler could complain of 'the languid spirit and taste for music in the metropolis [i.e. Edinburgh] at present'.[1] The Edinburgh Musical Society had to be wound up in 1798, and the Aberdeen one followed in 1801. Scotland began to fall seriously behind the Continent again, and her contributions to the European musical scene came to an end almost at once.

The corresponding characteristics of classical music and folk music may be summarized as follows. The classical music is common to Europe, the folk music peculiar to Scotland, though most of the left-hand column would probably hold for folk music of other nations:

FOLK	CLASSICAL
transmission oral	transmission notational
no definitive texts	definitive texts
composers soon forgotten	composers recorded
limits of complexity set by powers of memory	limits of complexity set by powers of intellect

[1] Tytler, p. 510.

FOLK	CLASSICAL
monodic	polyphonic or harmonized
dependent on amateur performers; few professionals	dependent on professional performers and composers
inexpensive, non-commercial	expensive, uncommercial, requires patronage to survive
an unselfconscious part of the way of life	a selfconscious recreational activity for which the taste must be cultivated; not equally valued by all members of the community
can fit into all classes and ways of life; flourishes in poor communities with little leisure	cannot flourish outside an affluent spendthrift community
no formal education needed for its propagation	formal education necessary for all concerned with it—the more the better
repertory relatively static	repertory ever-changing; subject to fashion
widespread	localized in main cultural centres

If two parallel cultures can flourish in the same country without one dominating and absorbing the other, there must be some barrier which restricts their influence on each other. The common view as to how this occurs—at least among English readers who have been brought up on Cecil Sharp—is that the 'two species' are kept going by different groups of people, who are separated geographically (town–country) or socially (upper class–lower class) or possibly both. As these two groups of people never meet, their musics cannot come into conflict. This situation seems to have been true of England in 1900, when Sharp did his research. It is not true, however, of eighteenth-century Scotland, where to a considerable extent the same group of people ran both kinds of music simultaneously. One must assume since no assimilation took place that the two genres fulfilled different emotional needs, and so were not in competition with each other. The political and economic origins of these emotional needs may be left to a later chapter; but I shall here state as an axiom that the leisured and professional classes of Scotland, who were responsible for the propagation of classical music, were also very much in touch with folk music.

Selfconscious, wholesale documentation of the folk tradition did not begin until the 1780s; yet there is a certain amount of earlier evidence that the Scottish upper classes shared the folk culture with lower classes. A number of seventeenth-century manuscript-books have survived which include transcriptions of folk-tunes; and there are several manuscripts in existence dated *c*. 1700, whose contents are an intriguing mixture of classical and folk pieces. A typical one is James Thomson's music book, dated 1702; it contains pieces for solo recorder:[1]

> Emp[ero]r['s] March
> I love my love in Secret
> Minevit
> Richmond Ball
> Come sweet Lass
> Saw you my Love Migey Linken ower the Lee
> Happy Groves
> French Minevit (for recorder duet)
> Geld him Lasses
> Earish Ayre
> March
> Trumpet Tune
> Trumpet by Mr Shors
> Trumpet
> Shores trumpet minevit
> What shall I doe to show
> [etc.]

This gives a complete spectrum. At the classical end of the scale are 'What shall I doe to show [how much I love her]', a song by Purcell, and 'Trumpet by Mr Shors', which is Jeremiah Clarke's Trumpet Voluntary (as played by the London trumpeter John Shore). At the folk end are 'I love my love in secret', a reel-tune, and 'Saw you my Love Migey', an obscene ditty whose words were recorded by Burns ninety years later.

1 NLS MS. 2833.

Another music book, from Newbattle Abbey, Midlothian, dating from about 1680, suggests that Scots tunes were taught to upper-class children as instrumental practice exercises. The book is entitled *Lessones for y* *violin*, and includes a section of Scots airs alongside bourrées, marches, galliards, and minuets;[1] like many manuscripts of the period, it is written out in a mixture of hands: masters' and pupils'. Yet another music book, this one from Nisbet House, Berwickshire, and dated *c.* 1765, contains the tune of the traditional Border ballad 'Gil Morice' among minuets and songs by Arne and Hasse.[2]

It also seems to have been common practice for upper-class ladies in Edinburgh to sing folk-songs after supper. In 1723 Allan Ramsay published a collection of fashionable verse set to pre-existing popular tunes, the *Tea-table Miscellany*, which was an attempt to cash in on this custom. Ramsay printed no music, and his collection uses seventy-two different tunes; therefore one can suppose that the Edinburgh ladies had a large repertory at this time, which he knew he could rely on. (Incidentally, the publication was a great success.) An account of their singing at a slightly later period, in about 1760, has survived:

> The ladies of Edinburgh used to sing those airs ['Lochaber no more' and others] without any accompaniment (indeed they scarce admitted of counterpoint, or any but a slight and delicate accompaniment) at tea and after supper, their position at table not being interrupted as now by rising to the pianoforte.[3]

Upper-class ladies also sang traditional ballads. In 1755 'Edom of Gordon', 'an ancient Scottish Poem. Never before printed', was brought out by the Foulis brothers of Glasgow: it had been supplied to them by Sir David Dalrymple 'as it was preserved in the memory of a lady'.[4] An outstanding upper-class ballad singer was Anna Gordon, daughter of Professor Thomas Gordon of King's

---

[1] NLS MS. 5778. The book has been partly chewed away by mice.

[2] NLS MS. 5449.

[3] Mackenzie, p. 79. Mackenzie was born in 1745 and wrote these memoirs in 1831. The 'delicate accompaniment' may have been from a cittern, which could easily be played sitting at table.

[4] Dalrymple, p. ix.

College, Old Aberdeen, and wife of Andrew Brown, minister of Falkland in Fife.

Mrs Brown was born in 1747, and had learned most of her ballads, before she was twelve years of age, from her mother, her aunt (Mrs Farquharson, of Allanquoich, Braemar) and a maid in her mother's family—all Aberdeenshire born and bred.[1]

Mrs. Brown's ballads were taken down by a nephew, who sent them to Sir Walter Scott, who used them as a main source of material for his *Minstrelsy of the Scottish Border* in 1802.

A difference between upper- and lower-class approaches to folksong is that the upper classes may well have used pieces of paper in the initial stages of learning them. Francis Craigmile, a graduate of Marischal College, Aberdeen, wrote down the tune and first verse of 'Tibbie Fowler of the glen' in about 1823, and then added a shorthand of the other verses up the margin of the page:[2]

2 Ten come east &c. ten row. . . . . . / Twa com dn lg dkside, th 2 & 30 chor
3 Shes g pendles—cockleshells—Hyhh[d] shoes & sill tgs—& a the lds are w
4 Be a lassie eer so black if hae nm siller—Tintock tap
[5] Be a l— eer so fair

But this is clearly only an aid to memory, since it is not complete enough to make sense to anyone who did not already know what it meant.[3]

Even professional classical musicians had strong roots in the folk tradition. Every single professional violinist in eighteenth-century Scotland, apart perhaps from some of the foreign visitors, had to

[1] Greig, p. xvii.   [2] AUL, uncatalogued accession in January 1968.
[3] Cf. *The Scots Musical Museum* no. 440:

Ten came east and ten came west, ten came rowin o'er the water;
Twa came down the lang dyke side, there's twa-and-thirty wooin' at her.

Chorus

She's got pendles in her lugs, cockle-shells wad set her better;
High-heel'd shoon and siller tags, and a' the lads are wooin' at her.

Be a lassie e'er sae black, an she hae the name o' siller;
Set her upo' Tintock-tap, the wind will blaw a man till her.

Be a lassie e'er sae fair, an she want the pennie siller;
A flie may fell her in the air, before a man be even till her.

earn his living part of the time by playing folk-fiddle music.
William McGibbon (*c.* 1690–1756) and Charles McLean (*c.* 1712–
c. 1765) were both employed as professional violinists by the
Edinburgh Musical Society; McGibbon composed 18 trio-sonatas,
6 solo sonatas, 3 concertos, and an overture, while McLean wrote
12 solo sonatas; yet both also wrote many sets of fiddle variations
in the folk style. The same roots are noticeable with music publishers. William Thomson, James Oswald, and William Napier
all went to London and published collections of Scots tunes there.
Each of them included in his collections folk-songs, or versions of
folk-songs, which had not appeared in print before,[1] and no one
knows what their sources for this material were if not direct personal knowledge. It seems indisputable that they had learned the
songs years before, and taken them to London in their heads.

The folk tradition in eighteenth-century Scotland was thus
available to all classes of society; the reason why it was not documented earlier than 1780 must therefore have been, not that educated people were not interested in it, but that they knew it all
already. This should be borne in mind during the next four
chapters, where we shall temporarily separate folk and classical
music from each other, and consider them as different cultures.

---

[1] Thomson, *Orpheus Caledonius*, 1725: 'The carle he came o'er the craft', 'Willy's
rare and Willy's fair', 'The bonny earle of Murray', etc. Oswald, *The Caledonian
Pocket Companion*, 1745– : almost throughout. Napier, *A Selection of the most favourite
Scots songs*, 1790– : 'Gil Morice', 'Ay waking oh', etc.

Classical Music

2

MUSICAL CENTRES

I N this chapter we shall discuss the various establishments in eighteenth-century Scotland where classical music tried to flourish, and the degrees of success which it had in each. First, however, a preliminary note on classical musical instruments in use during the period.

MUSICAL INSTRUMENTS IN USE

Musical instruments are usually classified according to how they work physically, i.e. wind instruments are distinguished from string instruments, and so on. But an alternative form of classification, more appropriate to this study, is also possible: according to social use. From this point of view eighteenth-century instruments can be distinguished as 'professional' or 'amateur', and amateur ones can be subdivided into 'male' and 'female'.

The 'professional' instruments included all brass and percussion, and all wind instruments except recorder and flute; learning these would have been beneath the dignity of an upper-class amateur player. In Scotland such instruments had a place only in theatre and army bands, and when used in amateur concerts they were always played by imported professionals.

The 'amateur' instruments in eighteenth-century Scotland were as follows: recorder (up to about 1740), flute (from about 1725), violin, cello, viola da gamba (the last up to about 1740), harpsichord, spinet, virginal, clavichord (these last two up to about 1740), piano (from about 1780), and cittern (throughout the century but with a period of special popularity between 1755 and 1780). The harp and guitar did not reach Scotland until about 1810.[1]

---

[1] Mackenzie, p. 80.

Of these, recorder, flute, violin, and cello were played only by gentlemen;[1] gamba and keyboard instruments were played by both sexes, the latter becoming increasingly 'female' as the century progressed; and cittern was played only by ladies.[2] This distribution reflects a society where the men go out to work and meet each other while the women stay put in their own homes—for the 'male' instruments are the sociable ones which fit together into orchestras and chamber ensembles, whereas the 'female' instruments are lone and harmonically self-supporting. The fact that ladies, as well as gentlemen, played gamba seems to break this rule, until one remembers the existence of 'division viol' playing, a style of playing chords as well as melodies on the gamba to make it harmonically complete on its own; this was a seventeenth-century technique which may well have lasted into the eighteenth century in Scotland. A male/female distinction also held in singing, for ladies typically sang solos in their own homes, while gentlemen sang together away from home—glees in the tavern, or choruses of Handel's oratorios in the concert hall. For women, music-making was an individual activity; for men, it was a group activity.

A further point arises from this approach to instruments. When an instrument becomes obsolete and a new instrument arises to take over its social function, it often also takes over the old name. Thus *flute* can mean both recorder ('common flute') and transverse flute ('German flute'); *guitar* both cittern ('English guitar') and the modern instrument ('Spanish guitar'). A more confusing doubling of this kind, which several scholars have come to grief over,[3] is *treble viol*, a name used in Scotland at the beginning of the eighteenth century to mean 'violin'. This fact can be established from a manuscript tuning-chart, written probably in Aberdeen in about 1715, which instructs the player to tune the four strings of the 'Trible viol' to g d' a' and e''.[4] A derived term *violer*, meaning a folk fiddle player, was used in Scotland throughout the eighteenth

---

[1] Smollett, vol. 2, p. 235: 'The Scots are all musicians—Every man you meet plays on the flute, the violin, or violoncello.'

[2] Topham, p. 95.

[3] e.g. Collinson, *Traditional and national*, pp. 202-3.

[4] Bound with NLS copy of Nicoll's *Twelve Tunes for the Church of Scotland* (Aberdeen, 1714): H.29.e.40.

century, and is recorded in Jedburgh as late as 1816.[1] At what date the actual treble viol went out of use in Scotland is not known, but the name carried on, applied to the new Italian instrument which took its place.

GREAT HOUSES

Aristocratic great house culture was the most important musical tradition which the eighteenth century inherited from the seventeenth. Historically speaking, it was a fragmented relic of the court culture which had vanished from Scotland in 1603 with James VI's removal to London. During the seventeenth century the Scottish great houses tried to preserve what they could of this lost court life. Their attempts to behave like miniature individual courts were, however, seriously hampered by lack of money; for most of them it was out of the question financially to maintain professional musicians permanently on the household staff.[2] The musicians that might be found running the musical life at a country house, therefore, teaching the laird's children during the day and playing music with the laird at night, were probably only a governess, a private tutor engaged for the summer months, and possibly the local minister.[3]

But perhaps the phrase 'great house culture' is misleading here. The musical life of the great houses in the seventeenth century was almost static. The aristocrats had, it was true, European connections: they travelled on the Continent and brought back musical scores, they ordered harpsichords from Antwerp and organs from London. But they did not integrate with each other to form a living cultural élite. Until the rise of concert-giving there was no central musical activity in the country to stimulate them: they had no characteristic shared musical repertory except the madrigals

[1] Campbell (MS.): 'Hunter, the resident fiddler (or *violer*) in Jedburgh.'

[2] The situation may have been different in the Highlands. Dunvegan Castle, Skye, certainly made regular payments to professional musicians. See Collinson, *Traditional and national*, p. 203 n.

[3] One such minister was Robert Edwards of Murroes parish, Angus, known to have been in touch with the cultural life of nearby Panmure House. His commonplace-book, the outstanding record of aristocratic poetry of the time, is now NLS MS. 9450. For further information see articles by Kenneth Elliott and Helena Shire in *Scottish Studies*, vol. 5, pt. 1 (1961).

and lute-songs which survived from the old Scottish court. As far
as is known, there was no great house composition at all in the
seventeenth century, apart from a few songs by Beck, a German
music tutor employed at Balcarres House, Fife, in the 1690s.

But during the eighteenth century great house culture gained a
new sense of direction. Many aristocrats acquired fine libraries and
collections of musical instruments, some of which are still intact
today in their original settings, uncatalogued. More work will have
to be done before a full picture of aristocratic home musical life
emerges; but some notes on a few establishments may be valuable
meantime.

Mellerstain House, Berwickshire, was the home of Lady Grisell
Baillie (1665–1746), patroness of the arts and authoress of several
excellent Scots lyrics. She was fond of music, and went to considerable trouble to secure a musical education for her two daughters,
Grisell and Rachel. I give below a number of entries from her
household account-books, concerning musical matters. The entries
date between 1701 and 1714. (It should be explained that Scotland had a dual monetary system at this time—it used both English
coinage and its own. A pound Scots was worth a twelfth of a pound
sterling. Lady Grisell's accounts begin in Scots money, but change
to sterling during the course of 1710.)

For Grisies quarter with Crumbin	19	7	0 [Scots]
To Crombin for a quarter to Grisie	17	8	0
To Grisies singing master Krenberg	14	4	0
For Grisies singing to Mr Krenberg	7	8	0
For Grisies singing book	1	9	0
For a si[n]ging book to Grisie	1	9	0
To Mr Kramberg, Grisells singing master for the mounth past	7	8	0
To Mr Crumbin Grisies playing master for a quarter past 6 dollers and a doller for tuning	20	6	0
To Grisie to goe to a consert	0	14	6
To Mr Crumbin for a month to Grisie	7	8	0
To Crumbin for a book	1	4	0
To a consurt fro Grisie	1	9	0

To the pip and drum £2 16*s*
To Grisis singing master Cremberg £7 8

For a flute £6 a quarter with Crumbin 6½ doll.	25	1	0
For mounthes at the violl to Grisie with Sinc-kolum	12	0	0
For mending her violl	2	0	0
To John Steall singing master, for 2 mounthes to Grisie	24	0	0
To a raffile for herpsicords by Grisie	14	4	0
To hoboys £1 9s.			
For tickets to Steals consurt	7	2	0
To Crumbin for a quarter throwgh bass to Grisie 2 guinys	25	16	0
For 2 mounth to Grisie with St Culume on the vyoll, etc.	15	3	0
For binding the operas 14s.			
To the pip and drum at this moneths fair	2	18	0
To Mr Crombine half a moneth	0	10	0 [Sterling]
For tickets to consorts 7s.			
To a man from Edinburgh to tune the spinits and virginells	0	15	6
To musick	0	5	0
To the ho boys	0	2	6
To fidlers 2 sh. 6d.			
To the fidlers	1	1	6
To the pyp and drum for 2 fairs	0	9	4
To Mr Steall for Grisie	0	12	0
For mending the fine virginall at London	12	10	0
For Fraught of them cariing out of Edn	2	0	0[1]

From this it will be seen that Grisie, Lady Grisell's elder daughter, was taught singing, keyboard, viol, and figured bass, all more or less simultaneously. The family possessed at least two keyboard instruments ('virginals' can be singular), and probably more, and it was necessary to send one of them all the way to London for repairs, even though the instruments could be tuned from Edinburgh. They also possessed several operatic scores, probably in manuscript, and made regular payments to local musicians. I shall return to these accounts at various later stages in the book.

Penicuik House, Midlothian, was also a musical household at

---

[1] From Baillie, pp. 8–26.

this time. The continental travels of Sir John Clerk of Penicuik (1676–1755) have already been mentioned: he returned from them in 1699 having learned to appreciate 'pictures better than became my Purse, and as to Musick, I rather performed better, particularly on the Herpsecord, than became a Gentleman'.[1] Clerk brought back various manuscript compositions of his own, and no doubt other pieces of music also: during his lifetime he built up a fine music library.[2] Penicuik House possessed a harpsichord, which Sir John played regularly until his late forties when his eyesight began to fail, and probably a chamber organ also.[3]

Thunderton House in Elgin was also a musical household. A letter has been preserved dated 30 January 1710, in which a prospective governess, Jean Chein of Huntly, offered her services to Lady Thunderton. Her accomplishments, she wrote, included the ability to 'play on the Treble and Gambo Viol, Virginelles and Manicords';[4] this gives us some idea what instruments a tutor at a great house might be expected to play.

Kilravock Castle, near Nairn, also had a musical tradition in the eighteenth century. The musical evenings of Hugh Rose, Lord Kilravock, were described by his daughter in these words:

> My delight was to stand behind his chair, and turn the leaves of Pergolesi's *Stabat Mater*, or the *Passione* of Jomelli, while he played the symphonies and the prettiest passages in the songs to me, showed me the various cliffs, the niceties in time, the difference of keys.[5]

One of Lord Kilravock's musical evenings went down in history, for Bonnie Prince Charlie was entertained at Kilravock Castle with the laird's violin playing, on 14 April 1746, two days before the battle of Culloden.

MUSIC SCHOOLS

Burgh music schools were similar to great houses in having a musical tradition which went back to the end of the sixteenth

---

[1] Clerk, p. 36 n.   [2] A contents-list is given in Appendix II.
[3] A composition of Clerk's with organ continuo is among the Clerk Papers in the Scottish Record Office, Edinburgh.
[4] Dunbar, p. 15. 'Treble Viol' here means violin; 'Manicord' is another name for clavichord.   [5] Innes, p. 462.

century, but they stood very much lower in the social scale. A brief account of their scope has already been given in Chapter 1. They were financed and governed by the town councils, and it appears that any boy with a good singing voice could become a pupil at one, either at nominal fees, or else free. The following gives a useful picture of the school at Aberdeen:

THE SAID DAY The Magistrates Represented that . . . they had drawn up ane Advertisement anent the Vaccancy of the Musick Master's Office of this Burgh, which they had caused insert in the Mercury several times, Desired all persons who had a mind to compete for the said office to appear at Aberdeen the Eighteenth instant, to undergo tryal for the said office, And that Charles Macklean Musician at Montrose had appeared and undergone Tryal for the forsaid Office before proper Judges, and was by them found Qualified, WHICH being considered be the Magistrates and Council forsaid, They Nominated and Elected the said Charles Macklean to be Master of the Musick Schooll of Aberdeen dureing the pleasure of the Council allennerly. In terms of the following Regulations signed by him of date the Nineteenth of May instant. VIZ. PRIMO The Sett Sallary payable to him by the Town is Three Hundred merks pannum. SECUNDO That he is to teach publickly in the Schooll Vocal Musick, as also Instrumental Musick on the Spinet, Harpsicord, Violin, German flute, common flute. TERTIO That he be obliged to attend the Schooll at the following hours VIZ from eight to nine in the morning from ten to twelve in the forenoon, and from two to four in the Afternoon. QUARTO That the fies and honoraries after mentioned be payed to the said Master by the Schollars VIZ By those who are taught Italian Musick and all other parts both of Vocal and Instrumental Musick Three pound Scots monethly, And by those who are only taught Church Musick, Scots Tunes and the lower pairts of Musick Thirty Shilling Scots monethly. QUINTO That the said Master shall always behave himself in a virtuous Moral manner as becomes a publict Master and teacher of youth, And to be subject to the Rules, Directions and Instructions of the Magistrates and Town Council, who are to be sole Judges of his Moral Deportment, behaviour and Conduct, And that the said Master attend Divine Worship in the Established Church in this Burgh on Sabbath days both forenoon and afternoon, So as to give good example to the Youth under his Instruction. SEXTO When the principal

Master imploys and calls ane Assistant or Doctor to the Musick
School, He shall be a person who shall be approven of by the Magistrates and Council, and setled by their Direction. AND ITS hereby
declared that the Magistrates and Council shall be sole Judges over
the said Master without any appeal to any other Judicature what-
somever.[1]

This account is interesting in several respects. It shows what instruments were being taught at Aberdeen in 1737—spinet, harpsichord,
violin, flute, and recorder; by comparison, the music-school
master at Haddington in 1728 played 'hautboy, bass-viol, and
German flute', while at Dunfermline 'virginalls and monicords'
were taught up till 1745.[2] The inclusion of 'Scots tunes' among
the cheaper part of the instruction course suggests that music-
school pupils were taught folk-tunes as instrumental practice pieces.
This would corroborate the evidence given in Chapter 1 for
upper-class children also doing this.

Furthermore, it shows what rates of pay a music-school master
might expect. A merk was worth 13*s*. 4*d*. Scots, so McLean's basic
salary was only 200 lib. Scots a year, in addition to which he could
take 30*s*. or three pounds, as appropriate, off each pupil per month.
Some of his pupils, however, would be attending the school free,
so he would not be able to charge them. He could, of course, try
sending in the bill for those pupils to the town council who had
approved their free education, but it would probably be ignored.
In the circumstances, he would have to take additional private
pupils to eke out his living.

In this way the music-school staffs and the private tutors to
great houses turn out to be the same set of people doing two jobs.
The 'Crombin' who taught harpsichord to Miss Grisie Baillie of
Mellerstain between the age of eight and seventeen was in fact
Henry Crumbden, master of the Edinburgh music school.[3] Crumbden's salary from Mellerstain seems to have fluctuated a little,
but averages about seven pounds Scots a month, more than twice
the three pounds per pupil allowed to McLean for his school

[1] Aberdeen Burgh Records, 20 May 1737.
[2] Grant, p. 378; and see ibid., pp. 374–84 for details of other music schools.
[3] Crumbden (or Krumbein) was a Swede. He died in Edinburgh in August 1720.

lessons. Crumbden had an extensive private practice, and used to put on concerts in Edinburgh in the 1710s, at which his best young ladies performed.[1] An interesting letter has survived, dated 25 November 1734, to Sir John Clerk of Penicuik from his sister, recommending 'Mr Sharreter organist & Musick Master in Aberdeen' as a private tutor to the family.[2] John Schereter was on the staff of the Aberdeen music school just before McLean's time.[3] Doubtless many more examples of this duplication of jobs could be found.

In some towns the council tried to make amends for the meagre salary offered to the music-school master by banning other music teaching within the burgh—so that their man would have the monopoly of any lucrative private teaching that was going. In Montrose in 1703, for example,

the council . . . [forbade] any other person than John Gillies to teach vocal and instrumental music under 'the falzie of 100 merks for each quarter's contravention'; two years later the same teacher complains that some women have taken upon them to teach music to the great prejudice of the public school, and craves redress of the abuse; a vote, after serious consideration, was taken, as to whether the council should suppress the private music-schools, or only put an 'imposition upon them'; the latter motion was carried.[4]

Such measures saved the town council from having to raise the music-school master's salary to a living wage, and also prevented the number of professional musicians in the town from rising. The over-all effect would be to limit the total amount of money spent on music within the town—an interesting piece of socio-musical ecology.

But the rise of concert-giving and the movement of the aristocracy into the towns for the winter upset this delicately balanced economic system. Perhaps the subsequent actions of Charles McLean may be taken as symbolic of the new order supplanting the old. McLean was clearly dissatisfied with his Aberdeen job—even though it was regarded as the top music-teaching post in

[1] Tytler, p. 509 n.   [2] Clerk Papers, Scottish Record Office, Edinburgh.
[3] Walker, *Commonplace-book of Andrew Melville*, pp. xl f.
[4] Grant, p. 374. The quotations are from Montrose Burgh Records.

Scotland—for in 1737, the same year as his appointment, he published a set of violin sonatas and dedicated them to the Edinburgh
Musical Society. Having thus brought his name to their notice, he
absconded from Aberdeen, and by June 1738 was on the payroll
of the Edinburgh Musical Society with a salary of £10. 10s. sterling
per annum.[1] Equivalent to 126 lib. Scots, this was nearly two-
thirds of his basic Aberdeen salary, with no duties attached
except turning up every Friday night to play violin in a scratch,
unrehearsed concert. He would thus have all his days free for
private teaching, and in Edinburgh his chances of obtaining private
pupils at large fees would be much better than in Aberdeen. It is
not surprising that most music schools in Scotland shut down
around this time, or were reduced to ordinary parish schools.
Musicians could earn a better living elsewhere.

EARLY CONCERTS: EDINBURGH

Public concerts in Edinburgh started in 1693. Most of the first
ones were put on largely for fun, in their spare time, by musicians
who already held positions in the existing music-school-and-
private-teaching network: there can have been no suspicion that
concerts were about to change the face of Scottish music completely.
The first known Edinburgh concert-series was run by Beck,
whom we have already met as music tutor to Balcarres House, and
some friends. It says much for Scottish attitudes to the arts that
the only reason why this series is recorded at all was that Beck
was prosecuted by the Master of Revels, one William McLean,
for not paying him a licence fee. The case came up before the Court
of Session on 10 January 1694, and caused some difficulty, as it was
without Scottish precedent; a decision had to be reached by analogy
with continental practice. The Master of Revels lost his case.[2]
The fact that the situation was unprecedented makes it very likely
that no public concerts had been given in Scotland before. It
was normal in England, however, for concerts to begin in mid-
November, so Beck's series had probably started two months
before, in November 1693.

[1] EMS minute-books (MS.), accounts, 1739.
[2] Lauder, p. 590; Chambers, *Domestic annals*, vol. 3, p. 89.

The grand concert on St. Cecilia's Day 1695 has already been described in Chapter 1.

A weekly series was given on Saturday afternoons between November 1699 and March 1700 in the house of William Badham, a dancing-master;[1] and the singer John Steill gave a concert, also in 1700, in St. Mary's Chapel in Niddry's Wynd.[2] Steill seems to have been successful as a concert-promoter, for further concerts of his are recorded in 1707[3] and 1711, by which time he had teamed up with Adam Craig (violin) and Henry Crumbden (harpsichord). Concerts run by Messrs. Steill, Craig, and Crumbden continued at St. Mary's Chapel throughout the 1710s.[4]

After 1719 Steill seems to have retired, and bought or inherited a tavern in the High Street, the 'Cross Keys'. His tavern was fashionable[5] and it was there that the Edinburgh Musical Society held their meetings in the 1720s. It is to the Edinburgh Musical Society that we must now turn our attention.

MUSICAL SOCIETIES: EDINBURGH

The Edinburgh Musical Society was formally constituted in 1728, but it had been in operation, under a variety of names, for many years previously. It seems to have started during the 1690s, for the programme of the concert held on St. Cecilia's Day 1695 has a signature at the foot, 'James Chrystie of Newhall, Preses':[6] 'Preses' was the ordinary term in use at the time for the president of a learned society. This is backed up by another piece of evidence; for there was also a St. Cecilia's Day concert in 1701, followed, according to this report, by an annual general meeting:

Edinburgh, November 22. This being *St. Cecilia's* Day the Society of Musicians of the Kingdom, Noblemen and Gentlemen met at the Skinners Hall, where they had an Excellent performance of Musick

---

[1] *Edinburgh Gazette*, weekly advertisements throughout the period; Dunbar, vol. 1, p. 14.

[2] From an untraced 'scrapbook of musical advertisements' in EPL, quoted in Willsher (MS.), vol. 2, p. 30.

[3] Mellerstain account-books, quoted above: 'To tickets for Steals consurt'.

[4] Transcription from St. Mary's Chapel session-books in Laing (MS.).

[5] Chambers, *Traditions*, 'Taverns of Old Times'.

[6] Tytler, p. 507.

of all kinds before a great number of Nobility and Gentry of both Sexes; And thereafter went to the Ship Tavern, where they had a Noble Entertainment, elected their Stewards for the ensuing year, and closed the day with Musick.[1]

So by 1701 a musical society was in existence which gave, at any rate, an annual concert on St. Cecilia's Day. In 1721 Allan Ramsay wrote an address 'To the Musick Club',[2] which especially mentions the members' liking for the works of Corelli. By this time the number of meetings had increased to one a week:

> Several gentlemen, performers on the harpsichord and violin . . . formed a weekly club at the Cross-keys tavern [*author's footnote:* Kept by one Steil, a great lover of musick, and a good singer of Scots songs], where the common entertainment consisted in playing the concertos and sonatas of Correlli, then just published; and the overtures of Handel.[3]

By 1727 the society had expanded to over sixty members and the 'Cross Keys' was becoming crowded, and in March 1727 the then Preses, Alexander Bayne of Rives, arranged for the meetings to be moved to St. Mary's Chapel, where Steill's concerts had been held ten years before. In March 1728 the society was formally constituted, and its minutes began to be recorded in a series of books which are now preserved in Edinburgh Public Library. It was still very much an amateur society at this stage, with a small annual financial turnover. During the 1726–7 season the treasurer took in sixty-one subscriptions of £1 (sterling) from members, and paid out three guineas each to three violinists 'Will: McGibbon, Adam Craig & Alex^r Stewart for performing last winter Session'.[4] Soon the society began to acquire solid assets: some members went to the auction sale of the property of Lord Colville of Ochiltree, who had died in March 1728, and bought his harpsichord for £4, and a selection of his music library for £8. 13s. 3d.[5] They also encouraged the violinist William McGibbon's efforts at composition by buying seven sets of parts of his first set of trio-sonatas, as soon as they were published

[1] *Edinburgh Gazette*, 21-24 November 1701.   [2] Published in *Poems*, vol. 1.
[3] Arnot, p. 379.   [4] EMS minute-books, accounts, 1727.
[5] Ibid., minute, 13 December 1728.

in 1729,[1] and ten copies of his second set in 1734. By 1736 the society's music library was becoming large and had been dispersed all over Edinburgh by members; Alexander Stewart was ordered to recall the volumes and draw up a catalogue.[2]

The society's concerts were held every Friday night at 6 p.m. They were divided into three parts (known as 'acts'), each including one piece for orchestra and one solo vocal item. At the end of each concert the committee got together and drew up the programme for the next week's:

> The Governour and Directors have Resolved that a plan be made by the Directors present at every Concert of Musick to be performed against the Concert the week thereafter, and that the plan name the person who is to play the Leading Fidle. But that it be left to Mr Benedetto to sing what songs he pleases himself.[3]

We see from this that members took turns at leading the band, though the singer was professional and engaged for the season.

Normally the concerts were quite unrehearsed, and indeed many of the programmes as drawn up leave scope for last-minute alterations. 'Overture by Lord Kellie' appears frequently in the society's programmes around 1770, implying that the exact choice of overture was not made until the concert began. 'Haydn's Overture in E♭ if the Bassoon is there if not the Overture in D' appears in the programme for 21 November 1783, and 'if Mr Butler comes an Alteration will be made' in the one for 30 December 1785.[4]

A number of times a year the society put on special concerts:

> Besides an extraordinary concert, in honour of St. Cecilia . . . there are usually performed, in the course of the year, two or three of Handel's oratorios. . . . An occasional concert is sometimes given upon the death of a governour or director.[5]

The society was especially fond of the oratorios and large choral works of Handel, and even wrote to Handel himself in December 1753 to ask for 'a Copy of the Recitatives and Choruses to some of his oratorios' to complete their library. For these special

---

[1] Ibid., accounts, 1730. This is the only evidence for the date of McGibbon's first set of trio-sonatas, as the title-page has no imprint.
[2] Ibid., minute, 28 January 1736.   [3] Ibid., minute, 3 July 1733.
[4] EMS plan-books (MS.).   [5] Arnot, p. 380.

performances a choir was got together and rehearsed in advance: the altos, tenors, and basses were drawn from the members of the society, and the trebles were imported from George Heriot's school.

So far the Edinburgh Musical Society had followed very much the pattern of similar societies in provincial parts of England. But by the mid century it began to be subject to peculiar social and financial pressures. The original idea of the society was that all members should be performers, either amateur or professional ('we the Members of the Musical Society held weekly in Marys Chappell in Niddry's Wynd . . . Agree to assemble our Selves weekly in the said place for the performance of Concerts of Musick'),[1] but things did not stay that way long. Non-performing members began to join the society in large numbers, and the meetings were infiltrated by gate-crashers and ladies. The directors attempted to restrict ladies to special nights, but were unsuccessful. The concerts started to be a fashionable place for meeting members of the opposite sex, to the great annoyance of lovers of Corelli and Handel. The tones of irritation come over well in the following extracts from the minute-books; the directors were clearly having a hard time keeping the situation under control:

Resolved that henceforth the Masters Shall meet at the Chappell a Quarter befor Six O Clock every Friday Night under the penaltys formerly agreed on.—And that the Same be recomended to the performing Members.—That their Shall be a Director appointed for the Night which Office the Directors shall take by turns who shall give the proper orders for the Night. That the time for beginning the Acts Shall be at Six O Clock a Quarter before Seven & a Quarter befor Eight to be Intimate by an Alarm on the Harpsicord which Every performer Shall obey Instantly—That one be appointed by the Director for the Night, to Sitt at the Door of the Orchestra to prevent any person comeing in there, Except Directors & performers. —That the Directors agree to restrict themselves to give only 3 Mens tickets Each Concert Night dureing the Session and 5 in time of Vacance. And that there shall be no more given unless signed by 3 Directors assembled—That after the 1st of December Nixt tickets shall be given to the Ladys in the ordinary Night not exceeding 80.

<hr />

[1] EMS minute-books, constitution, 29 March 1728.

That each member may Call for 3 tickets any time betwixt Nine and One o clock on friday to be answerd in their order till the Number is Compleat and if that after that hour there are tickets remaining undisposed of, the Same may be given to any member tho he may have already taken 3.—That the Treasurer prepair a proper advertisment to prevent Speaking in time of performance—That the Door keepers shall upon no Account call out a Director to the Door to admitt any person after the Company is mett.

It was found that the Master of Napier and Capt Halden (son of Coll: Halden) had come in to the Concert upon tickets which had been Erased and alter'd in the Date and not Designed for those Gentlemen nor for that Concert. Therefore the Directors Resolve that for the Space of one Year no tickets shall be given to either of the said Gentlemen.[1]

Edinburgh, as has been said before, was full of music-loving aristocracy, and the Musical Society was constitutionally limited to a membership of seventy. Later this was increased to 100. As a result, there was always a long waiting-list for admission; members were expelled promptly if they forgot to renew their subscriptions; and the committee were able to pick and choose from the highest in the land to fill any vacancies that occurred. The social tone of the society rose steadily, and the standard of performance at the concerts was forced to rise to match. The new members, and their female relations and friends, wanted not an amateur gut-scraping session but a worth-while evening's entertainment. To meet their demands the committee found themselves having to order the latest music from London and the Continent, to employ more and more professional stiffening for the orchestra, and to persuade really outstanding singers to come and live in Edinburgh. All of which cost money. Eventually the subscription had to be put up—to three guineas in 1758—but before that other means were explored of raising income:

The Governour . . . accquainted the meeting, that as the funds of the Society were small and a Great number of Masters on the Establishment it would therefore be necessary to incress the number of

---

[1] Ibid., minutes, 7 November 1749 and 26 January 1750. 'Dureing the Session' meant while the Court of Session was in progress.

Members. That as we had gott a Considerable Subscription for a new Room which must take place very soon, at which time we would be necessited to enlarge the number Considerably . . . we should Extend the number to 130 members.[1]

The 'Masters on the Establishment' at the time were:

	£	s	d
By Mr Passerini as one years Sallary in full to the 1st April 1752	130	—	—
By Mr Stewarts Do for 1½ years to 1st March	22	10	—
By Mr Mcphersons Do for 1½ years to Do	30	—	—
By Mr McGibbons Do for one year to Do	25	—	—
By Mr Pollani's Do for one year to 1st June	20	—	—
By Mr Marin's Do for one year to 1st March	5	5	—
By Mr Mcdougals Do in full to Do	7	7	—
By Mr Rochetti in full of his allowance from the Director	27	10	—
By Mr Jo. Mcdougal's allowance pr agreement for teaching	16	16	—
By Do in part of his Sallary	6	6	—[2]

Salaries that year cost £290. 14*s*.—a considerable difference from the £9. 9*s*. paid out to professional musicians in 1727.

Trying to pack more and more people into an already over-crowded building cannot have been fun. In 1753 the concerts moved out of St. Mary's into temporary accommodation in the Assembly Hall, while the musical society and the directors of the Assembly tried to reach an agreement about building a new hall jointly, to serve for both concerts and dances; but the scheme came to nothing.[3] The musical society then approached the Royal College of Physicians with proposals for building a hall jointly with them.[4] This too proved fruitless. Finally the musical society went ahead and built a hall on its own, at the bottom of Niddry's Wynd, twenty yards down the street from St. Mary's Chapel. It was opened at the end of December 1762, having been paid for by subscription; the aristocratic tone of the society by this date is shown

---

[1] EMS minute-books, minute, 10 June 1752.   [2] Ibid., accounts, 1752.
[3] Ibid., minute, 18 February 1755.
[4] Royal College of Physicians of Edinburgh minute-books, minute, 7 February 1758.

sufficiently in the fact that the subscription-list contains the names of twenty-one earls. Appropriately, it was named St. Cecilia's Hall.

The opening of St. Cecilia's Hall marks the beginning of the Edinburgh Musical Society's brief, but glorious, period of power. It had become, by gradual stages, modish and influential, the setter of standards of taste for the whole of Scotland, the centre around which aristocratic music-making revolved, as it had previously, two centuries earlier, revolved round the court. All worth-while private music teaching was now arranged during the course of its Friday night concerts: musicians coming to Edinburgh found it almost impossible to get upper-class pupils unless they were on the musical society's books:

The Salary here is nothing the character of belonging to the Musical Society Insures [musicians] of Bread directly . . . poor Pasquali who's merit was very well known Experienced this, he was Engaged to come from Dublin here by the managers of the play house and continued here for 6 or 8 months without any Scholler but no sooner did he apear in the Musical room then he had every hour Employed & continued so till his dying day.[1]

This meant that the society had taken over from the old music schools the function of employment exchange for private music teaching.

After 1762 the society had a London agent, the publisher Robert Bremner. The Deputy Governor from 1767 on was the Earl of Kelly, 'the first man of taste in the musical line, of any British subject', who was often acting Governor in the 1770s in Lord Haddington's absence. These two men were the most eminent and successful musicians that Scotland produced in the whole century —thoroughly European in outlook, at home in London, with no traces of provinciality in their dealings with the outside musical world—and with such informed administrators it is not surprising that the society prospered artistically.

By this time performers were being invited to come to Edinburgh, not merely from London, but from far-off places like Rome and St.

---

[1] EMS minute-books, copy of letter, 27 February 1759.

Petersburg; the concerts were featuring new symphonies and concertos written by composers resident in Edinburgh; the directors were engaged in constant squabbles with foreigners who could not understand that to legally minded Scots a contract was a contract, and an agreed-upon fee not the same thing as a preliminary offer;[1] and St. Cecilia's Hall was frequently 'crowded to excess by a splendid assemblage, including all the beauty and fashion of [the] city'.[2]

Unfortunately this state of affairs did not last. Successful classical music always tends to spend money faster than it earns it, and by 1776 the society's financial problems were becoming acute. Salaries to performers that year amounted to £641. 18s. 6d. (compared with £290. 14s. in 1752, and £9. 9s. in 1727). The management of the society had up till then been conducted on the assumption that more and more money could always be found for music: that increased expenditure would result in a higher quality of music being produced, which in turn would elicit increased public patronage. But the limit to which the public in Scotland was prepared to support classical music seems to have been reached by 1776. Arnot drew attention, three years later, to the musical society's 'strict oeconomy', and said that it was 'one of the most elegant . . . establishments, conducted upon the most modest expence, of any in Britain';[3] but though this was doubtless true (that is to say, that subscribers were getting good value for their money in relation to current prices) the fact remained that the society had overstepped the mark. Needless to say, it lived well up to its income, and had no margin of capital over to allow for mistakes. Various measures were put into operation to reduce expenditure—cutting professionals' salaries was the first—but after the mid 1770s the society never recovered its balance.[4]

Various social changes had a general adverse effect on classical music all over Britain at this time. The aristocracy rather suddenly became less willing to spend years and years learning to play instruments thoroughly, and town night-life extended further and further into the small hours, making concert-going seem rather a tame

[1] Gray, pp. 206–22.   [2] Chambers, *Traditions*, 'St. Cecilia's Hall'.
[3] Arnot, p. 381.   [4] Gray, pp. 236–42.

way of spending the evening.[1] During the 1780s and 1790s the musical society's income dropped rapidly, and it was eventually closed in 1798.

Concert-life in Edinburgh in the eighteenth century can thus be seen to have three distinct periods: (*a*) sixty years' expansion in the face of Scottish philistinism; (*b*) twenty years' flowering; (*c*) twenty years' decline due to changing social conditions. Though the middle period between 1760 and 1780 was so short, it has a precarious beauty about it, since it might quite easily not have happened at all had, for example, concerts taken eighty instead of sixty years to reach a flourishing state, or had the Industrial Revolution hit Scotland twenty years earlier than it did. As it was, Scotland enjoyed a brief musical renaissance. (It may be mentioned here that neither the Rebellion of 1715, nor that of 1745, seems to have had any effect whatsoever on the progress of classical music.)

I have described the rise and fall of the Edinburgh Musical Society in some detail, as it seems to me that it was the outstanding musical institution in the country, and the inspiration behind all other progressive musical activity of the period. Its concerts were planned within a yearly budget, subscriptions being paid in advance, so that the programme-planners could introduce new music to the members without worrying immediately about its 'commercial' aspects. The concerts were given by a mixture of amateurs and professionals, who could thus meet each other on equal terms; and opportunity was given for members to discuss and argue about music as well as play it. Concerts were places where ideas could be exchanged.

There were, of course, members who resisted being educated, like the gentleman whom George Thomson met at the Edinburgh Musical Society in about 1788, who said to him:

'Whase music is that, now?' 'Haydn's, sir', said I. 'Poor new-fangled stuff' he replied: 'I hope I shall never hear it again!'[2]

---

[1] Thom, vol. 2, p. 200.
[2] Chambers, *Traditions*, 'St. Cecilia's Hall'.

But George Thomson's own education undoubtedly profited enormously from his contact with the Edinburgh Musical Society; he continued to keep up with modern trends for some time even after it closed down. Thomson is remembered as the person who enlisted successively Pleyel, Kozeluch, Haydn, Beethoven, Weber, Hummel, and Henry Bishop to harmonize Scots folk-tunes; he was also an avid chamber-music player, and wrote to Beethoven in 1813 to say how impressed he had been by the first Rasoumovsky quartet:

> I lately spent some days in the country with a little select coterie of amateur friends, where among other things we performed your first Rasoumoffsky quatuor, and the quintuor in C. We repeated them every day with increased pleasure. . . . What an immortal theme, that adagio! . . . But alas! my friend, we have not in Scotland a dozen persons (professionals included) who could take a part in these quatuors, and not one who could play *correctly* the violino [primo] part of any of the three![1]

This was only five years after the quartet had been published; and when we consider the lukewarm reception that it met with at its first performance in Vienna, we see that Thomson's musical taste was advanced for his time. This almost certainly would not have been so had not his mind been opened to new music by his membership of the Edinburgh Musical Society in the 1780s and 1790s.

There were other concerts in Edinburgh than those run by the musical society. These were mostly 'benefit concerts', i.e. concerts put on by professional musicians as a private enterprise, with the prospect of large profits to themselves if a good audience turned up. But for various reasons such concerts were largely under the thumb of the musical society—partly because the musical society had a controlling interest in all the halls in town, partly because the musicians were felt to be first and foremost musical society employees, who had come to Edinburgh only by official invitation. The Edinburgh Musical Society was well aware of its power: on a number of occasions it 'allowed' a professional performer an extra benefit concert instead of a rise in salary, or as compensation for a cut in salary.

MUSICAL SOCIETIES: PROVINCIAL

There were musical societies in other Scottish towns, but they were all founded subsequently to the Edinburgh one and took their tone from it. Concert-giving seems to have spread slowly north and west from Edinburgh as the eighteenth century progressed. An Aberdeen Musical Society was founded in January 1748 by three professional musicians, Andrew Tait, master of the Aberdeen music school and organist of St. Paul's Episcopal Chapel, Francis Peacock, dancing-master, and David Young, music copyist, and by four amateurs. Its earliest regulations included

that a Plan be laid down every Night of the Musick to be perform'd at the next Meeting . . . that the Plan be . . . divided into three Acts, in each of which some of Corelli's Musick shall be performed: each Act also, if a Voice can be had, to end with a Song; and the whole so contrived as to end at Eight o'Clock at Night, and not to exceed two Hours in Continuance.[1]

This reads so similarly to the Edinburgh society's resolution of 3 July 1733 (quoted above), that there is little doubt what the Aberdeen society was modelling itself on. Like the Edinburgh society, it began its concerts at six in the evening; like the Edinburgh society, it built up a music library which members could borrow from for home use.[2] And when on 28 July 1750 'Lord Pittenweem, Mr Craig & Mr Dure (who are Members of the Musickal Society at Edinburgh)' arrived unexpectedly in Aberdeen, its officials ran round deferentially and organized a special concert for them; Andrew Tait himself called on the visitors the same day with free tickets.[3]

Interestingly, the social pressures which attacked the Edinburgh society around 1750 also made themselves felt in Aberdeen. The Aberdeen society started off, as the Edinburgh one had done, as an

---

[1] Aberdeen Musical Society minute-books, minute, 29 January 1748.
[2] Ibid., minute, 31 May 1771; cf. EMS minute-books, 28 January 1736.
[3] Aberdeen Musical Society minute-books, minute, 28 July 1750. Lord Pittenweem (later Earl of Kelly) was then aged seventeen.

essentially *performing* body; but in 1752, when it had barely been going four years, the non-performing members demanded rights of election on to the committee, and the whole character of the society was changed. After September 1753 every concert became a ladies' night, and overcrowding became a problem, as it had been in Edinburgh.[1] But despite such tendencies towards social exclusiveness and professionalism, the Aberdeen Musical Society remained subordinate to the Edinburgh one. Its annual subscription was always much less than Edinburgh's (5s. compared with two guineas, at one point in 1752), so it could hardly have afforded to pay the salaries of first-rate foreign performers, even if any had been found who were willing to go and live so far north. The relative status of the two societies is demonstrated by Alexander Udny of Udny, Aberdeenshire, who belonged to the Aberdeen society as his local establishment, but was also a member of the Edinburgh society, as the national one.

The other Scottish musical societies are badly documented, and no minute-books or other records of them are known to survive. Concerts were given in Glasgow from the mid 1740s, though a musical society as such was not founded until as late as 1799.[2] There was a musical society in Dundee by 1757, which, like the Edinburgh and Aberdeen societies, had its own music library.[3] Falkirk had concerts in 1775; a visitor to the town wrote that he had been 'admitted to a Monthly concert held at the Inn. The performers are gentlemen of the town and neighbourhood, most of them indifferent.'[4] There were probably concerts in Peterhead in the 1770s and 80s during the months of July and August, since many upper-class families migrated there for the summer from Aberdeen.[5] There were also concerts in Forfar in 1792, and in Greenock in 1793,[6] while we know that Perth had a musical society in the 1790s from the title-page of a collection of dance music published at that time.[7] There were probably concerts in

---

[1] Farmer, *Music making*, pp. 31–4.
[2] Farmer, *Concerts in 18th century Scotland*, pp. 107–9; Marr, p. xxx.
[3] Ibid., p. ix. [4] Neville, entry for 3 October 1775.
[5] Beattie, pp. 15–16. [6] Sadie (MS.), p. 72.
[7] John Clark's *Collection of New Strathspey Reels and Country Dances . . . dedicated to the Musical Society of Perth* (Perth, c. 1795).

several other Scottish towns during the last twenty years of the eighteenth century: Stirling, Dunfermline, Montrose, and Dumfries seem likely places, but so far no evidence has come to light.

THEATRES: EDINBURGH

The theatre in Edinburgh had a musical tradition which was quite separate from the Edinburgh Musical Society.

Drama seems to have been active in Edinburgh from the 1680s onwards, though it was frowned upon, and periodically closed down, by the church. After about 1730 the theatre in Edinburgh was obliged to maintain a standing orchestra, so it thus provided a certain amount of stimulus to the musical life of the town.

The resident orchestra was made necessary by a piece of bureaucratic hypocrisy. With the passing of the Censorship Act of 1737 it became illegal to perform plays except in a building licensed as a theatre. Edinburgh had no licensed theatre at the time, and no prospect of obtaining one without a special act of Parliament—an elaborate and costly business: so the matter was shelved for thirty years until 1767, when the theatre patent was slipped through Parliament with the bill authorizing the construction of Edinburgh New Town. Meanwhile the theatre proprietors got round the law by advertising their plays as *concerts*, in the following manner:

We hear that on Monday the 21st [February 1743], at the Taylors Hall, Cowgate, at the Desire of several Ladies of Distinction, will be performed a Concert of Vocal and Instrumental MUSICK. After which will be given gratis, *Richard the Third*, containing several historical Passages. To which will be added gratis, *The Mock Lawyer*. Tickets for the concert (on which are printed a new Device called the *Apology* and *Evasion*) to be had at the Exchange and John's Coffee Houses.[1]

Indeed the Canongate Theatre, which was in use from 1747 till 1769, was known officially through most of its life as 'the Canongate Concert Hall'. In such circumstances a resident band was clearly essential to the company.

The exact size of the band can be worked out by circumstantial evidence. In December 1733 the Edinburgh theatre company

---

[1] *Caledonian Mercury*, 17 February 1743.

performed the '*Tempest*; or, *Inchanted Island*, with all the musick, sinkings, risings, new scenes, and other decorations proper for the performance'. Nine months later, in August 1734, the company visited Dundee with 'hautboys and other musick'.[1] Purcell's incidental music to Shadwell's version of Shakespeare is scored for oboe and strings, so between them these two notices would imply a band of not less than 2 oboes, 4 violins, 1 viola, and 1 cello, if one assumed that two players would be required on each violin part.

During the 1757–8 season the band came out on strike against West Digges, the manager of the Edinburgh theatre, after he had tried to discharge the leading violinist, to whom he owed arrears of salary. A heated public argument followed, in which both sides circulated printed leaflets to put forward their point of view. One of the leaflets happens to give the names of all the members of the band at the time; there were eight of them: Mr. [James] Marine (leader), Mr. [John] Reoch, Mr. [John] Thomson, Mr. [John] Smeitton, Mr. [Philip] Kercher, and Messrs. Napier, Stewart, and Muggersland. It is not specified who played what instrument. The leaflet also gives their rates of pay: between 2*s*. and 5*s*. a night.[2]

For opera productions the band situation seems to have been somewhat different. Advertisements for opera in Edinburgh regularly announce that 'the Orchestra will be enlarged' for the occasion, and a harpsichord added.[3] (This is interesting, as it shows that a harpsichord was by no means a standard item in an eighteenth-century orchestra.) In 1772 Robert Fergusson published a retrospective poem about the Canongate Theatre before its closure in 1769; his description of the music clearly refers to these opera productions with 'enlarged' band:

> Here shepherds, lolling in their woven bow'rs
> In dull *recitativo* often sung
> Their loves, accompanied with clangor strong
> From horns, from trumpets, clarinets, bassoons;
> From violinos sharp, or droning bass,
> Or the brisk tinkling of a harpsichord.[4]

[1] Dibdin, pp. 43–5.   [2] Ibid., pp. 97–9.   [3] Ibid., pp. 65, 120, 125.
[4] Fergusson, vol. 2, p. 59: 'The Canongate Play-house in Ruins'

The only other Edinburgh theatre band-lists I have seen are early nineteenth-century ones, commencing with the opening of the New Theatre Royal in 1810.[1] By that time there were twelve regular musicians in the band, and in 1817 their instruments were as follows: 4 violins, 2 horns, and 1 each of flute, oboe, clarinet doubling viola, bassoon, cello, and double bass—that is, two players each on first and second violin, and one on each other part.

It cannot be said that the Edinburgh theatre did as much for classical music as could have been hoped. It was too chancy, too dependent for its success on the individual efforts of a few managers and star performers, to provide the solid continuity which classical music seems to need in order to flourish. Seasons of opera were short, and occurred at irregular intervals. English opera, apart from *The Beggar's Opera* and *The Gentle Shepherd*, was first given in Edinburgh in 1751, and Italian opera reached Scotland in 1763, when there was a whole season of it at the Canongate Theatre. But Edinburgh never reached the point at which it could support operas written by its own resident composers: with a few possible exceptions. Lampe's *Dragon of Wantley* was performed in Edinburgh six times in 1751, while Lampe was resident; but the piece had become famous in London years earlier, before Lampe moved north. Allan Ramsay's Scots ballad opera *The Gentle Shepherd* was performed many times in the course of the century; its music, however, consisted entirely of arrangements of folk-songs, so it hardly counts as classical music at all. Andrew Shirrefs's *Jamie and Bess*, performed three times in Edinburgh in 1796, is a direct imitation of *The Gentle Shepherd* and comes into the same category. On the other hand, there was a 'whimsical Farce' called *The Enraged Musician; or, the Tempest Rehearsed*, written and acted by Pasquali, based on Hogarth's print, which was given in the Canongate theatre on 2 February 1753. It was advertised as 'the first time of Signor Pasquali's attempting to speak on any stage',[2] and there is a strong likelihood that it contained pieces of specially composed music; if so, it would be the first home-grown Scottish opera ever. There was also a mysterious *Britannia Triumphant; or, the*

---

[1] Dibdin, pp. 500 f.   [2] Ibid., p. 73.

Spanish Disappointment, given at the Theatre Royal, Edinburgh, on
21 March 1778, which is said to have had music by Alexander Dasti,
a composer and violinist who lived in Glasgow and Aberdeen.[1]
Certainly no dramatic piece of that name was staged in London,[2]
so it is likely that it was written locally. If so, it and Pasquali's
Enraged Musician are the only known examples of eighteenth-
century operas composed specially for the Scottish stage.

It is strange that the Earl of Kelly never wrote opera, since he
was friendly with the opera-singer Tenducci and with the actor
Samuel Foote. Kelly's concert overtures were played extensively
as preludes to other people's operas in England as well as Scotland,
and two of them were nicknamed 'The Maid of the Mill' and
'Ezio' after the London productions in which they had been used.
He also wrote a Hasse-like concert aria for Tenducci to sing; it
would seem that he had all the necessary talents for the genre.

There were theatres in Glasgow, Dundee, and Aberdeen in the
eighteenth century, but they seem to have been run mainly as
sidelines by the various Edinburgh companies, and so are of little
importance in themselves.[3]

ASSEMBLIES: EDINBURGH

The Edinburgh Assembly, or aristocratic dancing-club, met
regularly on Thursday evenings during the winter season from
1723 on. It provided a further, if minor, platform for classical
music. It had a band, which in 1746 consisted of four violins (John
Reoch, James Cameron, John Wilson, Robert Hutton), two oboes
(Thomas Robertson, Charles Calder), and one bassoon (John
Thomson).[1] The lack of a harpsichord is again noticeable, probably
for reasons of space as much as expense—the dances were always

---

[1] Farmer states this, with no supporting evidence, in *History of music*, p. 306. But
he quotes the title of the piece inaccurately, and in the same sentence ascribes Shield's
Siege of Gibraltar to Urbani, and Dibdin's *Wives Revenged* to Corri. He also dates the
Edinburgh performance of *The Siege of Gibraltar* wrongly (1785 instead of 1783).
His statements cannot be relied upon too heavily.

[2] It is not listed in Nicoll.

[3] Dibdin, pp. 118, 182; Kennedy, vol. 2, p. 279. This section of the chapter
is indebted to Armstrong (MS.), who gives a complete catalogue of Edinburgh
theatrical productions from 1715 to 1820.

[4] Jamieson, p. 49.

packed tight. What music was played at the Edinburgh Assembly earlier in the century is not known; but in the 1760s Lord Kelly was writing minuets and dedicating them to the young ladies of fashion who frequented the dances. That these minuets were actually played at the Assembly is made clear by their subsequent wide manuscript circulation; those that survive in score are mostly laid out for two clarinets, 1st and 2nd violins, and bass, sometimes with an additional two horns in E flat. This, apart from the horns, would fit the band listed above, provided that the violins were used two to each part—as in the theatre orchestra—and that the oboes could double as clarinets.

Daniel Dow followed Kelly's example in minuet-writing. His pieces are only known to survive in keyboard reductions,[1] but the predominance of the key of E flat makes it likely that he composed originally, like Kelly, for a band with B flat clarinets and E flat horns.

Assemblies spread north and west from Edinburgh to other towns in a pattern similar to the spread of concerts. Dancing became an immensely popular national pastime in the 1770s. But hardly any composition of classical dance music took place outside Edinburgh, though a vast number of reels and strathspeys in the folk style were written by local composers.

CONCLUSION

Classical music in eighteenth-century Scotland is thus seen to have had four main branches—upper-class home music-making, concerts, theatre-music, and dance music; to have been strongly centred on Edinburgh; to have improved in quality and quantity in Edinburgh up to 1780; and to have attempted, with some success, to spread to other towns.

But despite the undoubted improvements in Scottish musical life during the eighteenth century, certain signs of poverty, of a precariously balanced economy, of the community counting its pennies and trying to get as much music for as little money as

[1] *Twenty Minuets . . . for the Violin, Harpsichord or German Flute* (Edinburgh, *c.* 1770).

possible, continue. The eight members of the Edinburgh theatre band in 1757–8, listed above, overlap by four with the ten professionals employed that season by the Musical Society, and even by two with the seven members of the Assembly band of 1746, so that one gets the impression of a very few professional musicians, overworked, underpaid, rushing round Edinburgh from one job to the next with no time for practice or relaxation. These are not the circumstances which favour composition; the aspirant composer needs leisure, as well as stimulus from contact with other people's music. How composition fared in Scotland during this period we shall see in the next chapter.

3

MUSICIANS

WHEN we turn from the study of music as a culture to the study of musicians as individuals, we are struck by a paradox: the best native Scottish musicians left Scotland as soon as they could and did not return, while the best musicians working in Scotland were immigrants who had come from elsewhere.

On the face of it, it would have seemed simpler if they had all stayed put where they were, instead of moving around. The movement was, in fact, quite complex: the Scottish musicians who emigrated all went to London, but the immigrants were drawn not only from London but also from the north of England, Germany, and Italy; it was not a direct exchange with another country but an interchange which involved Scotland with the rest of Europe.

Nor did the native Scots musicians who stayed in Scotland remain in one place. Charles Scheniman, Robert McIntosh, and Alexander Campbell, all of whom worked in Edinburgh in the 1780s, came from Banff, Tullymet (Perthshire), and Callander (Perthshire) respectively, while John Fergus, organist in Glasgow at the time, came from Huntly (Aberdeenshire).[1] So there would seem to be within Scotland itself a drift of musicians from country areas into the big towns, especially into Edinburgh.

Scottish people tend to be depressed by the thought of rural depopulation and emigration. There is a feeling that if only foreigners wouldn't come to Scotland, it wouldn't be necessary for the natives to leave in order to find work, and that this situation is all the foreigners' fault. So I should state that this kind of migration, at least as far as classical music is concerned, is perfectly normal and indeed healthy. Classical music flourishes in cultural

---

[1] Farmer, *History of music*, pp. 272–3; Baptie.

centres and is common to the whole of Europe; so it is obviously sensible for a musician brought up in a small village to move to his country's artistic capital as soon as possible, and for musicians from one cultural centre to migrate to others from time to time, to find out whether the art is practised there with unaccustomed refinements which would be worth learning.

There are further advantages in moving to a new place. Willingness to uproot oneself is itself the mark of an ambitious, opportunist person; but a newcomer to a place tends also to discover opportunities which the established inhabitant overlooks. An outstanding example of this in eighteenth-century Scotland is given by Johann Friedrich Lampe. Lampe arrived in Edinburgh with a small opera company on 5 November 1750, and during the nine months between then and his premature death on 25 July 1751, he put on the first season ever of English opera, and started open-air concerts in Heriot's Gardens.[1] Anyone in Edinburgh could have taken this initiative—but they left it to Lampe, who came from Dublin and sized up the possibilities of the place with a fresh eye.

It should thus have been to the general advantage that some Scottish musicians should emigrate from Scotland, and others immigrate to take their places. But in actual fact Scotland gained considerably on the deal; both the quality and the quantity of the musicians coming into Scotland were far higher than of those going out. This meant that Scotland was in the strange position of being prepared to support more classical music than she was capable of producing—not the usual definition of an 'unmusical' country, but nevertheless a true one; since conversely a 'musical' country is one which produces more music than it is capable of supporting, and so has a surplus of trained musicians. Scotland had a deficiency of trained musicians.

The reason for this is quite clear: the almost complete lack of music teaching in Scottish schools. That Scottish people are not inherently unmusical is shown by the abundance and excellence of their folk music. But the only sections of the community which received a classical music education in eighteenth-century Scotland were (a) children of musical upper-class families, who had private

[1] Harris, pp. 265–7.

tutors, and who became the next generation of patrons; (*b*) children of professional musicians, who got their education at home; and (*c*) any pupils at music schools which were not defunct at the time.

It might have been expected that Scottish schools would have succeeded, at least, in teaching all school-children to sing the twelve authorized Scottish metrical-psalm tunes. These were morally uplifting (therefore commendable from an official point of view) and technically easy; the reader may remember that church music was one of the elementary parts of McLean's curriculum in Aberdeen in 1737. Louis de France, who came to Edinburgh in 1684 in search of work, clearly thought that teaching psalm-singing to children was an exercise which school governing boards would be prepared to pay for. He wrote to the magistrates of Edinburgh, as governors of Heriot's School, that he was 'readie and willing' to

instruct the scholars in the grounds of musick, and the four parts of the psalmes, at least a competent number that may be fitt and able to attend the severall precenters in the churches of Edinburgh, to assist and bear up the true melodie in the four parts of the psalmes to the praise of God . . .[1]

Many years later, in 1762, Robert Bremner suggested that ten minutes of school time a day in parish schools should be given over to teaching church music from staff notation.[2] But such attempts were in the long run a dismal failure, and this can be shown by the fact that nearly all the top church music posts in eighteenth-century Scotland were held by Englishmen, that is to say, that even church music was not taught well enough to propagate itself without continual outside assistance. Andrew Tait, organist at St. Paul's, Aberdeen, up to the mid 1770s, was a Scot; but his two successors, Robert Barber and John Ross, both came from Newcastle. Stephen Clarke, organist at the New Episcopal Chapel, Edinburgh, when it opened in 1771, came from Durham, as did Cornforth Gilson, whom Edinburgh town council employed to teach church music in the city in 1756. Glasgow town council had, the previous year, fetched Thomas Moore up from Manchester for

---

[1] Maidment, vol. 2, p. 263.   [2] Bremner, *Rudiments*, 2nd edn., p. xv.

the same purpose. The organist at the Episcopal church in Dundee in 1760 was Dr. Heighington, an Englishman who originally came from Durham. The north of England seems to have produced a surplus of church musicians at this time, which Scotland absorbed.

If even church music was in such a sorry state, it is hardly surprising that classical music also needed massive assistance from immigrants. When we investigate who the individuals were that made important contributions to the Scottish classical music scene at the time, we find that most of them were indeed immigrants from England and the Continent; that the best of them were not prepared to spend the rest of their lives in Scotland, but returned to more favourable climates after about ten years; that, in consequence, few of them died on Scottish soil; that many were composers; and that those who did stay longer than ten years in Scotland tended to deteriorate into second-rate musicians.

FRANCESCO BARSANTI was born in Lucca in about 1690. He went to London in 1714, where he supported himself playing flute and oboe; later he published sonatas for flute and for recorder. In 1735 he migrated to Edinburgh, and stayed there for some years. He wrote his best compositions in Edinburgh: twelve concerti grossi were published in 1742, and nine overtures followed probably a year later. The concerti grossi are particularly fine; six are set for two horns, timpani, and strings, the other six for two oboes, trumpet, timpani, and strings, and all are distinguished by closely argued, brilliantly effective, contrapuntal writing. But Barsanti eventually tired of Scotland, and decided to go back to London; in 1743 he sold a pair of timpani to the Edinburgh Musical Society, presumably to pay the expenses of removal. But by this time he had lost his place in London musical life. He failed to regain it, and is said to have ended his days in poverty.[1]

NICOLO PASQUALI was born in 1718; he went to London in about 1743. From there he moved to Dublin and then to Edinburgh, arriving in Edinburgh in the autumn of 1752.[2] Pasquali was young

---

[1] Hawkins, vol. 5, p. 372; EMS minute-books, accounts, 1735–43.

[2] Burney, vol. 4, p. 672; EMS minute-books, copy of letter, 27 February 1759.

and energetic. He played violin in both the Canongate Theatre and Edinburgh Musical Society orchestras; he wrote and acted in a 'whimsical Farce' called *The Enraged Musician* in 1753; he wrote an 'Overture Stabat Mater' and two cantatas 'Tweedside' and 'Vineyard';[1] he composed minuets which passed into general circulation among folk-fiddlers round the country;[2] and he had published a set of twelve overtures before he left London. Pasquali's chief claim to fame, however, was a figured-bass instruction book, *Thoroughbass made easy*, published in Edinburgh in 1757, which became the standard textbook on the subject. A sequel, *The art of fingering the harpsichord*, was ready for the press by the autumn of 1757; but Pasquali died, very suddenly, on 13 October, leaving Bremner to bring the book out posthumously. Pasquali's brilliant career was thus cut off before he reached forty.

ROBERT BARBER, an organist and composer from Newcastle, went to Aberdeen in 1774 to take charge of the music at St. Paul's Episcopal Chapel.[3] He seems to have had a successful and interesting time in Aberdeen, for a harpsichord concerto of his is known to have been performed on 3 April 1778, and a month later two more of his compositions were done, 'a Harpsichord Trio, on a new Octave and pedaled Harpsichord' and an 'Organ Concerto, with the favourite Air of "Come, live with me, &c" made into a Rondo'.[4] He also kept in touch, from Aberdeen, with various London music publishers. Nevertheless he, like Barsanti, had had enough of Scotland after about eight years. His successor, JOHN ROSS, was aged just twenty at the time of his appointment, and was, like Barber, a native of Newcastle. According to one account,[5] Ross was 'called to' the post, and 'recommended to the managers of St. Paul's Chapel' by his teacher in Newcastle, Matthias Hawdon. Reading between the lines, one suspects that it was actually Barber who arranged for this bright, unknown young man from back home to take over the job, in order to escape from Aberdeen himself. Ross was a less ambitious person, and much more the kind

---

[1] Listed in EMS library catalogue, 1765 (MS.).
[2] A minuet of Pasquali's is recorded in NLS MSS. 808 and 3346.
[3] Aberdeen Musical Society minute-books, minute, 5 November 1774.
[4] *Aberdeen Journal*, 30 March, 8 May 1778.
[5] Joseph Robertson's, printed in Laing, p. lxxix.

of organist the chapel wanted. He settled down comfortably and married Jean Tait, the niece of Andrew Tait, Barber's predecessor,[1] and when he retired in 1836, fifty-three years later, the minister of the chapel presented him with 'a splendid edition of Bagster's large Bible'. Ironically, Ross's career as a composer was far more successful than Barber's, at least financially; but Barber did produce one fine work after he left Aberdeen, which he would probably not have written if he had stayed, and which goes far beyond the scope of any of Ross's compositions. This is *Thomson's Hymn to the Seasons*, published in London in 1788, a cantata in about twenty movements for choir, solo singers, and orchestra with obbligato wind, horns, timpani, and organ. It is basically in Handelian style but with some modern traits; one wonders whether Haydn could have heard it during his London visit of 1791.

JOHANN GEORG CHRISTOFF SCHETKY was a prime example of the shrewd and ambitious foreign immigrant. Born in Darmstadt, he came to Edinburgh on 28 February 1772;[2] he was then thirty-two, with an already established European reputation. He became overnight the best cellist in Scotland, and the second best composer—the other composer being the Earl of Kelly. He had been engaged for the Edinburgh Musical Society by Robert Bremner, whom he met accidentally the previous year while giving a concert in Lisle. He had not wanted the job but, being unable to find work in London, had accepted it *faute de mieux*.[3] Once in Edinburgh, he set about improving his position, and during the next five years published his ops. 1–6 with Bremner in London—six string trios,[4] six duets for violin and cello, six piano trios, six cello sonatas, six

---

[1] According to Robertson, Mrs. John Ross was Andrew Tait's *daughter*. But Smith, p. 212, shows that there was a Jean Tait baptized at St. Paul's Chapel on 18 August 1760 (probably the same person whom John Ross married, also in St. Paul's, on 12 December, 1787) whose father was *Charles* Tait. *Andrew* Tait was, however, a witness at the baptism, so he may well have been another relative, perhaps uncle; this would explain Robertson's mistake.

[2] *Edinburgh Evening Courant*, 29 February 1772.

[3] S. F. L. Schetky, p. 8; EMS minute-books, copy of letter, 7 February 1772.

[4] Schetky's op. 1 is undated, but can be shown to have been published by 1773 from an item in the EMS accounts for that year: 'To Mr Schetky for Six Setts of his Trios £3. 3/-'. The advertised price on the printed copy is 7s. 6d., which does not tally, since one-sixth of £3. 3s. is 10s. 6d. Perhaps Schetky persuaded the musical society to take his trios at a special patrons' rate. His op. 6 is dated 1777.

flute duets, and six string quartets. One would have expected a man of this calibre to have stayed in Scotland only a few years, and then to have pushed off in search of fresh pastures. Instead, the unexpected ha ppened. Almost the first friend Schetky made in Edinburgh was Joseph Reinagle, the state trumpeter, a musician of Austrian extraction whose eldest four children were Alexander, Maria Theresa, Joseph, and Hugh. In January 1774 he married Maria Theresa, who was then aged about sixteen, at the Episcopal Chapel. They had eleven children.[1] Schetky presumably could not face moving from Edinburgh with a large young family, and by the time his family had grown up, his wife had died, and he was fifty-five and too old to start again in a new place. So he stayed in Edinburgh until his death, at the age of eighty-five, in 1824. He continued to compose until late in life (in 1808 he set two songs from Walter Scott's *The Lady of the Lake*), but as far as one can tell, the quality of his compositions deteriorated fairly rapidly after the string quartets op. 6. The quartets try out octave doublings between various instruments, and contain passages of harmonic experiment in the manner of Haydn and Dittersdorf: though severely cramped by the technical limitations of the Edinburgh amateurs he was writing for, Schetky's European background is still very much in evidence at this date. But by the 1780s he had succumbed to turning out facile drawing-room music in the British style. It cannot be said that his continued residence in Edinburgh did him much good. He also wrote overtures and cello concertos in Edinburgh during the 1780s,[2] which may have been of higher quality; but as they have not survived, it is impossible to tell.

DOMENICO CORRI is another example of an ambitious foreigner. He arrived in Edinburgh, from Rome, on 25 August 1772, with a wife whom he seems to have married specially in order to secure the post which the musical society offered.[3] During the 1770s he wrote operas for London as well as fulfilling his engagements in Edinburgh. He started various publishing exploits in Edinburgh and then, leaving other people to tidy up the mess behind him, moved to London permanently, having stayed in Scotland, off

[1] S. F. L. Schetky, p. 10. [2] EMS plan-books (MS.).
[3] Corri; EMS minute-books, minute, 7 May 1771, accounts, 1773.

and on, about fifteen years. In London he went into publishing
again, this time in partnership with J. L. Dussek, to whom he
married his sixteen-year-old daughter, doubtless in order to cement
their business relationship. The firm later went bankrupt. Corri
seems to have thrived on arranged marriages and imminent
financial disaster, for he lived to the ripe old age of seventy-nine,
and at sixty-four wrote an immensely cheerful and rather inaccurate
account of his own life. His younger brother NATALE CORRI
followed him to Edinburgh some time before 1784. Natale, however,
lacked Domenico's flair, and it is indicative of his less energetic
personality that he was content to stay in Edinburgh for the next
thirty-six years, almost until his death. Natale ran the Corri Concert Rooms in the Theatre Royal from 1803 on, but they did not
prosper, and he told Sir Walter Scott gloomily one day that 'if
I became a baker people would give up using bread'.[1]

Another foreigner who stayed in Scotland too long was
GIROLAMO STABILINI. He came to Edinburgh from Rome in
1783, at the age of twenty-one, and was recognized at once as an
outstanding violinist and composer. On 14 May 1784 he performed
his own violin concerto in D at a musical society concert; a fortnight later a sinfonia concertante of his was done; and after that he
appeared at St. Cecilia's Hall playing solos almost every week.[2]
Only two of his concertos have survived, in E and A, and even then
only in the piano quartet arrangements which the composer published in the late 1790s; but their strong main themes mark them
out as fine works, though one can have no idea of the original
scoring. Stabilini's most famous concerto is not extant; it had a
rondo finale based on the Scots tune 'We'll gang nae mair to yon
town'. Stabilini performed it 'with great applause' during his
lifetime, and after his death it was revived and played to George
IV, when he visited Edinburgh in 1822.[3] Clearly, Stabilini had
achieved everything Scotland could offer him within a few years
of his arrival in the country, and he should at that point have moved
on. Stabilini spoiled his career, not, like Schetky, by getting married,
but by taking to drink. As a result he became incapable of taking

---

[1] Lockhart, vol. 7, p. 145.   [2] EMS plan-books.
[3] Stenhouse, no. 478; Harris, p. 92.

any initiative with regard to further migration. He died 'much broken down by dissipation' in Edinburgh in 1815.[1]

So much for immigrant musicians, who had the advantage of arriving in Scotland already fully trained in their art. How did native Scottish musicians fare, in view of the poor opportunities for musical education which Scotland had to offer?

It must be admitted that the outstandingly successful native Scots of the period were all music *publishers*—that is, they were artists in big business and legal intrigue with music as a sideline. James Oswald and Robert Bremner made good in London, while Neil Stewart, James Johnson, and John Hamilton were the backbone of music publishing in Edinburgh. It is hard to tell, in the absence of eighteenth-century gramophone recordings, how Scottish execu- tant musicians compared with foreign ones. The foreign performers were more in the limelight in Edinburgh, but there were certainly good native performers too—the singer William Thomson, for instance, who was a great success at the court of George I in the 1720s.[2] William McGibbon must also have been an outstanding violinist if he could play his own variations on Scots folk-tunes. But as composers of classical music, the native Scots were mainly woefully inadequate.

Some of the amateurs received training in composition abroad, but had no time to compose after returning to Scotland because of other commitments. JOHN CLERK of PENICUIK, whom we have already met, is a good example: he had thrice-weekly lessons in composition and violin from no less a person than Corelli, in Rome, between September 1697 and December 1698.[3] His work during this period shows great promise, and one of the pieces he wrote then, a solo cantata 'Odo di mesto intorno' for soprano, two violins, and continuo, is noted as having been 'made by me at the Duke of Bedfoords desaire. The poesie was made by one of his servants an Italian, & performed by Correlli, & other musitians befor his grace & many of the Roman nobility'.[4] On return to Scotland Clerk's

---

[1] Chambers, *Traditions*, 'St. Cecilia's Hall'.   [2] Burney, vol. 4, p. 647.
[3] Clerk, p. 28 n.
[4] Manuscript in Clerk Papers, Scottish Record Office, Edinburgh.

time was taken up by getting married, being called to the Bar, becoming member of Parliament for Wigton, managing the Penicuik estate, and bringing up a family; the few pieces he composed subsequently are all short, and show retrogression from Italian classical to Scots folk style.

DAVID FOULIS was born near Edinburgh in 1710. He studied medicine at Leyden in Holland in the early 1730s and probably picked up some musical training there at the same time. He succeeded better as a composer than Clerk, through having no children, and being a professional man rather than a landowner. He became a Fellow of the Royal College of Physicians of Edinburgh in 1737, and was physician to George Heriot's school from 1741.[1] He belonged to the Edinburgh Musical Society from 1737 until 1753. He published six violin sonatas in about 1770 which, though marred by technical defects (such as frequent consecutive octaves between the violin and bass), have a freshness and tunefulness which show that he was by no means untalented.

General JOHN REID is another interesting amateur composer of the period. He was born at Straloch, Perthshire, in 1721. Of his opportunities for studying music nothing is known: he read law at Edinburgh University around 1740, and went into the army in 1745.[2] He was basically a flautist who composed for his instrument —his works comprise two sets of six flute sonatas, about twenty minuets, and about twenty marches.[3] It is likely that he had help with the harmonization—at least—of the sonatas, probably from James Oswald.[4] Reid's marches are definitely tinged with Scottish folk style: 'March for the 70th Regiment' owes a lot to the tune 'Corn riggs', while 'March for the 76th Regiment' has melodic shapes in common with 'The last time I came o'er the moor'.

---

[1] Innes-Smith, p. 88; Foulis Papers, EPL, family tree.
[2] Tullibardine, pp. 391 f.
[3] A description of Reid's flute-playing is given in Cockburn, p. 81.
[4] The second set (1762?), by 'I. R. Esq.', are reattributed in a later edition (*c.* 1775) to 'J. Oswald'. Oswald died in 1769, so it would seem that the reattribution was made by Reid himself as a confession of how large a part Oswald had had in the composition of the pieces. Both Oswald and Reid belonged to 'The Temple of Apollo', a secret society made up of musical London Scots: one of the activities of this society was writing music under other people's names. See Kidson, *James Oswald*.

His 'Highland March' ('In the garb of old Gaul'), dedicated to his own regiment, the 42nd, is justly famed; it was one of the best tunes written in the century.

The native professional composers were generally at a disadvantage to the native amateurs, since they came from a lower social class, had received fewer years of formal education, and had even less free time to spare for writing music outside their other occupations. WILLIAM MCGIBBON came from a musical family, for his father, Malcolm McGibbon, was a professional oboist in Edinburgh, and he studied violin and composition in London with William Corbett.[1] But what is known of his music is disappointing; he seems incapable of writing counterpoint which is also good harmony, and vice versa, and one's over-all impression is of a talent undeveloped through simply not having done the requisite amount of hard work.[2]

The early education of CHARLES MCLEAN, McGibbon's younger contemporary, is unknown. His father may have been William McLean, the Master of Revels in Edinburgh in the 1690s,[3] in which case he would have received at any rate as good a musical education as Scotland could provide. His twelve sonatas op. 1 are technically uneven, not to say erratic, but show a lively mind and one capable of responding to all sorts of different influences: the twelve sonatas are by no means identical, either in form or style. No other sizeable compositions of McLean's are known to exist.

JAMES OSWALD's background is quite unknown. He was a man with more flair than either McGibbon or McLean—he was in turn dancing-master, singer, composer, and publisher—and he rarely bit off more than he could chew. He published some minuets and a sonata in Edinburgh in 1736;[4] nothing can be said of their quality, as no copies are extant. But he also wrote Scots tunes in the folk

---

[1] Tytler, p. 510 n. Tytler gives McGibbon's father's Christian name as *Matthew* by misreading the abbreviation 'Mal.' as 'Mat.'.

[2] This is certainly true of the second set of trio-sonatas of 1734. The flute duos of 1748 are more fluent but duller. McGibbon's other recorded compositions—twelve further trio-sonatas, six violin sonatas, three concertos, and an overture—are lost, or extant only in part. Their recovery might, of course, alter this assessment considerably.

[3] Farmer suggests this in *History of music*, p. 331.   [4] Laing, pp. xlviii f.

style, which were very successful; by the time he left Edinburgh for London in 1741, it was a standing joke all over town that certain tunes recently become popular, which had been presented to the public as 'by David Rizzio', were actually Oswald's own work.[1] Oswald did well in London as a publisher of popular music; he was good at gauging what the public wanted. The sonatas of his own that he brought out in London are, if charming rather than adventurous, at any rate thoroughly competent, and it is probable that he overhauled his composition technique drastically to suit London standards after he arrived there. He is certainly in a different class from the other Scots composers of the period.

Oswald knew his limitations; but there were other Scottish musicians who had no conception of their provinciality compared with London standards. An example of this is ROBERT McINTOSH, a red-headed, bad-tempered violinist and composer from Perthshire, who habitually gave offence to people he came in contact with. He lived in Edinburgh from 1773 (or earlier) to 1785, and from 1788 to 1803,[2] and spent the intervening years in Aberdeen. His op. 1, brought out in 1783 and containing a solo violin sonata and pieces for theatre band, shows him to have had old-fashioned taste and been proud of the fact. The sonata is like decadent Corelli, while the airs for band are full of Handelian 9–8 suspensions, many of them suspended in mid air as a result of being incorrectly prepared. He also wrote at least one concerto, and a 'Solo in the manner of a Rondeau, with harmonic tones' for violin, which he performed at a concert in Aberdeen in 1786.[3] His music is efficient in its own way, but out of touch with the contemporary developments that really mattered. He went to London in 1804 and died there, having met with no success, in 1807.

ANDREW SHIRREFS is an even sadder case. He came from a well-to-do Aberdeen business family and seems to have had no idea of the qualities necessary for success in the arts. He took an M.A. degree at Marischal College in 1783, and then dabbled in journalism and bookselling. He wrote both words and music of a

---

[1] *Scots Magazine*, October 1741, 'An Epistle to James Oswald'.
[2] *Edinburgh Directory*; *Caledonian Mercury*, 13 December 1788.
[3] *Aberdeen Journal*, 27 February 1786.

ballad opera, *Jamie and Bess,* which was staged in Edinburgh in
1796. Of the music to it, only the overture is original, the other
numbers being arrangements of folk-songs, and it is quite the
worst piece of music to reach publication in the century. Shirrefs
went to London in 1798 to make his fortune and was not heard of
again. He is thought to have died there in penury in 1801.[1]

The brothers ALEXANDER and JOSEPH REINAGLE were
different again: they were second-generation immigrants, and were
brought up in Edinburgh, where their father was state trumpeter.
Alexander had been born in Portsmouth in 1756, Joseph probably
in Edinburgh in 1762. They spent their formative years being
taught a selection of instruments by their father, and by Schetky,
who became their brother-in-law in 1774. By the early 1780s
Alexander had several published compositions to his name and was
playing harpsichord concertos regularly at the Edinburgh Musical
Society concerts, while Joseph had become leading violin in the
band at the Theatre Royal. But in 1784 both left Edinburgh, never
to return: Alexander went to the United States, where he founded
opera-houses in New York and Philadelphia; Joseph made a career
for himself as a cellist in Oxford. A third brother, HUGH
REINAGLE, promised great things as a cellist, but died of
consumption in 1786, aged twenty-one.[2]

Assuming that a musician was resident in Edinburgh or Aberdeen,
and technically capable of writing classical music, what incentives
were there for him to do so? As one can see by examining catalogues
of contemporary libraries,[3] the classical music played in Scotland
in the eighteenth century had nearly all been composed elsewhere,
and imported. Composers were thin on the ground in Edinburgh
up to 1770, and in Aberdeen throughout the century. Edward
Topham, who visited Edinburgh in 1775, wrote that there were
'very few Composers of modern Music, notwithstanding the great
encouragement it meets with',[4] but he was not quite right. In
fact the number of composers per head of population changed

---

[1] Walker, *Bards of Bon-Accord,* pp. 300 f.
[2] Krohn; Sainsbury, 'Reinagle, Joseph'; EMS plan-books.
[3] e.g. those given in Appendix I and II. [4] Topham, p. 373.

fairly abruptly in Edinburgh from low, in 1760, to rather high, in 1780, and these two situations must now be considered separately.

Up to about 1770 in Edinburgh, and later in Aberdeen, there was no particular demand for home-composed classical music, and no significant amount of money to be made out of it. Enlightened interest was, however, taken in the few composers active in the community, and modest patronage was extended to them all indiscriminately—foreign or native, competent or incompetent. The Edinburgh Musical Society purchased, in turn, McGibbon's trio-sonatas of 1729 and 1734, Oswald's minuets of 1736, Barsanti's concerti grossi of 1742 and overtures of *c.* 1743, and Pasquali's overtures of 1751; and they possessed manuscript parts of three unpublished concertos and an overture by McGibbon. Provided one was prepared to take the trouble to get one's friends to subscribe for copies, it was even quite easy to have one's compositions published: the subscription-lists of McGibbon's trio-sonatas of 1734, of McLean's solo sonatas of 1737, and of Barsanti's concerti of 1742, show who in the community was prepared to pay up.

It is interesting to see that the Barsanti subscription-list contains the names of a number of private individuals who could have had little practical use for a set of orchestral parts. Most contemporary Scottish performances of Barsanti's concerti grossi would have taken place at the Edinburgh Musical Society's concerts by special arrangement: the 'concertino' group would be played by the two oboists from the theatre and the state trumpeter, with the composer on kettle-drums, while the 'ripieno' would be rendered by the gentlemen amateurs. They were probably not very good performances, even by eighteenth-century standards. To Barsanti as composer, then, Edinburgh in the 1740s had such incentives to offer as: local kudos, warm personal appreciation, indifferent performances, publication (with luck), and no money— and all these were to be shared on equal terms with inferior composers like McGibbon. One thing strongly in favour of Edinburgh musical life at this time, however, was that as no large sums of money were involved, composers were not discouraged from writing difficult, 'uncommercial' works, and so artistic standards could be quite high.

After 1770, however, there was much more money to be made out of classical music in Edinburgh, and far more composers were trying to make it.[1] The atmosphere became competitive and ruthless, and the better-trained composers won. The different musical genres became arranged into a sort of hierarchy, with quality music at one end, and commercially profitable music at the other, as follows:

1. Opera
2. Oratorio
3. Works for orchestra alone
4. Works for orchestra and soloist
5. Chamber music for strings
6. Chamber music for keyboard and optional strings
7. Drawing-room songs and flute duets
8. Easy solo keyboard music: dance tunes, folk-song variations, and exercises for beginners.

Composers began to be influenced strongly by financial considerations; to a much greater extent than hitherto, they wrote what they thought would sell.

Opera, as we have already seen in Chapter 2, never got properly started in Edinburgh at all. Only one home-composed oratorio is known to have been performed in Edinburgh during the period; this was Domenico Corri's *Betulia Liberata*, a setting of an English translation of Metastasio, which the musical society sponsored and performed on 11 February 1774. They do not seem to have paid Corri directly to write the work, but they made sacrifices on its behalf—they paid Corri's brother to copy it out and forwent their usual performance of Handel.[2]

As to orchestral music, only Kelly's and Schetky's was performed at Edinburgh concerts in the 1770s, as far as I can tell: the Edinburgh Musical Society had become snooty, and would not

---

[1] I have collected information on forty-five composers of classical music originating from or resident in Scotland during the eighteenth century: of these, over two-thirds worked in the last third of the century. Scotland therefore had, relatively, four times as many composers after 1767 as before it.

[2] *Edinburgh Evening Courant*, 12, 26 February, 1774; EMS minute-books, accounts, 1774.

F

listen to just anybody's compositions. It is not known which other
Edinburgh composers were writing orchestral pieces at the time—
John Addison, Charles Scheniman, and Stephen Clarke possibly,
John Collet and Robert McIntosh almost definitely—but the
musical society seems to have neglected them completely.[1]
During the 1780s Butler and Stabilini joined the ranks of the
privileged few whom the society accepted. And publication was
remote by this date, even for them. None of Schetky's orchestral
music reached print, nor did at least half of Kelly's, and the works
are now lost as a result; while Stabilini's violin concertos were
published as piano quartets, that is to say, they were demoted in
terms of the table above from grade 4 to grade 6. The Edinburgh
presses were fully occupied in printing music in the lucrative
grades 6–8, and had no time for music in the uncommercial grades
3–5. London presses were not much better. It is unlikely, for
example, that Barsanti would have managed to get his concerti
grossi published at all if he had lived in Edinburgh in 1782 instead
of in 1742.

As to the commercial music at the bottom of the scale, it was
a free fight, open to anyone interested in making money, to see
who could write the most effective trash. Domenico Corri and
Schetky did well at this, as did John Ross, but perhaps first prize
should go to Thomas Butler, whose *Favourite Rondo for the Piano
Forte* on the tune 'Lewie Gordon', in the style of early-Beethoven-
and-syrup, went through no fewer than nine editions between 1785
and 1800.

Many composers were unsuccessful. A common pattern at the
time was for a young composer to bring out an adventurous opus
1 at his own expense, and then, having lost as much money as he
could afford, either to give up composing altogether or to turn to
commercial grades. Natale Corri's piano and violin sonatas op. 1

[1] But the evidence is incomplete. The EMS plan-books are not extant for the
years 1772–7, so there is a gap covering the whole of Collet's residence in Edinburgh;
also some entries are ambiguous, e.g. 'Harps^d Concerto Mr Scheniman' (16 January
1778) could conceivably mean that Scheniman was the composer of the piece as
well as the player. But it is significant that the EMS did not bother to purchase
Collet's Six symphonies op. 2 (London, 1764) when Collet became an EMS employee
in 1772. Twenty years earlier they had purchased Pasquali's Twelve overtures as
soon as Pasquali arrived in town.

(*c.* 1790), John Ross's piano concertos op. 1 and songs for voice and orchestra op. 2 (*c.* 1790), Alexander Campbell's *Twelve Songs* (*c.* 1790), and William Clarke's piano and violin sonatas op. 1 (1802) all show promise which was never fulfilled. The commercial grades of music which some of them ended up writing gave them little scope—Mozart, J. S. Bach, and Bartók each managed to write masterpieces for beginners at the keyboard, but such talent is unusual. But worse than this was the fact that the whole tradition had silted up. By this time no music of worth-while quality was being written anywhere in the country, nor possibly could be written in the circumstances. And once the musical societies closed down, there were no platforms left for uncommercial new music, even by the most talented of the resident composers.

By the end of the eighteenth century Scottish classical music had choked itself to death. The composers left or died, and by 1830 there was hardly one to be seen anywhere in the country.

4

THE EARL OF KELLY

THE way of life of a composer in eighteenth-century Scotland was a badly defined track studded with pitfalls and traps. As we have seen in Chapter 3, many composers set out along it and few reached the end intact. Foreign immigrant composers had their inspiration dry up through lack of stimulus; native professional composers were too hardworked playing and teaching to fulfil themselves; and native amateurs were sidetracked (looking at it from a musical point of view) into marriage and non-musical careers. Between 1760 and 1780 the environment improved for composers, and society responded by suddenly producing far more of them than before; but the change was only temporary, and after 1780 the situation deteriorated again, leaving the community full of unwanted composers, and with a general atmosphere of despondency and failure.

It is thus with some relief that we turn to the one Scottish composer who, in these unpromising circumstances, succeeded— namely, Thomas Alexander Erskine, Lord Pittenweem, Viscount Fenton, sixth Earl of Kelly. Though Kelly's music went out of fashion soon after his death and has not been successfully revived since, there is no doubt as to the high esteem in which his contemporaries held it. His music was played extensively in England and even gained some popularity on the Continent. Charles Burney wrote in 1789:

The late Earl of Kelly was possessed of more musical science than any dilettante with whom I was ever acquainted. . . . Indeed, he had a strength of hand on the violin, and a genius for composition, with which few professors are gifted.[1]

[1] Burney, vol. 4, p. 677.

The *Gentleman's Magazine* was equally warm. (I should point out, by the way, that this was a London periodical with no Scottish nationalist bias.)

His lordship was one of the first musical composers of the age, and esteemed by the cognoscenti as the first man of taste in the musical line, of any British subject, and ranked all over Europe in the first musical form.[1]

Why Kelly succeeded where everyone else in Scotland failed is an intriguing question.

Kelly's working life, to begin with, coincided exactly with Edinburgh's flourishing period of 1760–80. Kelly returned to Scotland from continental travels in 1756, and his first set of symphonies was published in Edinburgh in 1761. He died in 1781. He was fortunate in living at exactly the right time in history, but this may not be complete coincidence: the brief renaissance was largely due to the efforts of the Edinburgh Musical Society, especially as regards the building of St. Cecilia's Hall in 1762, which contributed enormously to classical music's morale and social prestige. Kelly was on the musical society committee from 1757, and must have been its youngest, most energetic, and best informed member. The architect of St. Cecilia's Hall, Robert Mylne, was also a young man, and had been a class-mate of Kelly's at the Edinburgh High School.[2] This fact is suggestive. Is it too much to suppose that Kelly, by his work on the musical society committee, helped to create the conditions in which he could survive as a composer?

His peculiar personal character also contributed to his success. The typical eighteenth-century gentleman led a fancy-free, irresponsible existence into his early twenties, and then settled down to carry the burden of the *status quo*; the social pressures on him to do this were particularly strong if, like Kelly, he was the eldest son of a landowning family. Any creative musical talent that he might have generally died at this point, as with Sir John Clerk, whose career I have outlined in Chapter 3; and to act any differently

---

[1] October 1781, obituary notice.   [2] Farmer, *Kellie.*

called for considerable resistance to public opinion. Kelly, who was descended from two eccentrics, his father the fifth Earl, and his maternal grandfather the poet Archibald Pitcairn, had such resistance in abundance. The accepted upper-class careers of the day were politics, the army, and law (or any combination of these); followed by the acquisition of land if there were none in the family already, marriage, and the breeding of an heir to inherit the estate. All these things Kelly systematically rejected. Politics was closed to him because of his family's known Jacobite sympathies. The army was virtually impossible for the same reason. (Both Kelly's younger brothers went into the army—Andrew came out again promptly, but Archibald stayed in for twenty-six years, during which time he rose only to the rank of major, the Jacobite stigma having prevented further promotion.)[1] He was not well enough educated to go into law, and this was partly his own fault, as he could probably have gone to university instead of doing the Grand Tour if he had wished. He inherited his father's estate, but sold it all off except the castle and a few fields, and lived a life of pleasure in Edinburgh and London on the proceeds. He did not marry, though there is no reason to suppose his life was celibate. He is not known to have had any children.

He was unique and unmistakable. He cracked outrageous puns in a loud voice with a Fife accent in the best eating-places in Edinburgh;[2] he consorted with people of the theatre long after the permitted age of twenty-five, and actually seems to have enjoyed their company, unlike most gentlemen, who only cultivated actors because it was the fashionable thing to do.[3] He wrote minuets for the Edinburgh debutante types, but not all his relationships with such girls were formal:

We had a splendid ball at the Abbey of Holyroodhouse. . . . Lord K— danced with Miss C—, by the fire of whose eyes, his melodious lordship's heart is at present in a state of combustion. Such is the declaration which he makes in loud whispers many a time and oft.[4]

[1] Gleig.
[2] Mackenzie, pp. 81, 176–8; for the Kelly family's Fife accent see Boswell, *London Journal*, entry for 1 January 1763.
[3] Farmer, *Kellie*, anecdote about the actor Samuel Foote and the cucumbers.
[4] Erskine, letter of 22 January 1762.

Even at concerts his behaviour drew attention to itself:

In the midst of a turbulent and tumultuous movement of a symphony in twelve or fourteen parts, if any instrument failed either in time or tune, though playing a different and difficult part himself, he instantly prompted the erroneous performer with his voice, by singing his part without abandoning his own.[1]

And strangely, society accepted him on his own terms. James Boswell's reactions to him are worth noting. To Boswell in 1764 Kelly was a *bête noire*, a figure alternately repulsive and fascinating, a boor who should have been ostracized for his uncultivated manners and whose social success was inexplicable and frightening. Boswell was eight years Kelly's junior, the best friend of Kelly's brother Andrew, and rather desperately trying to win a place in society himself:

Madame . . . bid me by all means avoid being impolite. I asked her if I had been really so sometimes. She said 'It must be admitted that sometimes you have been extremely rude'. I explained to her how it proceeded from a flow of vivacious humour. But that will not do. Lord Kellie has the same. Let me then be master of myself.[2]

By the 1770s Kelly was one of the acknowledged leaders of Edinburgh society. Topham's description of Edinburgh in 1774–5 includes a section on Kelly the composer, but we hear first of all of Kelly the socialite. Topham was served haggis at a dinner and, when he expressed his dislike of it, was reprimanded and told that it had been 'applauded to the skies by my Lord Kelly, and other knights of the trencher'.[3]

In effect, Kelly was prolonging his youth into middle age. Amateur composers tended to write only as young men, and then to give up composing under pressure of other work. Kelly's urge to compose was so strong that it led him to shirk normal adult responsibilities and to strike out on a path of his own, in which composition and other youthful, pre-settled-down habits were

[1] Rees, *Kelly*.
[2] Boswell, *Grand Tour*, entry for 16 September 1764; and see p. 84 n. 4.
[3] Topham, p. 157.

preserved. Edinburgh in the 1770s was a good place for such a person. The town was already full of intellectual eccentrics (including several Court of Session judges), and music was in vogue and highly respected. As a result, society accepted him with open arms. Nevertheless, Kelly's life cannot have been entirely happy. He drank heavily. It seems likely that the stresses and strains inherent in pursuing an eccentric way of life had a detrimental effect, finally, on his mind. His brother Andrew, who was an excellent poet and in some ways similar to Kelly in character, finally committed suicide by drowning himself in the Firth of Forth. It is certain anyhow that Kelly's way of life affected his physical constitution. By 1780 his health was ruined. He went abroad to Spa, but the treatment was unsuccessful and he died in Brussels on the way back. He was then aged just forty-nine.

Kelly's education is known in some detail. He was born at the family seat, Kellie Castle, Fife, on 1 September 1732, and it seems probable that Samuel Thom, the family chaplain, gave him his first lessons on the violin. He was known as 'fiddler Tam' in Pittenweem, the nearby fishing-burgh where the Kellys had a town house. Later he spent two years at the Edinburgh High School, but his formal education was brought to a halt by Bonnie Prince Charlie, who, the month before Tam's thirteenth birthday, set up his standard at Glenfinnan in Moidart, and reduced Scotland to a state of chaos. Tam's father, the fifth earl, came out on the Jacobite side; he was the only gentleman in Fife to do so. The fifth earl had 'a merry temper which never deserted him', and was regarded as being not altogether right in the head. He tried to raise a regiment for the prince, but could only get together four men—himself, his manservant, his chaplain, and an old lieutenant-colonel. After the Rebellion failed, he was imprisoned in Edinburgh Castle awaiting trial for treason, while the countess ran round buying up incriminating documents and encouraging the story that the fifth earl was insane. Finally the Government decided to take no further action against him, and he was released in 1749.[1]

What Tam did during these years is not known. He probably lived in Edinburgh, but he did not go back to school, or on to

[1] Wood, pp. 262–3; Howie; Farmer, *Kellie.*

university. There is an interesting minute in the Edinburgh Musical Society minute-books for 27 December 1748:

As there are some Young Gentlemen who are Performers and thereby useful to the Society, The Treasurer is hereby Authorized to Sign a Ticket for each of them (to serve for themselves only) which Ticket shall continue in force till the eleventh day of June next.

Tam was at the time sixteen and a half, an aristocrat, and played the violin, so he may well have been one of the 'Young Gentlemen who are Performers' intended; if so, this minute records his first contact with orchestral music. By June 1750 he was a full member of the Edinburgh Musical Society;[1] and the following month he visited the Aberdeen Musical Society in the company of two other Edinburgh members, Mr. Craig and Mr. Dewar. His early education was therefore adequate as far as music was concerned, and deficient in just about everything else.

In about 1753 he went abroad on the Grand Tour, and furthered his musical education with Johann Stamitz:

According to Pinto, before he travelled into Germany, [he] could scarcely tune his fiddle, [but he] shut himself up at Manheim with the elder Stamitz, and studied composition and practised the violin with such serious application, that, at his return to England [*sic*!], there was no part of theoretical or practical Music, in which he was not equally versed with the greatest professors of his time.[2]

Kelly returned to Scotland in 1756, an ardent convert to Mannheim orchestral music: indeed he was the first British composer to write in the Mannheim style. His father had died while he was away, and he was now sixth earl. The novelty of his compositions soon attracted attention. Bremner brought out his Six Overtures op. 1 in Edinburgh in 1761, and reissued them in London a year later. His music began to be played extensively in theatres: a 'grand overture' of Kelly's was used for the Edinburgh production of Carbonini's *Il Giocatore* on 27 June 1763;[3] a 'concerto' was played

---

[1] EMS minute-books, membership list, 13 June 1750: 'Lord pittenweem'.

[2] Burney, vol. 4, p. 677. Thomas Pinto did not come to Edinburgh until 1771, so this estimate of Kelly's fiddle playing as a teenager is at least third-hand, and may well be quite inaccurate.

[3] Dibdin, p. 126.

before *Tartuffe* at Kassel on 26 October 1764;[1] *Ezio*, a pasticcio given at the Haymarket Theatre, London, on 24 November 1764 had a Kelly overture,[2] as did Samuel Arnold's *Maid of the Mill*, which opened at Covent Garden on 31 January 1765. Doubtless many more examples like this could be found. Furthermore, the Mannheim style caught on rapidly: by the mid 1760s several other British composers—Thomas Norris, James Hook, John Collet—were writing in it. An interesting collection of orchestral music, containing many pieces in the Mannheim style, was put together in 1770 for Henry Dashwood Esq. by Welcker of London,[3] and shows how far Mannheim music had become accepted in Britain by that date. Kelly was recognized as the native British leader of the movement.

The Edinburgh Musical Society made him Deputy Governor in 1767, which, with his aristocratic connections, put him into a position of considerable power and prestige. He used his influence to obtain the post of state trumpeter for Joseph Reinagle.[4] He conferred with Abel in London about the advisability of engaging Schetky for the musical society.[5] It was probably through him that John Collet, whose Six Symphonies op. 2 were dedicated to Kelly, came to Edinburgh in 1772.[6] And in 1774 he was invited to write minuets for one of the most splendid social gatherings of the century —the five-day-long *fête champêtre* which Lord Stanley held at his country seat, The Oaks, near Epsom, Surrey, to celebrate his marriage to the daughter of the Duke of Hamilton.[7] Kelly's extremely high personal social status continued to the end of his life.

[1] Boswell, *Grand Tour*, entry for 26 October 1764: 'At six I went to the *comedie*. On entering the house I was surprised to hear the *orchestre* play one of Lord Kellie's concertos. They, however, played it very ill. The pretty, slow parts they made a country dance of. The piece was *Tartuffe*, and pretty well performed.'

[2] An unknown, non-extant 'Overture in Ezio' appears many times in the EMS plan-books, e.g. on 5 May 1769. This is the only *Ezio* production I can find which fits the dates.

[3] Now in the Bodleian Library, Oxford, Mus.221.c.57. See also Cudworth, *English Symphonists*.

[4] Sainsbury, 'Reinagle, Joseph'.

[5] EMS minute-books, copy of letter, 11 February 1772.

[6] Ibid., accounts, 1772.

[7] A detailed description of the *fête champêtre* is given in F. J. Hudleston, *Gentleman Johnny Burgoyne* (New York, 1927), p. 234.

Kelly's achievement as a composer is difficult to assess exactly, as a large part of his work is not extant. No original manuscripts have survived: indeed we have hardly any specimens of his hand-writing at all except a few signatures in the Edinburgh Musical Society minute-books. Our knowledge of Kelly's music is restricted almost entirely to what reached print during his lifetime, and this selection may well be unrepresentative. It is at most a half, more likely only a sixth, of his total output: it contains none of his wind-band music, and nothing of major importance written after the age of thirty-five. Thus the last fourteen years of Kelly's life are un-accounted for, though there is evidence (discussed below) that he continued to compose steadily through the 1770s, and that this later music was performed and enjoyed, in Edinburgh at least.

It seems strange that Kelly did not have his later music published. Possibly it was more conservative in style than his earlier music, and not as attractive a proposition to a publisher, but this is hardly an adequate explanation; Kelly knew all the right people in the country, and for an old friend like Robert Bremner to turn down anything Kelly sent him would have been unthinkable—especially since Bremner accepted six opuses of Schetky's at this time. The reason must have been Kelly's own negligence. The earl saw no reason to behave like a professional composer; he had a reputation for carelessness with his manuscripts:

> Whenever he met with a good band of wind instruments, he was seized with a fit of composition, and wrote pieces in the moment, which he gave away to the performers, and never saw again; and these, in his own judgement, were the best he ever composed.[1]

Another piece of youthful irresponsibility, with tragic results this time; for the missing manuscripts have not reappeared yet, nor have those of (I would estimate) ten or fifteen symphonies in his most mature style.

What remains of his music, however, shows him to have been the genuine article, a composer with real exploratory urges: not merely a follower of fashion, and certainly not an amateur dabbler. The important part of his extant work was all written within about

[1] Robertson, p. 436.

ten years (*c.* 1757–67), yet it falls into three distinct periods; also, Kelly's development was unusual, that is to say, the periods do not come in the order one might expect.

Kelly began as a pure orchestral composer, who conceived his music in coloured masses of sound. The themes in his early works are mostly formulas, and when he does write an individual tune (in the finale of the overture op. 1 no. 2, for instance) he seems not to know how to harmonize it properly: the important things are the texture, the timbre, the dynamic contrasts, the 'sound', rather than the outline. His violin parts are full of tremolo and crashing chords, and his horns are high and blaring. His wind section is limited to two oboes and two horns in these early works, but he has a way of using violas as a functional wind part (that is, having them play in passages which would otherwise be wind solos) which suggests that he would have liked more wind instruments. These materialize in the later works ('The Maid of the Mill' overture: 2 oboes, 2 horns, 1 bassoon; *Periodical overture no. 17*: 2 flutes, 2 clarinets, 2 horns, 1 bassoon). The style is pure Mannheim, and Kelly's dependence on Johann Stamitz is shown by the fact that the first twenty-two bars of his op. 1 no. 4 are lifted direct from Stamitz's op. 4 no. 6.

Kelly's early works are by no means all revivable: most of them contain at least one bad movement, and the slow movements are generally too long for what they have to say. But at his best (for example, the first movements of op. 1 no. 2 and op. 1 no. 4; the finale of *Periodical overture no. 25*) Kelly achieves an excitement and sense of pace which put even Stamitz in the shade. It was this which appealed to Thomas Robertson, a contemporary of Kelly's, who wrote:

> In his works the *fervidum ingenium* of his country bursts forth; and elegance is mingled with fire. . . . While others please and amuse, it is his province to rouse, and almost overset his hearers. Loudness, rapidity, enthusiasm, announce the Earl of Kelly . . .[1]

The works that fall into Kelly's early period are the *Six Overtures op. 1*, no. 4 of *Six simphonies in four parts by J. Stamitz, his pupil*

[1] Page 436. It is curious that Robertson regards Kelly's Mannheim style as a Scottish national characteristic.

the *Earl of Kelly, and others*,[1] and *The periodical overture nos. 13 and 25*.[2]

The next period is represented by *The periodical overture no. 28* ('The Maid of the Mill'). Kelly has by this time added considerably to his technical range. The first movement is, for the first time, in sonata form with a fully worked-out development section. The slow movement has soft wind holding-chords (learnt from J. C. Bach) and individual melodies with a popular English flavour (learnt from Arne):[3]

[1] It is difficult to tell on internal evidence who wrote which of the *Six symphonies*. No. 4 is, however, ascribed to Kelly in two early nineteenth-century sources, a set of parts which the Royal Artillery Band, Woolwich, owned in 1811, and C. K. Sharpe's *Minuets &c. Composed by . . . Kelly* of 1836. See Farmer, 'Royal Artillery concerts', and *History of music*, p. 335.

[*See overleaf for notes 2 and 3*

Kelly's third period is marked by his discovery of counterpoint as a new means of expression. His counterpoint often looks academically naïve on paper, as though he had never had any lessons in how to do it, but it sounds remarkably good to the ear. The important aspect of it is the rhythmic imitation, which creates a quite new kind of dramatic forward movement. In the following passage, from the finale of *Periodical overture no. 17*, the bass instruments imitate the rhythm of the first violins: bars 4 and 8 of the example have, as a result, a most original phrasing effect which could have been arrived at in no other way:

In the first movement of *Periodical overture no. 17* there is a wind passage where the clarinets imitate each other's rhythms in a

---

² *The periodical overture in 8 parts* was a regular series put out monthly by Bremner, consisting of new British overtures and recent continental ones. Kelly was one of the composers featured, along with the Stamitzes and Haydn. Musical societies probably subscribed for the whole series in advance.

³ Editorial additions and emendations are not shown in these musical examples.

somewhat similar way. The clarinet parts could almost be by Corelli, though the wind-blend and the idiosyncratic, beautiful vertical spacing of the chords give the passage a modern sound:

Around this time Kelly also wrote a minuet for a Miss McLeod which is strikingly unusual: it is canonic. The contrapuntal imitation is even more surprising for coming in a piece written primarily to be danced to:[1]

[1] This is an editorial reconstruction from a piano arrangement in J. Clarkson's *Complete collection of much admired tunes* (Edinburgh, *c.* 1800). Ascription to Kelly is also editorial, but is supported by position in the book as well as by style.

While the fourth of his six trio-sonatas of 1769 has the following elegant imitative opening:

These examples should be enough to show that Kelly's counterpoint was no academic throwback but a stylistic development arising from creative necessity. With the counterpoint came an interest in chamber music, a medium which he had neglected up to that time. Kelly published six trio-sonatas in 1769 and also wrote some string quartets which are not extant. The trio-sonatas are disappointing as a whole, but contain some passages of great beauty; the movement I have just quoted above also has a short section in fragmentary texture, where the harpsichord is temporarily dropped out of the ensemble. This kind of line-drawing is far removed from Kelly's orchestral style of ten years earlier (for the sake of clarity I have realized the harpsichord part in this example):

But at this exciting point in the story the extant works suddenly peter out, so we have no means of telling how Kelly's style developed subsequently. Topham wrote in 1775 that Kelly's 'talents and genius' had been 'corrupted and restrained by his poorly copying the compositions of other masters . . . [and by] too close an observance of the Italian manner'. He preferred Kelly's earlier compositions where

his proper genius has broke forth, where his imagination heated by wine, and his mind unfettered by example, has indulged itself in all its native freedom.[1]

But the Edinburgh Musical Society continued to play new compositions of Kelly's through the 1770s, so it is to their records that we must now turn for information about Kelly's lost works.

[1] p. 374. Topham, like Robertson, regards Kelly's Mannheimisms as something characteristically Scottish.

The musical society's library catalogue for 1782[1] gives the following list under 'Kelly':

no. of copies					Horns
4	Kelly's	6 overtures—op: 1st × 20 × 21 × 22			26
	Dos —	overture—No 1---	30	31	
———		———— 2---	—		
———	Symphony---	3---	—	—	
———		———— 5---	31	39	
———	Concerto ——	6---	—	—	
———	Sinfonia ——	7---	—	—	
———		———— 8---	—	—	
———		———10---	—	—	
———		———11---	39		
———		———12---	39		
———		———13---	—		
———		———14---	—		

The first entry refers to four printed sets of the Six Overtures op. 1, and the shelves, or cupboards, where the different parts of the sets were kept. The other entries refer to works in manuscript, presumably under Kelly's own numbering system. They form a series, from which nos. 4 and 9 are missing. Perhaps nos. 4 and 9 were unsatisfactory works which Kelly had withdrawn, or for some reason he kept the parts of these works at his home in Bell's Wynd rather than in the library at the hall in Niddry's Wynd. But it is difficult to make any more sense of the list. 'Overture', 'Symphony', 'Concerto', and 'Sinfonia' were fairly interchangeable terms at this date, and it is probable that some of this series of fourteen orchestral works were printed, and are the overtures that we already know about. But many of them must be works which are now lost.

The Kelly entries in the Edinburgh Musical Society plan-books are more illuminating. They are too numerous to be given here in full: Kelly's works were played at St. Cecilia's Hall at a rate of about one per fortnight during his lifetime. Entries of particular interest, however, are:

[1] The 1765 catalogue contains a duplicate list.

15 April 1768	Quatuor Lord Kellie
6 May 1768	Quatuor Lord Kelly No 11
26 August 1768	New song Sig^r Tenducci by Ld Kelly
3 February 1769	Quatuor Lord Kellie
10 March 1769	Overture Lord Kellie manuscript
5 May 1769	Overture in Ezzie by L. Kellie
2 March 1770	Overture in Ezio Ld Kelly
„	Written Overt of Ld Kellie
15 February 1771	New Overture Lord Kellie
9 August 1771	over. the Maid of the Mill
„	Quartto. Lord Kelly
15 November 1771	Concerto Lord Kelly with Clarinitt[s]
22 November 1771	Dead March By the Earl of Kelly With French horns and kettle-drums
13 December 1771	MSS. Overture by Lo/ Kelly with Clarinett solos
30 April 1779	Overture in Ezio Lord Kelly
7 April 1780	Concerto Lord Kelly wt Clarinets
5 May 1780	Ouverture Lo/ Kelly—Tenore oblig°
21 December 1781	Funerall Concert for Lord Kelly

'Quatuor No 11' suggests that Kelly wrote, around 1768, two sets of six string quartets. The 'Overture in Ezio' was probably written for the London pasticcio of that name in 1764. The 'New song [sung by] Tenducci' was probably an aria 'Death is now my only Treasure' subsequently published in *A Collection of favourite airs in score sung . . . by Tenducci* (London, *c.* 1775). 'Concerto wt Clarinets' might be a description of *Periodical overture no. 17*, and 'Ouverture—Tenore oblig°' (i.e. with obbligato parts for violas) might be any of the overtures op. 1, but it is at least as likely that they were new works using, and developing, the same kinds of instrumentation. The 'New Overture' of 15 February 1771 had certainly only just been written. (This can be proved from the way that phrase is used elsewhere in the programmes; the plan-books also list a number of unknown Schetky orchestral works, distinguished as 'new overtures' and 'last overtures'—'last' meaning Schetky's most recent piece but one which, nevertheless, had been in circulation for some months.)

The 'Dead March' opened a funeral concert given in honour of

Sir Robert Murray. This concert had a printed programme, a copy of which is inserted in the manuscript plan-book. There is an accompanying manuscript draft programme, however, which gives the first item of the concert as 'Dead March in *Saul*', and shows that the society had originally intended to play Handel instead. Kelly must therefore have decided to write a new Dead March at the last minute, just before the programme went off to the printers. It is not known what music was played at the funeral concert put on in memory of Kelly himself: the programme-book has only a blank page with a heading.

Edinburgh in the 1780s must, what with one thing and another, have been full of Kelly manuscripts. 'Part of his works is still unpublished; and not a little probably lost', wrote Robertson in 1784. It is ironical that the opportunity to put together a Kelly manuscript collection should have been missed, at a time when the antiquarian folk movement in Scotland was beginning in earnest. But there is a chance that the lost manuscripts may turn up yet; someone may even have formed a Kelly archive in the 1780s which has subsequently been mislaid. There may be more to say about Kelly in the future.

Folk Music

5

MUSIC IN A STABLE SOCIETY

One's overwhelming first impression of Scottish folk music, on coming to it from the study of classical music, is its stability and unchangingness. Classical music is an art which evolves continuously and ruthlessly; one period hardly reaches maturity before it is undermined and superseded by the next. It changes beyond recognition in the space of two centuries, and considerably even during one person's lifetime, so that the pieces which any individual is taught in youth are likely to be outmoded by the time he dies. Only a very few works of classical music, out of the total produced, survive to be heard by later generations.

Folk music is altogether different: it has little inherent desire for change, and if the society where it flourishes remains stable, it will stay the same for an indefinite period of time. Successive generations of people will sing the same songs and play the same kinds of instrument quite contentedly, so that pinning individual folk-songs down to specific dates is an impossible, and indeed pointless, task. Between 1790 and 1830, for example, many collections of oral Scottish folk-songs were published by such people as Robert Burns, Walter Scott, William Motherwell, and Peter Buchan; the typical collector's story about a song is that he took it down from a woman of eighty, who had learned it in the same form in childhood also from a woman of eighty, who had known it since *her* childhood —giving the song a recorded, unaltered transmission of a century and a half. What the collectors were recording in 1800 was a folk-song corpus which had largely been current in 1650.

There was, actually, some change in the total folk-song repertory between these two dates. The collections of 1790–1830 tend to be biased in favour of old songs, for old songs were what collectors at that time were primarily interested in, and they collected from

old singers in preference to young ones, and from country people
rather than townspeople. Nevertheless folk-singers were generally
conservative, and it is likely that a large proportion of the songs
orally current in 1800 had been sung in the same burghs, villages,
and uplands for one, two, or even four centuries.

Folk instruments also remain the same for long periods. In
1548 a book was published in Edinburgh entitled *The Complaynt
of Scotland*; a socio-political survey of contemporary life, it includes
a dream-sequence in which the author wanders through the Lothians
and meets a group of shepherds playing musical instruments.
The instruments consist of 'ane trump, ane corne pipe, ane pipe
maid of ane gait horne . . . ane quhissil', among others.[1] Two and a
half centuries later, in 1801, the book was edited and republished
by a young Edinburgh antiquarian, John Leyden, who added a
large scholarly introduction to it, in which he commented on this
passage as follows:

> The *trump*, or Jews' harp, is chiefly confined to boys; yet I have
> heard a peasant occasionally play on it with no unpleasing effect,
> while others danced to its sounds, in the absence of more perfect
> instruments.
>
> The *corne pipe* . . . is still formed by shepherd boys, and its compass
> varies with the ingenuity displayed in its formation. I have heard
> tones produced from it in the Highlands of Scotland, which I have
> more than once mistaken for those of the bagpipe.
>
> The *pipe maid of ane gait horne* is the stock and horn . . . which gives
> a full and mellow expression to the sound.
>
> The reed or *whistle* was often formed of the excavated elder branch.
> . . . Shepherd boys display their dexterity in forming them of
> very different substances, from the perforated elder, to the green
> willow bough, part of the bark of which is skilfully taken off, and
> afterwards superinduced, when the ligneous part of the instrument
> is prepared.[2]

One reads this a few times before it suddenly dawns on one that
this part of Leyden's introduction is not scholarly at all: he knew
about folk instruments of 250 years earlier, not because he had

---

[1] *Complaynt*, p. 65. *Gait*: goat.
[2] Leyden, *Preliminary dissertation*, pp. 152, 169.

done research into the subject, but because they were still going strong in his own time. (Similarly, he was able to put together a glossary of sixtee th-century Scots words from his knowledge of contemporary Te iotdale dialect.)[1] The willow-tree pipe, for example, is clearly something he knows how to make himself: it is significant that his English style becomes stilted and awkward at this point—a manual skill with a penknife which you learned at the age of ten is not an easy thing to explain in words to the cultivated reader.

The elder-wood pipe, too, had a clear run of several centuries as a folk instrument in Scotland; other information about it exists. It is mentioned in the fifteenth-century poem 'Cockelbie's Sow' as a 'pype maid of a borit bourtre'. Helena Shire recently told me that she used to play elder-wood pipes in her childhood, in Aberdeen in about 1920:

'At the beginning of the summer each year, every child in the family was made a bourtree pipe by my father. The kind of pipe he made was about nine inches long, with three holes, and they played four different notes. You could only make them out of soft wood, at a certain time of the year; they shrivelled up after a bit. I expect children still have them nowadays.'

So in this department of life at least, very little has changed since the Middle Ages.

Folk music seems to require, in order to flourish in its most typical and characteristic forms, an almost static social setting; a society, in fact, which is so unaffluent that it has its work cut out not to recede economically, where every harvest is felt to be an achievement in itself if the standard reached during the living memory period is roughly maintained, where *development* of the community's resources is so far outside the realm of possibility that it is neither expected nor desired. Ideally such a society would have a static repertory of folk-songs, which people would learn during childhood and adolescence and then sing unchanged for the rest of their lives. In this way the songs would acquire invincibly strong emotional overtones. They would express, for adults, a

[1] Ibid., p. 291.

sense of belonging to the community, of the community's identity and permanence; they would connect people to the past and give them a sense of security; they would make them feel that life would continue as it always had done, and that they would die in the same society as that in which they had been brought up.

Eighteenth-century Scotland does not exactly fit this model. The most settled part of society was that employed on the land, but even rural communities were constantly losing and gaining members as individuals went off to foreign wars or on trade expeditions. Scottish agricultural methods, also, began to be revolutionized from about 1720 on, which led gradually to a break-up of the old country attitudes towards life.

It is impossible to assess to what extent Scottish folk music developed between 1700 and 1800; but it seems probable that at least half the repertory remained largely unchanged between these two dates. For folk music cannot work properly if it develops so fast that, say, the whole repertory is replaced during the course of one person's lifetime. Old people would tend to learn fewer new songs than young people, so that a probable effect of changing the repertory every fifty years would be to cut off a man of seventy totally from a man of twenty: they would have almost no songs in common at all. Folk music could then express not the community's identity, but only its fragmentation. (This is in fact what has begun to happen in twentieth-century Scotland, since the country began to become affluent; many modern folk-songs at present current in Scotland are known only to people under the age of twenty-five, and express not a sense of tradition, but a peculiar adolescent loneliness.)

In 1820, however, there were still large numbers of medieval ballads in circulation, which must have been preserved by some kind of anti-evolutionary force. How this operated is anyone's guess: the likeliest answer seems to me to be simply that old people encouraged young people to learn their own favourite songs, and objected very strongly to their singing anything new and unfamiliar; and that old people were respected, and their wishes, up to a point, heeded. This would have the effect of arresting the repertory's potential development.

To carry on a tradition unchanged requires a certain ingenuous-ness as well as a certain sensitivity. A folk-singer's attitude to a song's words is usually unthinking acceptance: he goes on singing the song even if parts of it are incomprehensible. (In modern society this situation is still found in people singing hymns in church.) It thus happens that corruptions and mistakes creep into folk-songs, which are ineradicable, since the corruption itself soon be-comes part of the tradition. Obsolete technical terms in songs which have survived from past epochs get rationalized, irrespective of meaning, into some contemporary words which sound vaguely the same. Different songs, relating to similar but quite distinct historical events which happened a century apart, get conflated into a single, non-historical narrative. The uneducated folk-singer's knowledge of the past stretches back only as far as the memory of the oldest person in the community: he has no means of spotting, and correcting, such mistakes. Thus folk-songs are often wildly unhistorical despite their 'sense of tradition'. Margaret Laidlaw, the mother of James Hogg the Ettrick Shepherd, once sang Walter Scott a song in which Leader-town was defended

With springs, wall stanes, and goad of ern.

Scott, with his knowledge of medieval fortifications, corrected it to

With springalds, stanes, and gads of airn.[1]

Quite recently, in 1963, a famous Scottish folk-singer sang to a gathering of people at the house of a Cambridge friend of mine. The recital included 'Tullochgorum', an eighteenth-century reel-tune with words by John Skinner, Episcopal minister of Langside, Aberdeenshire (1721–1807). The first verse runs:

Let Whig and Tory all agree,
Whig and Tory, Whig and Tory,
Let Whig and Tory all agree
To drop their Whigmegorum.
Let Whig and Tory all agree
To spend this night with mirth and glee,
And cheerfu' sing alang wi' me
The reel of Tullochgorum.

[1] Greig, p. xl.

After the recital the singer was asked what this song was about, and she offered the following explanation:

'Ah weel a wig—ye ken fit a wig is, a wig's that kinna fulse hair they used to wear, an' a tory, a tory's a bunnet wi' a toorie on it.'[1]

She thought it meant that the Reel could reconcile, not left and right political parties, but the upper and lower classes, symbolized by their headgear. Incorrect; but somehow more creative than the proper answer would have been.

For the unhistorical nature of folk-song is part of its strength: it is not a dead record of the past, but a living part of the present. In any folk-song repertory some songs will be of recent origin, and people will know where they came from; but if the culture is surviving well, the greater part of them will go back beyond the reach of living memory. The community accepts them, not because it necessarily understands them, but because they are traditionally sanctioned. Like life itself, they are familiar yet mysterious, and their origins will never be fully known.

It would be valuable to continue this chapter with a descriptive study of the different forms of folk music in eighteenth-century Scotland, parallel to the description of classical music which I gave in Chapter 2. For various reasons, however, this is hardly possible. There are almost no records of what happened; folk music is so unselfconscious an activity that people do not normally feel impelled to record it at all. (Here again, folk music and classical music differ radically.) Even what information there is is enigmatic: a certain person is known to have sung a certain song in a certain place on a certain day, but is this representative or significant? For another thing, folk music resists definition by its nature: would-be-recognizable forms, genres, texts, and periods merge into each other and become blurred at the edges. Much valuable work has been done on histories of individual folk-songs,[2] but a general picture of the whole repertory and its social uses has never been attempted. This is certainly impossible to do at all adequately at the present time, and will probably remain so.

[1] *Toorie*: tassel. Probably the singer had no idea of the song's origin.
[2] Stenhouse; Chappell; Child; Claude M. Simpson; Bronson.

Nevertheless, I shall here advance a few general propositions which the reader may find illuminating; they are all based on slender evidence, gleaned from a period of time covering four centuries, so I shall try not to push them too far. I believe, however, that these generalizations are valid as far as they go.

MONODY

Folk music in eighteenth-century Scotland was monodic. It consisted of single, unharmonized melodic lines, sometimes accompanied by bagpipe drones, or by percussion such as meat-bones clicked together; but in its orally transmitted state it did not have supporting harmony. This can be tested empirically by taking any folk-tune current in the eighteenth century and trying to harmonize it: generally it will be found impossible to do without damaging something vital.[1] Heterophony may have arisen accidentally when several instruments played a tune simultaneously, and decorated it in different ways; and it occurred deliberately in churches, due to a special method of singing metrical psalms which will be described in Chapter 9. But classical harmony remained outside folk music in Scotland until the nineteenth century. The concertina—the first naturally harmonic Scottish folk instrument—did not come in until about 1880.

SINGING STYLE

There was a special folk-singing style which differed markedly from the classical one. Scottish scholars around 1800 distinguish the two by referring to folk-singing as 'chanting', apparently an agreed-upon technical term:

In singing, or rather chanting, this ballad, the last two lines of every stanza are repeated. In 1786 I heard a lady, then in her 90th year, sing the ballad in this manner.
(William Stenhouse, 1820, *Illustrations*, no. 203, 'Gil Morice')

. . . these wild and monotonous strains so common in Scotland, to which the natives of that country chant their old ballads.
(Walter Scott, 1818, *The Heart of Midlothian*, ch. 15)

[1] This will be demonstrated in Chapter 8.

The most brilliant [historical] episodes are occasionally chaunted to monotonous legendary airs.

(John Leyden, 1801, *Preliminary dissertation*, p. 225)

It is also notable that Scott and Leyden agree in describing ballads as 'monotonous'. This cannot mean that the tunes literally consisted of one note, or of a few within a narrow range; recorded ballad tunes are generally distinguished by very wide ranges of well over an octave. It must, then, mean that the songs were sung in an undemonstrative, deadpan *manner*. Ballads were probably also sung slowly, in free rhythm with no discernible beat. The following tune for the ballad 'Lord John', given in Kinloch's *Ancient Scottish Ballads* of 1827, has very odd-looking rhythms in bars 3 and 4, showing the transcriber having a hard job making notational sense of rubato:

Lord John

More evidence about folk-singing style is given by Robert Bremner, in an essay published in 1762. Bremner was writing to encourage classical musicians to start parish church choirs in country districts, and he described the difficulties which such musicians faced. One was a 'common' but 'ridiculous' habit, which country singers evidently had, of breaking diphthongs in the wrong place—wrong, at least, by classical standards: they slid straight on to the second element of the diphthong at the beginning of the note with a kind of click, instead of holding the note on the first element, and then moving gradually towards the second.[1] Another difficulty was that country singers habitually flattened seventh degrees of the scale: in the psalm tune 'Dundee', for instance, rural congregations insisted on singing flattened sevenths, even when accompanied by an educated precentor singing the correct sharpened notes.[2]

[1] Bremner, *Rudiments*, 2nd edn., p. 54.   [2] Ibid., p. 36.

It does not seem to have occurred to Bremner, though it is fairly obvious to us, that country singers clicked their diphthongs and flattened their sevenths in psalms because that was how they sang folk-songs. Bremner had come up against the performance practice of an alien culture.

William Dauney also remarked upon flattened sevenths in 1838:

The use of the flat, instead of the sharp, seventh for the penultimate note, is an ancient ... practice ... the remains of which still subsist in the psalm—and even in the ballad—singing of the uneducated, in all parts of the country.[1]

These characteristics are all still present, in varying degrees, in present-day Scottish folk-singing, so it seems that the style has not changed so much as one might have expected.

INSTRUMENTS IN USE

Folk instruments in eighteenth-century Scotland can be classified into three social levels.

At the top level were town pipers; they were officially employed by many Scottish towns to walk round the streets every morning and evening playing a fife,[2] accompanied by an assistant with a drum. They were a means of public time-keeping in the days before public striking clocks; they woke the community up in the morning and told them when it was time to go to bed. In Aberdeen in 1574 the town council

ordanit Johnne Cowpar to pas everie day in the morning at four houris, and everie nycht at eight houris at ewyne, throu all the rewis of the toune, playand upon the almany quhissel, with ane servante with him playand upon the taborine, quhairby the craftismen, their servandis, and all utheris laborious folkis, being warnit and excitat, may pas to their labouris in dew and convenient tyme.[3]

[1] Dauney, p. 179 n.
[2] Some scholars seem to think that town pipers played *bagpipes*; see Dauney, p. 127, Collinson, *Traditional and national*, p. 168. But several town pipers in Border towns were *also* notable bagpipe players.
[3] Aberdeen Town Council Register, 24 November 1574; quoted in Maidment, vol. 2, p. 325.

Most sizeable towns had town pipers in the sixteenth century. But during the seventeenth century there was a general move to abolish pipers and employ only drummers; in 1630 the Aberdeen magistrates decided to

discharge the common piper of all going through the town at nycht, or in the morning, in tyme coming, with his pype—it being an incivill forme to be usit within sic a famous burghe, and being often fund fault with, als weill be sundrie nichtbouris of the toune as be strangers.[1]

Lanark lost its piper in the late sixteenth century, but its drummer continued until the eighteenth century; in 1661 we read that

Andro Weir were electit drumer till Michaelmas nixt . . . to goe throw [the town] at four in the morning and aught at night.[2]

In several Border towns the town piper survived to the end of the eighteenth century. The piper at Galashiels in about 1740 was named Donald McLean, while the Jedburgh pipers were all named Hastie. The Hastie family's ancestry was supposed to go back to a John Hastie who had piped the Borderers into battle at Flodden in 1513; the last of the line was Robert Hastie, who died in about 1790.[3] Campbell gives a delightful picture of Robert Hastie at work:

Mr Rob[er]t Shortreed, Sherriff Sub[sti]t[ute] of Roxburghshire told me that the office of Piper in Jedburgh had been suppressed some years since—that when the Piper, accompanied with the Town's Drummer played—especially in the evenings of the spring, summer & autumn, the joyful group of Matrons with their babies, & the little ones which followed the pipe & drum was delightful to behold.[4]

It could be argued that town pipers should be counted as classical musicians, since they enjoyed civic, and apparently also aristocratic, patronage; Lady Grisell Baillie's account-books list several payments 'to the pyp and drum', who were probably the town musicians at Kelso. But town pipers must have played almost exclusively folk-tunes, and so been an important factor in moulding the district's folk-song repertory. Robert Bremner noted in 1762 that

[1] Aberdeen Town Council Register, 26 May 1630; quoted in Maidment, vol. 2, p. 326.   [2] Lanark Burgh Records, quoted in Langwill.
[3] Campbell (MS.); Leyden, *Preliminary dissertation*, p. 142; Stenhouse, no. 356.
[4] Campbell (MS.).

the musical Genius of the People in some Towns is much stronger than that of others; and this may be owing to the having or wanting a Town-piper. . . . I am credibly informed that there is a Piper in a neighbouring Town that can only play one Tune; and was you to walk through every Corner of that Town, you would hear that Tune, and no other, in the Mouth of every Child and Servant there.[1]

Edinburgh differed from other Scottish towns, for it had a 'classical' form of public music: it kept a band of waits.

Waits were skilled musicians, traditionally oboe- and bassoon-players, who were employed by a town council; they were expected to play in the town streets at night and to be on call for civic functions. They were an established feature of town life in sixteenth- and seventeenth-century England,[2] but were rare in Scotland, being found only in Edinburgh, and then only at certain periods. The Edinburgh waits never numbered more than five; their duties were restricted to passing through the town morning and night— exactly the same as the town piper elsewhere—and to giving a daily recital in the middle of town starting at 12 noon; and many of them were English immigrants.

In 1607 the Edinburgh waits were led by 'Jhonn Orley, Inglishman'; at some time subsequently they were disbanded and replaced by a town drummer; in 1675 they were resuscitated, and 'Robert Wood, John Boll, John Smyth and Robert Mairteine Inglishmen' were granted

libertie . . . to goe throw the Citie in the morneing tymouslie be fore or fyve of the clock daylie and make use of that instrument that they use to play upon viz. cornets and sackbotts for giveing advertisements to the inhabitants that it is about that tyme of the day . . .

In 1679 the same team were fitted up with 'coats in the touns liverie', and waits were still in operation in 1696, when John Munro and Malcolm McGibbon, professional oboists in Edinburgh, successfully petitioned the town council to be allowed to teach the waits to play the modern French oboe and 'double curtle'.[3] It is not known how long they survived in the eighteenth century;

---

[1] Bremner, *Rudiments*, 2nd edn., p. 50.   [2] Woodfill, pp. 33 f., 74 f., 293.
[3] Edinburgh Burgh Records, 30 January 1607, 22 October 1675, 31 October 1679, 17 April 1696.

the office of leader of the Edinburgh waits was not abolished till 1804, but had been reduced to a nominal post probably several decades before.

Another form of public music in Edinburgh, which may be briefly dealt with here, was the carillon in the tower of St. Giles' Cathedral. It contained twenty-one bells, and was constructed by John Meikle between 1697 and 1699; in 1699 Francis Toward, professional violinist in Edinburgh, who had supervised the tuning and hanging of the bells, was engaged by the town council to play on them every day, except Sundays and holidays, for an hour starting at 11.30 a.m.[1] This seems to have replaced the daily recital given by the waits earlier in the seventeenth century.

Carillon recitals continued throughout the eighteenth century in Edinburgh. An English visitor to the town in 1726 remarked that the carillonist played 'Scots, English, Irish and Italian tunes to great perfection, and is heard all over the city'.[2] At that time the recital began at 11 a.m.; by 1770 it had been put back to 1 p.m.:

All the people of business at Edinburgh, and even the genteel company, may be seen standing in crowds every day from one to two in the afternoon, in the open street, at a place where formerly stood a market-cross . . . the company . . . are entertained with a variety of tunes, played upon a set of bells, fixed in a steeple hard by —As these bells are well-toned, and the musician, who has a salary from the city, for playing upon them with keys, is no bad performer, the entertainment is really agreeable.[3]

A further account was written in 1787:

In the tower of St. Giles' Church is a set of bells which are rung out, or played upon by the hand with keys, like a harpsichord, the person having leather covers to his fists, by which he is able to strike with the more force. They play all manner of tunes very musically; and a yearly salary is paid for playing upon them from one to two o'clock every day, Sundays and holidays excepted.[4]

It would be stretching a point to try to fit the Edinburgh waits and the St. Giles' bells under the heading of folk music; they both

---

[1] Edinburgh Burgh Records, 13 September 1699; Tytler, p. 507; Price, p. 212.
[2] Burt, vol. 1, p. 189.   [3] Smollett, vol. 2, p. 223.   [4] Kincaid, p. 159.

relied on classically trained professional musicians, and were both foreign importations—the waits from England, and the carillon from the Low Countries. But it is certainly true that they were part of the general life of the Edinburgh community at the time.

At the next level of folk-instrument playing came violins and bagpipes. I have grouped these two together because both required many years' practice to master, and because folk-fiddlers and bagpipers were generally established, secure members of the community; they were schoolmasters, tradesmen in country towns, factors on estates, personal servants of the aristocracy. Most of them could read and write musical notation.

The bagpipes in use in the Lowlands at the time were the Border pipes, now extinct, which were inflated by a bellows held under the player's left arm; they were soft-toned, and similar to present-day Northumbrian pipes.[1]

Violins were difficult to make as well as to play. But it seems that many fiddlers in country areas used to make their own instruments nevertheless; they probably borrowed, and measured, the laird's imported Italian model, and set to work laboriously to copy it. The job would take up a whole winter's spare time. Discussions about methods of violin manufacture formed a staple part of conversation whenever amateur fiddlers met; the tone of such discussions is well caught in William Honeyman's book *Scottish Violin Makers: Past and Present*, written in 1898 at the end of the great fiddle-making era.

Outstanding Scottish violin-makers in the eighteenth century were Joseph Ruddiman, who worked in Aberdeen from 1760 onwards, and Matthew Hardie, who worked in Edinburgh from 1790; and there must have been hosts of other makers whose work has been completely destroyed and forgotten. Honeyman put forward a plausible theory on the subject of damage to eighteenth-century violins:

[Ruddiman] appears to have repaired Niel Gow's *Gasparo da Salo* violin after it had been fractured by a fall on the ice at Stairdam in 1784, an accident to which violins were then more liable, as they

---

[1] Collinson, *Traditional and national*, pp. 169 f., has further information on Border pipes.

were carried in a green bag instead of in a fiddle-case as now. The owners also usually carried more whisky than they do now.[1]

It is likely that many were also smashed during punch-ups at dances.

At the lowest level were home-made folk instruments; some of these could only be constructed at certain times of year when the right material was available, and many would only play for a few hours before wearing out. A corn stem with notches in it; pipes cut from various tree branches or from hollow meat-bones; a cow's or goat's horn used as a sort of bugle: these instruments seem almost too improvisatory to deserve the title, but they were actually traditional designs, and capable of producing really musical sounds in the right hands. Leyden's remarks on the corn-pipe may be recalled: 'I have heard tones produced from it . . . which I have more than once mistaken for those of the bagpipe.'

The stock-and-horn was the most advanced of these 'peasant instruments', as Dauney called them. A kind of folk oboe, it was on the decline during the eighteenth century, but Robert Burns managed to acquire one in 1794, and sent a description of it to George Thomson. From his account we see that it consisted of three basic types of home-made instrument, all fitted together: a corn stem, plus a meat-bone with holes, plus a bugle.

I have, *at last*, gotten one; but it is a very rude instrument.—It is composed of three parts; the stock, which is the hinder thigh-bone of a sheep, such as you see in a mutton-ham; the horn, which is a common Highland cow's horn, cut off at the smaller end, untill the aperture be large enough to admit the 'stock' to be pushed up through the horn, untill it be held by the thicker or hip-end of the thigh-bone; & lastly, an oaten reed exactly cut and notched like that which you see every shepherd-boy have when the corn-stems are green & full-grown.—The reed is not made fast in the bone, but is held by the lips, & plays loose in the smaller end of the 'stock'; while the 'stock', & the horn hanging on its larger end, is held by the hands in playing.—The 'stock' has six, or seven, ventiges on the upper side, & one back-ventige, like the common flute.—This of mine was made by a man from the braes of Athole, & is exactly what the shepherds wont to use in that country.[2]

[1] Honeyman, p. 89.   [2] Burns, *Letters*, letter of 19 November 1794.

The stock-and-horn was an adaptable instrument, as the sections could be detached and played separately:

The *stock and horn* was so formed, that the parts could be easily separated, while the horn might be employed as a bugle, and the pipe, as a simple pipe or whistle.[1]

THE RISE OF THE VIOLIN

There was one major change in instrumental playing during the eighteenth century—the Border bagpipe gradually dropped out of use, and the violin took its place. 'The fiddle', wrote Leyden in 1801, '. . . has, in the Scottish Lowlands, nearly supplanted the Bagpipe.'[2] But one cannot date the change very exactly: the violin was being used to play folk-tunes as early as 1680,[3] and the bagpipe was by no means extinct as late as 1816.[4] It is no use assigning a date for the change if one has to make allowances of a hundred years each way. (Here again, classical music is contrasted strongly. It can be stated with some accuracy that the transverse flute took over the position of the recorder in Scotland between 1725 and 1740; people follow fashions punctiliously in classical music circles.) It is probable that the violin was introduced into Scotland by the upper classes, who got it from England as a classical instrument. There was probably also an existing medieval-fiddle tradition in Scotland, which the Italian violin joined forces with and stimulated.

VOCAL AND INSTRUMENTAL IDIOMS

It is pointless to draw a sharp distinction between vocal music, on the one hand, and instrumental music, on the other: many song-tunes ('airs') also appear in instrumental versions, and many instrumental tunes ('springs') have words to them. Because of the unhistorical nature of folk music it is generally impossible in any one case to say which version is the original. 'O let me in this ae

---

[1] Leyden, *Preliminary dissertation*, p. 155.   [2] Ibid., p. 158.
[3] 'Lessones for ye violin', a manuscript book of *c.* 1680 from Newbattle Abbey, Midlothian, contains many Scots tunes: it is now NLS MS. 5778.
[4] Campbell (MS.).

night' is a good example of this: it appears as a song in the *Scots Musical Museum* in 1792, as follows:

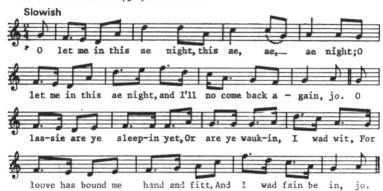

But it is also recorded as a violin piece, in two different versions, in a fiddle book of *c.* 1805:[1]

[1] Peter Macewen's music book, EPL. The second version was originally a tone higher, and is transposed to facilitate comparison.

These two versions differ from each other as much as they do from the song version, so it is likely that the song is the original here, and the fiddle pieces later variants. But other possibilities may be borne in mind: a decorative violin piece could well be simplified for singing. In some cases a multiple process can be traced, where a tune has been passed back and forth several times between poet and composer, singer and player. A striking example of such development is 'The Lowlands of Holland'. It was current as a song in about 1750 in this form:[1]

In about 1775 William Marshall rewrote it as a fiddle dance tune, 'Miss Admiral Gordon's Strathspey'. Marshall composed a second strain, so doubling the tune's length:[2]

[1] From *Scots Musical Museum*, vol. 2, 1788. See Stenhouse, no. 115.
[2] From *Scots Musical Museum*, vol. 3, 1790, with a few editorial rhythmic normalizations. See Stenhouse, no. 235. But cf. Glen, pp. 95–9.

Then in about 1789 Robert Burns wrote words to Marshall's strathspey, and turned it back into a song:

> Of a' the airts the wind can blaw,
> I dearly like the west,
> For there the bony Lassie lives,
> The Lassie I lo'e best:
> There's wild-woods grow, and rivers row,
> And mony a hill between;
> But day and night my fancy's flight
> Is ever wi' my Jean.
>
> I see her in the dewy flowers,
> I see her sweet and fair;
> I hear her in the tunefu' birds,
> I hear her charm the air:
> There's not a bony flower, that springs
> By fountain, shaw, or green,
> There's not a bony bird that sings,
> But minds me o' my Jean.

At a later stage, sometime in the mid nineteenth century, an anonymous composer seems to have simplified Marshall's tune and recast it in a more vocal idiom; the result was the well-known 'Bonny bonny banks of Loch Lomond':

> (continued by a chorus which is an almost exact repetition of the tune).

Interchange between vocal and instrumental idioms seems to be the main means by which a tune can develop.

DANCE MUSIC

Almost any form of music could be used for dancing. The fiddle was the dominant dance-music instrument in the eighteenth century, for dancing-masters traditionally played it to accompany their lessons; but if a fiddle was not available its place could be taken by the bagpipe, by any sort of whistle, by a jew's harp, singing, or diddling (a kind of vocalization in which the tune is articulated to 'dum-di-diddle-um' syllables). It was common in earlier periods for dancing, singing, and playing to proceed simultaneously. *The Complaynt of Scotland* gives a list of names of dance tunes current in 1548;[1] some of them are place-names which do not imply that the tunes had associated words ('ennyrnes', 'the loch of slene', 'soutra'),[2] but others are names of narrative ballads ('Robene hude', 'thom of lyn', 'ihonne ermistrangis dance'). This suggests that it was customary in the sixteenth century to dance while ballads were being sung, and it is possible that the practice survived into the eighteenth century in some parts of Scotland.

I shall discuss the dance music written specifically for fiddle in more detail in Chapter 6.

MUSIC AND ANIMALS

Music played an important part in controlling animals. The Scottish countryside was largely unenclosed up till 1750, so livestock had to be folded at night-time and taken out to pasture every day. In the sixteenth century it seems to have been normal practice to move animals from one place to another by walking behind them, blowing long wailing noises on the bugles made out of cows' horns which I have already described. These instruments were known as 'stock horns' or 'buck horns'. Here the author of *The Complaynt of Scotland* describes the scene:

i beheld mony hudit hirdis blauuand ther buc hornis and ther corne pipis, calland and conuoyand mony fat floc to be fed on the feildis.[1]

Once out at pasture, the animals had to be watched—a task usually given to junior members of the community. Rural children

---

[1] *Complaynt*, p. 65.

[2] 'ennyrnes' is Inverness; 'the loch of slene' is in Aberdeenshire; 'soutra' is a hill on the road between Edinburgh and Lauder. The custom of naming dance tunes after places was still common in eighteenth-century Scotland: witness 'The East Neuk of Fife', 'The Brig of Perth', 'Pinkie House', 'Tullochgorum'.

[3] *Complaynt*, p. 42. *Hudit hirdis*: hooded shepherds.

and adolescents spent hours and hours a week watching sheep and cows grazing. To alleviate boredom they played tunes on home-made pipes; the animals associated the music with the shepherd boy's presence, so that it prevented them from wandering away and getting lost.

Allan Ramsay included in *The Gentle Shepherd* a speech in which Roger, a young shepherd aged about seventeen, is threatening to smash his pipe because his girl-friend has insulted his playing—whatever the consequences to his flock of sheep. Despite the Arcadian literary convention this is fundamentally a realistic situation:

> When I begin to tune my stock and horn,
> With a' her face she shaws a caulrife scorn.
> Last night I play'd, ye never heard sic spite;
> *O'er Bogie* was the spring, and her delyte:
> Yet tauntingly she at her cousin spear'd,
> Gif she could tell what tune I play'd, and sneer'd.
> Flocks, wander where ye like, I dinna care,
> I'll break my reed, and never whistle mair.[1]

MUSIC FOR SPECIAL OCCASIONS

Several social occasions had their own special pieces of music. Some of these were focal points in the community's life-cycle—weddings, kirns, and leave-takings—others ancient festivals like Hallowe'en and New Year. Little is known of the actual songs used, and it is probable that they varied from one district to another. For example, in the south-east of Scotland in the eighteenth century a leave-taking (at the end of a party, or the night before some member of the community was due to go on a journey) was generally accompanied by the singing of 'Good night and joy be with you all':

> What I hae done for lack o' wit
> I never never can reca';
> I trust ye're a' my friends as yet,
> Gude night and joy be wi' you a'.

[1] Ramsay, *Poems*, vol. 1. *Caulrife*: unenthusiastic/ *spring*: instrumental tune/ *spear'd*: inquired.

Significantly, a number of Edinburgh-based editors of eighteenth-century Scots song books included this as the last song in their collections.[1] But a quite different song seems to have been sung at leave-takings in, for example, Aberdeenshire. And since the early nineteenth century, Burns's 'Auld lang syne' has been the dominant leave-taking song all over Scotland.

This survey of eighteenth-century folk music has been, unavoidably, brief and sketchy. Were more material on the subject to turn up it is probable that certain broad outlines would become apparent, for example regarding the development of the folk-song repertory: Border ballads might then be seen as the repertory's traditional backbone, and it might be possible to chart influxes of regimental march-tunes, English broadside-songs, and other alien modes. But additional material would probably also vastly complicate the over-all picture: one would be able to see hundreds of local variants and survivals from the Middle Ages. Even as things are, one can catch tantalizing glimpses of unexpected, strange genres: of work-songs peculiar to oyster-fishermen in the Firth of Forth;[2] of folk-plays in which 'guisards dressed up in a fantastic but military guise go round the country, they represent warriors such as Julius Caesar Robert Bruce Alexander the great and Sr Wm Wallace, they fight single combats accompanyed with strange rhymes';[3] and no doubt there were hundreds more.

I hope, however, that this survey, incomplete as it is, has given the reader some idea of Scottish folk music's vitality and richness, and prepared him for the next four chapters, where I shall discuss how folk music and classical music came into confrontation with each other.

---

[1] See Stenhouse, no. 600. [2] Collinson, *Oyster-dredging songs.*
[3] Letter from Sir David Dalrymple to Bishop Percy, 19 April 1764: Dalrymple, p. 75.

Cross-currents

6

FIDDLE MUSIC

Most people do not realize how far Scottish folk-fiddle music was influenced by classical music: it is usually thought of as an indigenous growth, untouched by civilization, transmitted by illiterate farm workers and vagrant players. But in fact folk-fiddle playing, as it exists in Scotland today, was almost entirely an eighteenth-century creation; and it was developed by educated musicians, most of whom were at home in the classical music culture.

Folk-fiddle music was in the limelight in the eighteenth century; unlike other forms of folk music, it had a place in the contemporary fashionable scene. There were a number of historical reasons for this. The violin had come to Scotland as a new classical music instrument towards the end of the seventeenth century; Scottish craftsmen learnt how to copy the Italian designs, and the instrument then caught on in folk-music circles, to such effect that the Border bagpipe, hitherto pre-eminent among Lowland folk instruments, became virtually extinct by 1800. Simultaneously there was an enormous boom in dancing in Scotland, which called into being a completely new repertory of fiddle dance music. But the violin continued as a classical music instrument, which could be used for playing Corelli sonatas and Haydn symphonies as well as folk-tunes; and by the end of the eighteenth century there were musical societies in most sizeable towns in the country, giving regular amateur classical music concerts. Thus every facility was available for the literate folk-fiddler to dabble in classical music, if he wished. Conversely, the classical violinist could dabble in folk music. As a result, the two categories of player became intermixed, and in the process folk music absorbed many elements of classical style.

Certainly there were illiterate fiddlers in many parts of Scotland at the time, who had no contact with classical music at all. Robert Burns describes a midget in his poem 'The Jolly Beggars', who was one of the regular down-and-out clientele of Poosie Nancie's public-house in Mauchline in the 1780s, and whose only occupation was playing violin at fairs, weddings, and kirns in the neighbourhood. It is clear from Burns's satirical use of classical music terminology that the midget was totally uneducated:

> A pigmy scraper wi' his fiddle
> Wha used at trysts and fairs to driddle. . . .
> He crooned his gamut, ane, twa, three,
> Then in an *arioso* key,
>   The wee Apollo
> Set aff wi' *allegretto* glee
>   His giga solo.[1]

But I do not see such players as this taking an important part in the transmission and development of the repertory. They were not the people who were building fiddles, or discovering ways of using classical instrumental technique in folk music: by 1760 they were definitely peripheral to the mainstream of the tradition. The players in the mainstream were the dancing-masters, the village and town craftsmen, and professional men such as schoolmasters and doctors—educated men of social standing. For fiddle music differed from other forms of folk music at the time in that it was transmitted, in its most developed form, not aurally but on paper.

It was customary for fiddlers to define their personal repertories by making up collections of tunes in small oblong manuscript books. Leyden wrote in 1800: 'it is . . . very common for Parochial schoolmasters and teachers of music to write out such collections for their own use',[2] and countless numbers of these books must have

[1] Burns, *Poems. Crooned his gamut, ane, twa, three* probably refers to the player tuning up:

```
    1  2  3
```

[music notation]

[2] Manuscript note dated Edinburgh, 5 March 1800, on front page of NLS Adv. MS. 5.2.14. Leyden was attempting in this note an erroneous comparison between

existed in the eighteenth century. A number have been preserved to the present day.

Aberdeen University Library, for example, possesses several: a book belonging to John Niven, a well-to-do Aberdeen citizen, dated 1761 and containing 227 tunes; a book belonging to James Massie, also of Aberdeen, dated 1777, containing 95 tunes; one belonging to an unnamed fiddler whose grandson, James Christie, was a lawyer in Banff in 1802, containing 130 tunes; one belonging to Alexander McLaren of Pitlochry, of *c.* 1830, with 429 tunes; and one belonging to James Webster of New Deer, Aberdeenshire, dated 1839.[1] The contents of these five books overlap to a significant extent; and some pieces occur in different books in so nearly identical a form that it seems certain that it was normal practice to copy straight from one book to another, without intervening aural transmission. A set of variations on the 'Reel of Tulloch', for example, appears in similar form in three of the five books, and also in two others which I have seen—Thomas Sheils's music book, written in Crieff in 1820,[2] and a book of unknown provenance of *c.* 1750.[3] This gives the piece a recorded life of about ninety years. Another set of variations, on the tune 'John come kiss me now', appear in almost identical form in four manuscripts dated between 1723 and 1768,[4] two of which were written in Edinburgh and one in Perth: a recorded life of forty-five years. These variations do not seem ever to have appeared in print, and both sets are too long and complex to learn accurately by ear; thus a manuscript transmission is indicated.

Publishers were not slow to realize that this had commercial possibilities, and various attempts were made to turn the hand-copying tradition into a paying game. Printed collections were brought out, on the same lines as existing home-made ones, to try and cash in on the market, and the following had some success:

eighteenth-century fiddle books and sixteenth/seventeenth-century madrigalian part-books; but his remark is perfectly valid as a record of current practice in his own time.

[1] AUL MSS. 2232, 795², 2422, 2424, and 2421. James Webster's place of residence is supplied from MS. 2427.

[2] In private possession of Mrs. W. J. Macaulay.

[3] NLS MS. 2086.   [4] NLS MSS. 1667, 2085, 2086, 808.

Henry Playford's (London, 1700); Adam Craig's (Edinburgh, c. 1725); James Oswald's (Edinburgh, c. 1740, and London, 1745 on); William McGibbon's (Edinburgh, 1742 on); Robert Bremner's (Edinburgh and London, various); and a whole spate after 1775. They were certainly successful in influencing the repertory: selections from them may be found copied out, without permission or acknowledgement, in many fiddle manuscript books. This was probably not, however, the kind of success which a publisher wanted.

A number of publications failed dismally. Alexander Stuart's *Musick for Allan Ramsay's Collection of Scots Songs Vol: First* (Edinburgh, c. 1726), a set of arrangements of folk tunes for fiddle and continuo, went through only one edition, and the projected subsequent volumes were never issued, even though its corresponding words book, Allan Ramsay's *Tea-table Miscellany* (Edinburgh, 4 volumes, 1723 on) was the best-seller of the century; the probable reason being that fiddlers in Edinburgh had most of the *Tea-table Miscellany* tunes in their manuscript books, or in their heads, already, and saw no point in spending money on Stuart's collection.

Publications of fiddle music had less effect on the tradition, therefore, than one might have expected. Several sets of variations for solo fiddle by McGibbon appear in the McFarlane manuscripts,[1] for example, which pre-date McGibbon's printed collections: this means that McGibbon's work must have been actively circulating round Edinburgh in handwritten copies by 1740, and shows that printing was not essential to transmission. Similarly a number of minuets by Robert McIntosh, the Edinburgh violinist, had found their way down to the remote village of Whitsome in Berwickshire, near the English border, by 1780,[2] even though McIntosh's first published collection did not come out until 1783.

It is not always known who the composers of the fiddle music were; the classical-music rule about ascriptions which I put forward in Chapter 1 ('when a . . . work is copied from one piece of paper to another, the name of the composer is . . . copied also') is often suspended in favour of the folk-music rule ('composers' names are soon forgotten'). Thus the same piece of music occurs in one

[1] NLS MSS. 2084–5.   [2] William Trotter's music book, EPL.

manuscript[1] under the title '[James] Oswald's Bass Minuet' and in two other exactly contemporary manuscripts[2] merely as 'The Bass Minuet'. Nicolo Pasquali's name is preserved in two manuscripts, but in somewhat mutilated form: 'Pasqualio's Minuet' in one, and 'Signo: Pissqualie's Minuet' in the other.[3] Many minuets by Daniel Dow and the Earl of Kelly appear in manuscripts of the 1765–85 period with no ascription at all, and one can only discover who the composers were by referring to printed collections.

Thus fiddle music was partly classical and partly folk. It was folk in so far as it was essentially unharmonized and based on the monodic folk-idiom with gapped-scale melodies; in so far as it forgot the names of its composers, was kept going by amateurs, and developed its repertory—by classical standards—very slowly. It was classical in so far as it was transmitted on paper, and was influenced by classical violin technique. The table of 'folk' and 'classical' characteristics which I gave in Chapter 1 may be consulted for comparison.

RECITAL PIECES

I suggested in Chapter 5 that the Italian violin was introduced into Scotland some time before 1680, and that there was an indigenous, medieval fiddle tradition in Scotland prior to that. The following piece, from a manuscript from Panmure House, Angus,[4] is a good example of pre-Italianate fiddle style; it was probably intended to be played on a 'folky' fiddle with a reedy, nasal timbre, with a bowing style favouring vigour rather than subtle nuance:

---

[1] NLS MS. 808.
[2] NLS MSS. 3327, 3346.
[3] NLS MSS. 3346, 808.
[4] NLS MS. 9454, *c.* 1680. Further fiddle pieces from this source may be found in *Early Scottish Keyboard Music*, ed. Kenneth Elliott (London, 1967).

The piece is a reel with a decorated repeat. Characteristic of the style are the leanings towards pentatonicism (the seventh of the scale does not occur at all, and the fourth only as an unaccented passing-note); the fact that the tune does not bother to end on the tonic; and the sequence pattern ♪♪♩♪♪♩, which moves downwards ignoring gaps in the scale, and treating tones and minor thirds as equivalents.

Fiddle music in the late seventeenth century seems to have been purely functional: it was used for dancing to. But early in the eighteenth century sets of variations began to be written for fiddle, which are clearly intended as 'recital pieces'. Most of these variations would be unsuitable for dancing, since they change speed between one section and the next; and it is in them that the first signs of Italianate technique appear. The variations on 'John come kiss me now' in Patrick Cuming's music book of 1723,[1] for example, have slurred bowings, trills, double-stops, changes of tempo and time-signature, and fast arpeggios across the string, and they use both flattened and sharpened sevenths with some awareness of the different harmonic implications of each.

Around 1740 David Young, writing-master and music-copyist in Edinburgh, made up a three-volume collection of fiddle music for Walter McFarlane Esq.[2] This collection contains many sets of

[1] NLS MS. 1667.
[2] NLS MS. 2084–5. Volume 1 of the set was lost in about 1800. Walter McFarlane became a brother-in-law of the composer Lord Kelly on his marriage to Lady Betty Erskine in 1762.

variations in which Italianization is taken much further. The
composers named as responsible are McGibbon, McLean, Disblair,
and Young himself; significantly, all four of them were deeply
involved with classical music. McGibbon and McLean we have
already met as classical composers in Chapter 3; 'Disblair' is probably
James Dyce of Disblair, who joined the Aberdeen Musical Society
in 1748;[1] and David Young, as we saw in Chapter 2, was one of the
Aberdeen Musical Society's founder-members. Another fiddle book
of the period[2] contains Disblair's variations on 'John Anderson my
Jo', which even go so far as to give the different sections Italian
titles: 'Vivace', 'un poco Largo', 'Andante', and so forth. One
can get the effect of the piece best by imagining a Corelli sonata
with very four-square phrasing and rather obvious thematic
connections between the movements, played senza basso.

Indeed, an experiment in 'sonatas on Scots tunes' had already
been carried out: A[lexander] Munro had published twelve such
sonatas, for flute and continuo, in 1732 under the title *A Collection
of the best Scots Tunes*.[3] 'Fy gar rub her [o'er wi' strae]' opens with
five allegro variations:

and then proceeds to a canonic adagio,

[1] Aberdeen Musical Society minute-books, minute, 4 March 1748.
[2] NLS Adv. MS. 5.2.25, *c.* 1750.
[3] For some unknown reason this collection was published in Paris. Munro seems,
however, to have been a native of Edinburgh.

a corrente, two gavotte variations, and a minuet:

Further developments in Italian technique appear in *A Collection of Favourite Scots Tunes . . . by the Late Mr Ch^s McLean and other Eminent Masters*, published in Edinburgh in about 1770. This collection includes fast scales used as melodic decoration, bariolage, skips across two strings, and up-bow spiccato. Many of the pieces are sets of variations which end with *gigas* resembling modalized Corelli; for example, the following:[1]

Later, in the 1790s, Robert Riddell published *A Collection of Scotch, Galwegian and Border Tunes*, which included Italianate fiddle variations on 'The Lee Rigg' by James Clark, schoolmaster at Moffat, Dumfriesshire. These variations are entitled 'Andante', 'Largo', 'Vivace', 'Tempo di Gavotta', 'Giga Allᵒ', and 'Presto'.

The movement towards Italianate folk-fiddle playing thus continued throughout the century. But many composers stuck out against it, James Oswald, for example. The pieces for solo fiddle in Oswald's *Curious Collection of Scots Tunes* (Edinburgh, *c.* 1740) are a fascinating study in style. 'To Dauntin me' has Italianate bowing and a few trills, but its rhythms are unsystematized and its melody lacks any classical sense of harmonic direction. There is

---

[1] 'Logan Water'. The basso part is here omitted.

even an old-fashioned 'gapped sequence' pattern in it, identical
to the one in the Panmure House reel-tune of sixty years earlier,
quoted above. 'When she cam ben she bobed', from the same collection, shows Oswald attempting to combine classical and folk
elements, and treating gapped-scale melodic shapes as interchangeable with harmonically directed ones. In one place he takes a
harmonic melodic shape [music], decorates it
pentatonically [music], and then balances it
symmetrically with the undecorated version:

This fusion of styles works rather well.

As one might expect, Italian techniques never caught on at all in
many parts of the country, particularly in the north. James Gillespie's fiddle book, written in Perth in 1768,[1] includes many pieces
in pure seventeenth-century style, for example 'The Coallier's
Daughter'. The same manuscript, however, contains much of the
most worth-while fiddle music of the century: which is, in my
opinion, music written along Oswald's lines, where classical
techniques have been absorbed but the result still has a folk
identity. I would cite 'Johnie Cope' and 'Duncan Gray' in the
Gillespie fiddle book as outstandingly fine examples.

A peculiarity of folk-fiddle playing which should be mentioned
here is the use of scordatura, or non-standard tunings of the strings.
Its origins are obscure: its use in eighteenth-century Scotland
does not seem to derive from classical music. The point of it is to
simplify fingering and to increase the number of useful open-
string notes. A classical musician would not wish to play a fiddle
like this because open-string notes differ in tone-quality from

[1] NLS MS. 808.

finger-stopped ones; but a folk musician would not mind the indiscriminate uneven tone-colour. Pieces to be played with scordatura are indicated in manuscripts and printed collections by a prefatory stave giving the pitches for retuning: the most common retuning is *a e' a' e' '*—the bottom two strings up a tone. Some tunes, such as 'My ain kind Dearie O', seem always to have been played with this tuning.

DANCE MUSIC

In order to understand fiddle dance music it is necessary first to know something about the history of dancing itself.

Dancing was disliked by the Church of Scotland. In 1649 the General Assembly passed an act prohibiting so-called 'promiscuous dancing' (i.e. in which men danced with women), and this act was reaffirmed in 1701. As a result there was almost no public dancing of any kind in Scotland in the seventeenth century; it had to be done surreptitiously, if at all.

Towards the end of the seventeenth century, however, dancing came out into the open again in Edinburgh as an upper-class recreation, stimulated by the visit of the Duke and Duchess of York in 1680. New dances came into vogue at this time, supplementing the traditional Scottish Reel: these were the Country-dance, an English type not hitherto known in Scotland, and the Minuet (pronounced 'minaway'[1] in the French manner). The church objected, predictably; pulpit-thumping sermons equating dancing with sexual permissiveness were frequently to be heard in Edinburgh churches during the first ten years of the eighteenth century. But times had changed, and the ladies of Edinburgh defied the church and danced on: a popular dance tune at the time was called 'The de'il stick the minister'. In 1723 an Assembly, or aristocratic dancing-club, was opened in Edinburgh which was to continue until nearly the end of the century.

The Edinburgh Assembly was in theory open to the general public, in practice confined to 'Persons of Quality, and others of Note'. But assemblies also opened in provincial Scottish towns, and

---

[1] So spelt in Agnes Hume's music book, 1704, NLS Adv. MS. 5.2.17.

dancing-masters set up teaching practices in areas remote from the capital. Topham remarked in 1775 how dancing-masters earned a good living by teaching large classes of pupils at small individual fees: it is probable that dancing lessons became cheaper as the eighteenth century progressed, so encouraging the spread of dancing downwards socially into the lower middle classes. Certainly there was a vast increase in the amount of dancing done in Scotland, until by the 1770s it had become a major national pastime.[1]

The Country-dances which had been imported from England soon became acclimatized. New dances of this type, designed to go with Scots folk-tunes, were invented, and experimented with at aristocratic country-house parties; indeed it is likely that many of the great houses had their individual dancing traditions during the period between 1730 and 1780.[2] Instructions for forty-eight new, native country-dances are preserved in a manuscript written by David Young in Edinburgh in 1740, which is entitled 'A Collection of the newest Countrey Dances Perform'd in Scotland'.[3]

The Reel also flourished during this period; and a new type of slow reel, the Strathspey, originating presumably from the Spey valley in Inverness-shire, appeared in the Lowlands during the 1760s and caught on very quickly.

Country-dances, reels, and strathspeys were all danced to *folk* music; and as the dancing-masters—the people largely responsible for setting the trends—normally accompanied lessons with their own fiddle-playing, it followed that the dance-music tradition centred itself round the solo fiddle. A number of other instrumentations were also in common use. A greater volume of sound could be obtained from two fiddles played in unison. Often dance music was provided by a 'band', consisting of two fiddles and a cello: in this case the fiddles played the tune together, and the cello played a rudimentary bass-line in steady crotchets, often consisting of no more than an alternation between tonic and flattened seventh, whose purpose was to keep the beat more than to supply classical harmony. The cello part in such bands has been well described as

---

[1] Topham, pp. 339 f.; Jamieson. [2] Flett, *Scottish Country dance.*
[3] Bodleian Library, Oxford, MS. Don.d.54.

'a kind of accented drone'.[1] The painting 'The Highland Dance' by David Allan (1744–96) shows open-air dancing accompanied by one violin and a cello; with a bagpiper, not playing, helping himself to refreshments in the background.[2]

Oboes were also sometimes used instead of fiddles: the tunes in David Young's dancing-instruction manuscript of 1740 are expressly 'adapted to the Violin, or Hautboy'; and payments to musicians in Lady Grisell Baillie's account-book in 1710 include 'to the ho boys' as well as 'to the fidlers'. At the Edinburgh Assembly in 1746 there was, as we saw in Chapter 2, a resident band of four violins, two oboes, and a bassoon. It is probable that the music there was harmonized and 'classicalized' to make it fit for the most genteel dancing establishment in the country. But on the other hand, a single fiddle was perfectly respectable for private dances, even in the highest society. It had to be: eighteenth-century houses were so cramped that there was often no room for more than one musician. This is vividly shown in a description of a dance which took place at the Edinburgh home of Mrs. Alison Cockburn, in about 1770:

On Wednesday I gave a ball. How do ye think I contrived to stretch out this house to hold twenty-two people, and had nine couple always dancing? Yet this is true; it is also true that we had a table covered with divers eatables all the time, and that everybody eat when they were hungry and drank when they were dry, but nobody ever sat down. . . . Our fiddler sat where the cupboard is, and they danced in both rooms; the table was stuffed into the window and we had plenty of room. It made the bairns all vastly happy.[3]

And of course in conservative country districts the fiddle would often be replaced by such ancient instruments as the bagpipes or the stock-and-horn.

The amount of dancing done in Scotland greatly increased between 1720 and 1780, and led to an increased demand for dance music; to meet the need, large numbers of folk-songs were rewritten

---

[1] Collinson, *Traditional and national*, p. 226 n. Alexander McGlashan's band employed Nathaniel Gow as cellist in the 1780s; the published keyboard arrangements of McGlashan's compositions give some idea of how his band sounded.

[2] Reproduced in ibid., pl. 16.   [3] Cockburn, p. 82.

as instrumental dance tunes and pressed into service. The rewriting caused problems. Most song-tunes were of only one strain, usually eight bars long, and most dance tunes were required to have two strains. (David Young's manuscript employs two different kinds of handwriting to show what steps are to be made to the first strain of the tune, and what to the second.) Thus a fiddler rewriting a song-tune had not only to transfer it from vocal to instrumental idiom, but often also to compose a second strain to bring it up to the right length. William Stenhouse, annotating the *Scots Musical Museum* in 1820, remarked of many of the songs that 'the second part or strain of this tune is a modern interpolation',[1] though he offered no explanation why this should have happened. It is clear, however, that adding second strains to tunes was a favourite occupation of educated fiddlers in the mid eighteenth century. A myth even grew up about it: it was said to be impossible to write a second strain to 'The Broom of Cowdenknowes', and that the famous Geminiani of Dublin had tried and been forced to abandon the task after 'blotting several quires of paper'.[2]

The advent of the strathspey in the 1760s set off a further wave of composition. William Marshall's reconstruction of the song tune 'The Lowlands of Holland' as 'Miss Admiral Gordon's Strathspey' has already been described in Chapter 5. Some tunes were turned into strathspeys which had already suffered conversion earlier in the century into country-dances. An example of this is 'O'er the muir among the heather', which appears both as a 'new Countrey Dance' in David Young's 1740 manuscript, and as a strathspey in the *Scots Musical Museum* in 1792:[3]

O'er the muir among the Heather (country-dance)

1 Stenhouse, nos. 21, 33, 55, 65, 69, 73, 94, 154, 172, etc. Alexander Keith also suggested that folk-songs were naturally 1-strain, and that 2-strain tunes had at some stage been tampered with by professional musicians. See Greig, p. xliii.

2 This story is told, e.g., in Shield, p. 31.

3 *Scots Musical Museum*, vol. 4, with a few editorial rhythmic normalizations. The strathspey is transposed up a tone to facilitate comparison.

O'er the moor amang the heather (strathspey)
Lively, but Slow

It is notable that both versions are in definite instrumental idiom—characterized by the large unvocal leaps and the wide over-all range—and that both have two strains.

The Minuet differed from the country-dance, reel, and strathspey in being a continental dance and based on *classical* music. The music used in Scotland for minuets followed the normal classical pattern of stylistic evolution: it was Purcellian (or French) up to 1710, then Handelian (or Italian baroque) up to 1760, and after that galante: it followed the stylistic trends of classical music in London about ten years late. Minuet tunes were either imported from London or written in Edinburgh by classical composers such as Oswald and Kelly; and they were intended to be played in harmony by a full band.

Outside the main assemblies and special occasions like balls at Holyrood Palace, however, the musical forces were not readily available. Accordingly, minuets were adapted for solo fiddle by playing only the violin 1 part and ignoring, or imagining, the rest of the score. Many of Kelly's, Dow's, and McIntosh's minuets may be found written into fiddle books like this, the first violin part sometimes making very little musical sense on its own. But they must often have been played in this manner to accompany minuets at dances in country areas.

Thus a new musical genre, the 'folk minuet'—consisting of an unharmonized pseudo-classical melody for solo violin—came into being. A manuscript of a 'folk minuet' apparently originally composed like this is preserved in the Scottish Record Office, Edinburgh.[1] It is a presentation manuscript, inscribed 'Composed at Kerriemuir May 1769 by A. Stewart', and dedicated to Lady Ogilvy of Invercarity:

1 GD 38/1/1244.

Lady Ogilvy of Invercarity's Minuet

Though intended for solo fiddle, the melody is made up entirely of clichés from harmonized classical music. Bars 9–12, for example, bear a strong resemblance to part of the minuet in Barsanti's overture op. 4 no. 5, published in Edinburgh *c.* 1743:

This shows what kind of music the composer in Kirriemuir was using as a model. His piece hardly counts as classical music; yet it is not 'folk' either, except in its instrumentation and social context. It is a hybrid.

We see therefore that fiddle dance music, like the recital pieces, was developed and experimented with in a spirit of conscious artistry, by groups of musicians who were in touch with the classical culture.

PROFESSIONALISM IN FOLK MUSIC

I put forward in Chapter 1 the axiom that classical music depends for its continued existence upon professional musicians, while folk music can get along quite happily without them; and a paradox arises that, though folk music is in Scotland the more successful culture of the two, in terms of providing enjoyment for a greater number of people, yet it is easier for a musician to earn a living in classical music, where the audience, though a minority one, are accustomed to paying for their entertainment. There were in fact no professional folk musicians in Lowland Scotland in the eighteenth century up to 1775; the nearest thing to them were dancing-masters (whose prime job was in any case to teach dancing, so they do not really count), and vagrant players such as the midget in Burns's poem.

Two more such players may be mentioned here. The first is Patie Birnie, 'the famous fidler of *Kinghorn*' in Fife, on whom Allan Ramsay wrote a mock elegy in 1721. Famed for his scruffy appearance, bad jokes, and bibulousness,

> Tho' baith his weeds and mirth were pirny. . . . . .
> The brown ale was his kirn ay
> And faithfully he toom'd his horn.

Patie's basic technique was to attach himself to travellers as they came ashore off the Leith–Kinghorn ferry-boat, and force them to listen to his fiddle-playing and stand him drinks.

> When strangers landed, wow sae thrang
> Fuffin and peghing he wa'd gang
> And crave their pardon that sae lang
>   He'd been a coming;
> Syne his bread-winner out he'd bang
>   And fa' to bumming.[1]

In the *Edinburgh Evening Courant* for 20 November 1773 we find the following notice:

Thursday died at Kinghorn, one Robert Davidson, a musician, who for a number of years has made it his practice to divert the passengers betwixt Leith and Kinghorn with his fiddle. He was formerly musician on board the Phoenix man of war.

The similarities between the two players are interesting. Both lived in Kinghorn, and both earned a living by playing to travellers on the main route north from Edinburgh. But the living must have

---

[1] Ramsay, *Poems*, vol. i, 'Elegy on Patie Birnie'. Patie's *bread-winner* is his violin.

been precarious in the extreme, and the job was hardly one a man would take on from choice. And this was the best kind of existence that society could offer to a would-be professional folk-fiddler.

Thus amateur players brought up in the folk tradition who wanted to go professional had no alternative but to switch to classical music in order to earn a decent living. This, I am sure, is what happened to James Oswald. Oswald started off in life as a dancing-master in Dunfermline, and by the age of thirty had made a sizeable contribution to the folk-fiddle repertory as a composer; and he must have decided that this was hopeless as a career. So he mastered classical music, and ended up composing and publishing in London; but his sonatas are all rather wistfully tinged with Scottish folk style. Robert McIntosh was another such: he tried to pursue a career in folk and classical music simultaneously. He wrote minuets, sonatas, and concertos, yet his classical composition style is old-fashioned and his heart was not really in the job. It is probable that McLean and McGibbon, too, felt from time to time unfulfillable urges to become professional folk-musicians; this may be why both wrote so much folk-fiddle music.

But during the 1770s the situation changed. I outlined in Chapter 2 how public expenditure on classical music in Scotland reached a peak in 1776; and at the upper limit of this affluence society also became willing to spend money on folk music. Accordingly, we find that a small class of professional virtuoso folk-fiddlers emerged at this time. (Interestingly, the situation has repeated itself in Scotland in the 1960s. With the foundation of the Edinburgh Festival in 1947 and of Scottish Opera in 1962, classical music has reached a peak comparable to that of the 1770s; and the virtuoso folk-musician has appeared once again, now making LPs and performing on television.)

The first of these players was Niel Gow. He was born at Inver, Perthshire, in 1727, the son of the village weaver, and had times not been ripe he would no doubt have become a weaver also, and kept his fiddle as a hobby. Instead he was able to play fiddle as a full-time occupation. He won a national fiddle-playing competition at the age of eighteen, was patronized by the Duke of Atholl, and in

due course set up a band which was much in demand for aristocratic functions all over Scotland. He specialized in playing reels,
hornpipes, jigs, and strathspeys of his own composition, and in
1784 started a publishing firm to market his own pieces as an
additional source of income.

Niel Gow's fourth son Nathaniel followed in the same path. He
broadened his scope by taking lessons in cello and trumpet
from various members of the Reinagle family, whom we met earlier
in Chapter 3; they were of Austrian extraction and firmly rooted
in the classical tradition. Nathaniel Gow's compositions show,
however, that he absorbed this classical training successfully into
the folk style. Apart from being one of His Majesty's Trumpeters
for Scotland he did not earn his living from classical music. His
band frequently played in London.

William Marshall was another outstanding composer-fiddler of
the time. He was born at Fochabers, Morayshire, in 1748, and
went into service at the age of twelve with the Duke of Gordon,
who patronized him and allowed him to have a career as a musician;
though Marshall never in fact left the duke's service. Marshall
published collections of his own pieces in 1781 and 1822, the latter
of which is perhaps the finest single collection of Scottish fiddle
music ever printed. In addition to dance music, Marshall wrote
recital pieces of a new type which he may have invented himself:
the Slow Strathspey. These are pieces in strathspey rhythm but
played too slowly for dancing; they are usually nostalgic in
character.

Many other folk-fiddlers made a bid for professionalism at this
time by publishing their own compositions: Angus Cumming of
Grantown-on-Spey, John Bowie of Perth, John Morison of Peterhead, Robert Petrie of Kirkmichael, Perthshire, Isaac Cooper of
Banff, and many others brought out collections of reels and strathspeys between 1780 and 1810.[1]

After 1810 or so the boom in folk-fiddle music began to slacken
off again. Over the preceding seventy years the fiddle repertory had
been transformed almost beyond recognition, as a result of the

[1] Collinson, *Traditional and national*, pp. 214 f., has further information on professional fiddlers.

professional attention paid to it, but the era was over, and this attention was now transferred to new types of dance, the Waltz, the Quadrille, and the Mazurka, none of which had any connection with Scottish folk music. Even so, folk-fiddle music was a going concern for a hundred years more: reels and strathspeys were listened to and danced to not only in country areas, but by fashionable society from Queen Victoria down, and provided a living for many near-professional fiddlers, until 1914 at least.

7

NATIONAL SONGS

W E must now turn to a genre which Francis Collinson has aptly called 'national', as opposed to 'traditional', music. Scottish national songs were invented early in the eighteenth century. They are a kind of pseudo-folk-song, designed for a genteel class of people who regard real folk-songs as crude and beneath their attention, and to which they can attach the feelings of tradition and national identity which other people express through the oral tradition. They were a kind of artificial substitute for the real thing. A national song is usually made by taking a folk-song and rewriting first the words and then the tune, bringing them into line with the latest fashion, until nothing is left of the original but the use to which it is put, like the spade with the new blade and the new handle. However, the dividing line between the two genres is sometimes indistinct, and it is not unknown for national songs to be sucked back into oral circulation and so become new folk-songs in their own right.

The man who, more than anyone else, was responsible for the creation of the national song genre was the poet Allan Ramsay; and to understand how this came about we must first go back to music in seventeenth-century London.

There was, in London in the 1680s, a flourishing genre called 'Scotch songs'; these were somewhat debased popular songs of allegedly Scottish origin, some with fake tunes, all with fake words, and Londoners liked them because they were refreshingly different from the classical productions of Purcell and Lully. They had a quality which the late eighteenth century would have called 'wildness'—that of breaking the accepted rules of the art and yet giving pleasure to the beholder. Dryden in 1700 compared the appeal of 'Scotch songs' to that of Chaucer's poetry:

The Verse of *Chaucer*, I confess, is not Harmonious to us; but . . . they who liv'd with him, and some time after him, thought it Musical; . . . there is the rude Sweetness of a *Scotch* Tune in it, which is natural and pleasing, though not perfect.[1]

It is not known how the genre originated: perhaps from the personal tastes of royalty, who after all were (from one point of view) third-generation Scottish *émigrés*. Royalty certainly liked 'Scotch tunes', anyhow:

The queen having a mind one afternoon to be entertained with music, sent to Mr Gostling . . . [and] to Henry Purcell and Mrs Arabella Hunt, who had a very fine voice, and an admirable hand on the lute, with a request to attend her; they obeyed her commands; Mr Gostling and Mrs Hunt sung several compositions of Purcell, who accompanied them on the harpsichord; at length the queen beginning to grow tired, asked Mrs Hunt if she could not sing the old Scots ballad 'Cold and Raw', Mrs Hunt answered yes, and sung it to her lute. Purcell was all the while sitting at the harpsichord unemployed, and not a little nettled at the queen's preference of a vulgar ballad to his music; but seeing her majesty delighted with this tune, he determined that she should hear it upon another occasion; and accordingly in the next birthday song, viz. that for the year 1692, he composed an air to the words, 'May her bright example chace Vice in troops out of the land', the bass whereof is the tune to Cold and Raw.[2]

The person in London who did best out of 'Scotch songs' was Thomas D'Urfey. D'Urfey was a glittering success figure: he was the author of the longest series of successful plays the London stage has ever seen, not even excepting Bernard Shaw; the editor of *Pills to Purge Melancholy*, the most popular song book of the day; and a personal friend of Charles II. He reduced the writing of 'Scotch song' lyrics to a fine art. He worked to a standard pattern. The subject-matter was either conventional sex-in-high-life comedy, or satirical comment on the current England–Scotland political situation. Characters were called Sawney/Jockey if male,

[1] John Dryden, *Fables Ancient and Modern; translated into verse* (London, 1700), preface.
[2] Hawkins, vol. 4, p. 6 n.

and Jenny/Moggy if female. As poetic diction he used a synthetic Scots dialect, consisting of English with Scottish flavourings, e.g. the phrase 'Gude faith!' (ejaculated by all Scottish people at regular intervals, cf. the modern 'Hoots, mon!'), Scottish place-names, inserted for local colour, and vaguely meaningless adjectives with provincial or obsolescent overtones, such as 'blithe' and 'bonny'. The following D'Urfey lyric illustrates the formula nicely; it is set to a fake folk-tune composed by Purcell:

'Twas within a Furlong of *Edinborough* Town,
In the Rosie time of year when the Grass was down;
Bonny *Jockey* Blith and Gay,
Said to *Jenny* making Hay,
Let's sit a little (Dear) and prattle,
'Tis a sultry Day:
He long had Courted the Black-Brow'd Maid,
But *Jockey* was a Wag and would ne'er consent to Wed;
Which made her pish and phoo, and cry out it will not do,
I cannot, cannot, cannot, wonnot, monnot, Buckle too.

Note that D'Urfey regarded the Scots word *canna* as a slurred-over form of *cannot* in English, and by analogy back-formed 'correct' spellings for *winna* and *mauna*. He clearly had no conception of Scots as a separate language with its own spelling conventions: he improvised his own.

But the social attitudes of the next two lines betray that these characters turning hay less than 220 yards from the Edinburgh town walls are not locals, but Londoners on holiday:

He told her Marriage was grown a meer Joke,
And that no one Wedded now, but the Scoundrel Folk;

Clearly, the 'Scotch song' lyric does not deserve to be taken seriously as a form of literature; it matches such popular beliefs about Scotland as that all Scotsmen live in the Highlands and go about in kilts with no underwear. That it might be an important influence on real Scottish song would seem incredible.

But Scottish literature in the early eighteenth century was in a neurotic state. After the Scottish parliament disbanded for the last time in 1707, Edinburgh awoke painfully to the fact that it had become, culturally and politically, a satellite of London. Edinburgh's men of letters looked round, rather desperately, for a new kind of literature which could be essentially Scottish and yet make its mark on the London scene: something that would beat London at its own game. There was, for example, a literary debate in progress in London in the 1710s as to the correct method for moderns to imitate the pastorals of Theocritus. Theocritus wrote in Doric, an ancient Greek dialect noticeably different from the Attic Greek which was taught to schoolboys. It was suggested that moderns should, as a parallel, write pastorals in broad Yorkshire or Devonshire. Allan Ramsay in Edinburgh jumped on this band-wagon with a resounding thud. He wrote a pastoral (later extended into the play *The Gentle Shepherd*) in Lowland Scots, which he surrounded with such an effective publicity campaign that Scottish intellectuals have ever since referred to Scots dialect, affectionately, as 'the Doric'.[1]

The London 'Scotch song' was an obvious next target. It was already established and fashionable, yet to Ramsay's way of thinking it was a genre which Scottish poets could not help but do better at than Londoners, by the mere fact of their being Scots. Also I suspect that Ramsay was personally jealous of D'Urfey's success.

In 1718 Ramsay brought out in Edinburgh a trial volume entitled *Scots Songs*, consisting of new lyrics set to specified traditional tunes. Comparison of the names of some of the tunes:

> The yellow-hair'd laddie
> Nanny O
> Bonny Jean
> The Lass of Livingston

with Ramsay's first lines:

> 'In *April*, when primroses paint the sweet plain'
> 'While some for pleasure pawn their health'
> 'Love's goddess in a myrtle grove'
> 'Pain'd with her slighting *Jamie*'s love'

[1] Ramsay, *Poems*, vol. 1, preface.

shows how far this was a divergence from the folk tradition. Emboldened by favourable public reception, Ramsay then set to work on *The Tea-table Miscellany*, whose first volume was published in Edinburgh on 1 January 1723. Like the earlier collection it consisted of new words set to folk-tunes, but this time on a larger scale: the *Tea-table Miscellany* was nothing less than an attempt to set up, single-handed, a complete new Scottish song repertory. As a piece of brazen effrontery it is unequalled in the cultural history of Scotland, and it is even more remarkable in that it succeeded. Scholars ever since have had great difficulty in forming a picture of Scots folk-song prior to 1723, largely because Ramsay's work obliterated the traces of it.[1]

The *Tea-table Miscellany* eventually comprised four volumes; it went through fifteen official editions and many more pirated ones; and many editions have disappeared completely, showing that the public used the books over and over again until they fell to bits. The collection deserves examination in some detail.

Ramsay's new repertory was made up of four main strands: first, new lyrics written to traditional Scots tunes by himself and his friends and correspondents; second, 'Scotch songs' by D'Urfey, lifted without acknowledgement from *Pills to Purge Melancholy*, with the mistakes in dialect corrected to make them fit for Edinburgh; third, genuine folk-songs, touched up to make them fit for London; and fourth, a group which has no bearing on this study and which I shall not discuss further, poems from the old Scottish court and seventeenth-century vernacular pieces, culled by Ramsay from such sources as the Bannatyne manuscript.

Of the first group, Ramsay said in the preface to the ninth edition of 1733:

My being well assured, how acceptable new words to known good tunes would prove, engaged me to the making verses for above sixty of them . . . about thirty more were done by some ingenious young gentlemen, who were so well pleased with my undertaking, that they generously lent me their assistance.

[1] See, for example, Leyden's discussion of 'John Leyden's lyra-viol manuscript' in *Preliminary dissertation*, p. 286, in which he dates the manuscript *c.* 1715 and remarks that it 'at least enables us to advance a step beyond Ramsay'.

I propose to take 'young gentlemen' literally in that statement, and to assume that Ramsay's assistants were both junior to and of higher social class than himself. One of them was David Malloch, an Edinburgh University student who later changed his name to Mallet and made a name as a playwright in London. The uniformity of their poetic style suggests that Ramsay kept a firm controlling hand on them.

The second group, the rewritten D'Urfey songs, are interesting, as Ramsay has in all cases tried to make them more realistic and down-to-earth; there are five songs in this group.[1] 'In January last' seems to have been an English folk-song originally, which D'Urfey Scotticized to bring it into line with current fashion. It tells the story of a gentleman who accompanies a strange girl across a moor and offers to make love to her; she says she has a lover already, so he retracts and apologizes, whereupon she laughs at him for being so easily put off. Ramsay corrected D'Urfey's Scots spelling and grammar and so improved the look of the song on paper, but in other ways he confused its over-all shape. One detail of his alterations is, however, significant; he changed D'Urfey's

> I spear'd o her, fair Maid quo I, how far intend ye now?
> Quo she, I mean a Mile or twa, to yonder bonny brow.

to

> I spear'd, My dear, how far awa
> Do ye intend to gae?
> Quoth she, I mean a mile or twa
> Out o'er yon broomy brae.

The broom was a traditional place for illicit love-making in Scots folk-songs,[2] so it is clear that Ramsay was trying, by altering

---

[1] 'She rose and let me in', 'In January last', 'As I sat at my spinning wheel', 'Young Philander woo'd me long', 'O Jenny, where has thou been?'. These songs have been the subject of considerable controversy over the last 150 years. The differences between D'Urfey's and Ramsay's texts have been explained in two ways: (1) Ramsay stole them from D'Urfey and altered them; (2) they were written in Scotland *c.* 1650, e.g. by Francis Sempill of Beltrees, imperfect texts reached D'Urfey in London, Ramsay had access to originals or to near-originals. Theory (1) seems to me much the simpler, and there is no doubt that Ramsay, who was a prominent Edinburgh bookseller, was aware of D'Urfey's work. No one has ever seen any Scottish, pre-D'Urfey, manuscripts of these songs.

[2] The symbol recurs in other songs, e.g. 'Low down in the broom', 'The broom of Cowdenknowes'.

'bonny' to 'broomy', to connect up the song to the folk tradition
and to give it rich overtones beyond D'Urfey's scope.

Another D'Urfey song begins:

> The Night her blackest Sable wore,
> And gloomy were the Skies;
> And glitt'ring Stars there were no more,
> Than those in *Stella*'s Eyes:
> When at her Father's Gate I knock'd,
> Where I had often been,
> And Shrowded only with her Smock
> The fair one let me in.

There is nothing particularly Scottish about this song except the
word 'bearn' ('child') in stanza four. William Chappell pointed out
that this was not the standard spelling of the word in Scots, and
that it might as well be Yorkshire or another local English dialect;[1]
but I am inclined to think that it *is* intended as Scots, and that
D'Urfey simply improvised the spelling, as usual. At any rate,
that was how Ramsay took it. He translated a few more words into
Scots, and removed the tautological 'blackest Sable' and the pun
between 'Stars' and '*Stella*'s'. It also occurred to him that 'Stella'
sounded like the class of woman who wouldn't be seen answering
the door in person in any circumstances, let alone wearing a nightie.
A one-word alteration put all that right,

> The night her silent sable wore,
> And gloomy were the skies;
> Of glitt'ring stars appear'd no more
> Than those in *Nelly*'s eyes . . . . .

and changed D'Urfey's sex-in-high-life conventional situation into
Scottish low-life realism.

If Ramsay's rewriting of London song to give it a Scottish folk
flavour was not entirely successful, his work in the reverse direction
—i.e. rewriting Scottish folk-songs to give them a London flavour—
was much worse. Some background information about folk-songs
is necessary here.

---

[1] Chappell, vol. 2, p. 510.

There were a number of songs in circulation in 1720 about Lowland girls abandoning their families and wealth and eloping with Highland lovers; the Highlander was supposed to possess greater sexual energy than the Lowlander, like the Negro compared to the White in present-day myth. One of these songs was printed on a broadside of the time; entitled 'The New Way of the Bonny Highland Laddie', it is a violent narrative about an Edinburgh girl who decides to leave home and walk north until she is stopped on the road and raped:

> I crossed *Forth*, I crossed *Tay*,
> I left *Dundee*, and *Edinborrow*,
> I saw nothing there worth my Stay
> and so I bad them all Good-morrow.
>
> > O my bonny, bonny Highland Laddie,
> > O my bonny, bonny Highland Laddie,
> > When I am sick and like to dye,
> > Thou'lt row me in thy Highland Pladie.[1]

Finally she finds what she wants:

> For on the *Cairnamount* I spy'd,
> in careless Dress a Highland Laddie,
> Who briskly said, were't thou my Bride,
> I'd row thee in my Highland Pladie.

Ramsay attempted a genteel, lyric, version of this song, but the subject-matter was so inherently bawdy that his efforts at refined treatment were largely a waste of time. He managed to reduce the bawdiness somewhat, but only by substituting prurience:

> If I were free at will to chuse
> To be the wealthiest lawland lady,
> I'd take young *Donald* without trews,
> With bonnet blew and belted plaidy.
>
> > O my bonny bonny highland laddie,
> > My handsome charming highland laddie;
> > May heaven still guard, and love reward
> > Our lawland lass and her highland laddie.

[1] NLS: Ry. III.a.10 (89).

Ramsay's 'Highland Lassie', however, is even worse. This is a
parallel lyric, to the same tune, in which a Lowlander is pursuing a
Highland girl. By transposing the sexes Ramsay breaks the tradition and cuts off the song's folk roots. That throws him back on
to his own inventive resources: in this case, watery sentimentality:

> Than ony lass in borrows-toun,
> Wha mak their cheeks with patches motie,
> I'd tak my *Katie* but a gown,
> Bare-footed in her little coatie.[1]

Another song which Ramsay tried his hand at was 'The Collier's
Daughter'. This was a popular tune in Scotland at the time, and
according to William Stenhouse, had words which began:

> The collier has a dochter,
> And, O, she's unco bonny;
> A laird he was that sought her,
> Rich baith in lands and money.
> She wadna hae a laird,
> Nor wad she be a lady,
> But she wad hae a collier,
> The colour o' her daddie.[2]

Coal-mine workers in Scotland at the time were serfs. They
belonged to the mine-owner for life, along with their wives and
children. It was not possible for their sons to escape from the mine,
and their daughters could do so only by marrying outside. But
such marriages were not usual, since the work which women were
forced to do down mines caused permanent facial and bodily
deformity, and they were regarded by outsiders with 'mysterious
horror'.[3] For a collier's daughter, then, to be 'unco bonny' and
courted by a landowner was extraordinary, and her rejection of
him was even more so. The rest of the song has been lost, but it is
clear that it had a strong, topical story-line, concerned with a
current struggle for survival. The same collier's-daughter/laird
situation recurs in other popular songs. A broadside of *c.* 1720
entitled 'The Coalier Lassie' describes the happy opportunities of

---

[1] *Motie*: speckled with dust/ *but*: without.   [2] Stenhouse, no. 47.
[3] The phrase is Lord Cockburn's. See Innes, pp. 498 f.; Smout, pp. 430 f.

... the Landwart Laird
that is the Coaliers Master
For he may speak a word with her
when she lyes down to rest her.[1]

and the version of 'The Laird of Cockpen' which David Herd published in 1776 has a stanza that runs:

And was nae COCKPEN right sawcy?
And was nae COCKPEN right sawcy?
He len'd his lady to gentlemen
And kist the collier lassie.[2]

Cockpen was an estate about ten miles south-east of Edinburgh, on the edge of the Lothian coal-fields, so its laird would be nicely placed for this kind of activity.

Clearly the subject had great possibilities. Ramsay, however, turned his 'Collier's bonny lassie' into a conventional elegant love-lyric, and simply threw all this rich, dramatic, folk-rooted material away:

The collier has a daughter,
And O she's wonder bonny,
A laird he was that sought her,
Rich baith in lands and money.
The tutors watch'd the motion
Of this young honest lover;
But love is like the ocean;
Wha can its depth discover?

He had the art to please ye,
And was by a' respected,
His airs sat round him easy,
Genteel, but unaffected ...

I see no need to quote any more of this rubbish. Yet the Edinburgh upper-class public—and subsequently the British general public—lapped it up; Ramsay was a good businessman if often an indifferent poet. And his 'Scots songs', though an oil-and-water mixture of London fashionable verse and Scots folk-song which rarely, if ever,

[1] NLS: Ry. III.a.10 (44).   [2] Herd, vol. 2, p. 206.

worked artistically, yet caught the public mood of the time, and did much to restore Edinburgh's self-esteem as a literary centre.

So far this chapter has been only about national songs as litera-ture; for Ramsay was musically naïve, and expected his elegant new lyrics to be sung to folk-tunes unaccompanied: his plans for reshaping the popular-song tradition did not go as far as tampering with the music. He received a shock, therefore, when on 1 January 1725, exactly two years after the first issue of *Tea-table Miscellany*,[1] William Thomson in London published *Orpheus Caledonius*, a collection of fifty Scots songs set for voice and continuo, thirty-eight of them lifted directly from the *Tea-table Miscellany*. Thomson must be given full credit for the settings, some of which are ex-tremely tasteful; the vocal lines are delicately ornamented, probably reflecting Thomson's own performance, for he was a professional singer of Scottish descent whose renderings of Scots songs were much admired in London. To Ramsay, however, Thomson's collection was no better than a pirate edition of his own—if one could possibly regard any large folio volume with handsome leather covers and a subscription-list of 300 persons headed by the Princess of Wales, as a pirate edition. Ramsay commented in his 1733 preface:

> From this and the following volume, Mr *Thomson* . . . cull'd his *Orpheus Caledonius* . . . dedicated to her royal highness. . . . This by the by I thought proper to intimate, and do my self that justice which the publisher neglected; since he ought to have acquainted his illustrious list of subscribers, that most of the songs were mine, the musick abstracted.

In fact the indebtedness was not so one-sided as Ramsay wanted the public to think. The other twelve of Thomson's fifty songs gave Ramsay several good ideas for *Tea-table Miscellany*, volume two, which came out shortly afterwards, probably in 1726. And to show London that Edinburgh was not so backward musically after all, he had the Edinburgh violinist Alexander Stuart[2] arrange *Musick*

---

[1] I presume this was the date of publication; the collection was registered at Stationers' Hall on 5 January. See Laing, pp. xli f.

[2] He was on the Edinburgh Musical Society payroll in 1726. See EMS minute-books, accounts, 1727, 'Alex^r Stewart'.

for Allan Ramsay's Collection of Scots Songs Vol: First for violin and continuo; this was also published *c.* 1726. *Orpheus Caledonius*, second edition, 1733, was expanded to a hundred songs, and milked *Tea-table Miscellany*, volumes one and two, still further; but Ramsay retaliated by swiping six songs from it for *Tea-table Miscellany*, volume four, published *c.* 1737, including the beautiful and subsequently famous ballads 'Willy's rare and Willy's fair' and 'The bonny earl of Murray', which Thomson had printed for the first time. So the relationship between the two collections is more complex than it appears at first sight.

It is interesting that while Ramsay's collection was intended as an injection of life-blood into the Edinburgh cultural scene, Thomson's was merely a foreign curiosity for the London public in the accepted D'Urfey-ish vein. Thomson's title, adapted from Henry Purcell's *Orpheus Britannicus* (London, several editions, 1698–1721) suggests that his collection had that function, while the introductory verse, which confuses the Scottish Highlands with the Lowlands and hints at the usual what-does-he-wear-under-his-kilt joke, makes it explicit:

> Love's brightest Flames warm *Scottish* Lads,
> Tho' coolly clad in High-land Plads;
> They scorn Brocade, who like the Lass,
> Nor need a Carpet, if there's Grass. . . . .
> Thus merrily they court the Fair,
> And love and sing in Northern Air.

Thus the same repertory of songs was performing two different social functions at once: bolstering Edinburgh's cultural self-confidence and tickling London's palate with foreign novelties.

By 1740 or so Ramsay's repertory had become established. It was regarded all over Britain as synonymous with the very idea of 'Scots song', and had begun to give birth to complicated classical music arrangements. The songs were sung by foreign vocalists, with orchestral accompaniment, at the Edinburgh Musical Society's concerts: the musical society's library catalogue of 1765 includes 'Banks of Forth', 'Lochaber', 'One day I heard Mary say', 'She rose and let me in', 'Tweed Side', 'The Braes of Yarrow', and 'The

Lass of Patie's Mill' among a list of 'songs whose parts are wrote out'. Barsanti in Edinburgh in 1742 arranged thirty of them for voice and continuo; Geminiani in Dublin in 1749 set four of them for voice with flutes and string quartet, and incorporated others into trio- and solo sonatas;[1] Pasquali in Edinburgh in 1755 wrote a cantata based on 'Tweedside', 'newly set in the Italian manner . . . with various symphonies of Violins and Flutes';[2] J. C. Bach in London in the 1770s set three of them for voice and orchestra and one—'The Braes of Ballenden'—for voice and virtuoso chamber ensemble, and incorporated two more into piano concertos;[3] and many Edinburgh and Aberdeen composers in the 1780s followed Bach's lead and used the tunes in sonatas and concertos, notably Butler, Stephen Clarke, Ross, Schetky, and Stabilini.

The tunes were also used, with new words, in English opera. Gay included a few in *The Beggar's Opera* in London in 1728; three Scots songs were added to Arne's *Artaxerxes* for its Edinburgh production in 1769; and Thomas Linley included Scots tunes, beautifully scored for horns and strings, in *The Duenna* in London in 1775.

The famous castrato Tenducci was a great champion of Scots song during the period, and probably helped, personally, to increase its popularity.[4] He was based in London but made regular visits to Edinburgh. He was a friend of J. C. Bach, and it was for him that Bach made his vocal arrangements of Scots songs; he sang in both *Artaxerxes* and *The Duenna*; and during Edinburgh visits he was always invited to sing at the musical society, where his renderings of Scots songs were greatly appreciated. George Thomson frequented the Edinburgh Musical Society concerts in the 1780s and heard Tenducci, and at a much later date imitated his manner of singing for the benefit of Robert Chambers:

About 1770, the Italian singer Tenducci made a great success in introducing ['One day I heard Mary say'] to his Edinburgh audiences;

---

[1] In Geminiani's *Treatise of Good Taste in the Art of Musick* (London, 1749).

[2] Listed in EMS library catalogue, 1765 (MS.); and see Dalyell, p. 286.

[3] Roger Fiske, 'J. C. Bach and Scots songs', broadcast talk, B.B.C. Third Programme, 24 January 1967.

[4] Campbell, p. 14 n.

and so lately as 1848, the editor had the pleasure of hearing a representation of that great vocalist's manner of singing this song, from a gentleman who not only remembered it well, but could imitate it with tolerable effect. As might be expected, a strong rise in passionate energy at 'Alas, my fond heart will break!' was the *tour de force* of the performance.[1]

All this time the repertory which Ramsay had laid down in the 1720s, in volumes one and two of the *Tea-table Miscellany*, was kept virtually intact. It had been canonized. A few new tunes had been added, such as Oswald's 'Roslin Castle' and 'Braes of Ballenden', and James Hook's 'Saw you my father',[2] and a few lyrics had been changed, but that was about all. The reason for this stability was probably that most of the composers we have just mentioned were *foreigners*: they had no Scottish folk roots, and no means of telling a genuine Scots folk-tune from a bogus one. Hence, when they wanted a 'Scots tune' to set, they tended to play safe and use one of Ramsay's already sanctioned ones. And these were the people who were setting the standards of cultivated taste.

By 1780, however, the national song corpus was beginning to look decidedly tattered. Society had changed over the preceding sixty years and many of the lyrics had gone, by imperceptible stages, out of date. For example, it had been normal Scottish farming practice in 1720 to milk ewes, and this custom is referred to in two of Ramsay's songs, 'Will ye go to the ew-bughts, Marion' and 'The yellow-hair'd laddie'; while an allied farming custom, the forcible weaning of young lambs in order to free the ewes' milk supply for human consumption, was the background to a third song, 'The wauking of the fauld':

> My *Peggy* is a young thing,
> Just enter'd in her teens,
>> Fair as the day, and sweet as May,
>> Fair as the day, and always gay,

---

[1] Chambers, *Songs of Scotland*, p. 347.

[2] The ascriptions of these tunes are all a little doubtful. 'The Braes of Ballenden' was ascribed to Oswald in 'An Epistle to James Oswald', *Scots Magazine*, October 1741; for 'Saw you my father' see Chappell, vol. 2, p. 731.

> My *Peggy* is a young thing,
> And I'm not very auld,
> Yet well I like to meet her at
> The wauking of the fauld.

But farming methods changed,[1] so that by 1780 these songs were no longer realistic pictures of the present, but nostalgic accounts of the past. Nostalgia is plainly apparent in Chambers's notes on 'The wauking of the fauld', written in 1862, and it had begun to set in before the end of the eighteenth century:

> In the old rural economy of Scotland, it was necessary for a shepherd and one of the female servants of the farm to keep up a nightwatch upon the ewe-bughts or fold, in order to prevent the weaned lambs from getting back to their dams. In the mild twilight nights of July, it was no great hardship to stay from eve to dewy morn in the open air, and when the pair were of congenial minds, still more if they were declared lovers, it was of course considered as a luxury. The occasion is commemorated in a charming song by Ramsay.[2]

Nostalgia also crept into the style of musical performance. Foreign singers decorated the tunes mercilessly in order to squeeze the last drop of sentiment out of them, and tempi were progressively slowed down until 'Scots songs' were nearly always slow songs. 'An thou wert mine ain thing' in the setting by Haydn in George Thomson's *Select Collection*, volume three, published in Edinburgh in 1802, is a good demonstration of the state which national songs had reached by that date. The excessive decoration and the slow speed are complementary:

Tune:

Haydn's introduction:

Haydn's conclusion:

Meanwhile a mounting volume of protest rose against the whole genre. An important spokesman was John Leyden, an intellectual Scot of humble origins, who was born in the village of Denholm in Roxburghshire in 1775, and spent the first fifteen years of his

---

[1] Trow-Smith, vol. 2, p. 208.   [2] Chambers, *Songs of Scotland*, p. 316.

life in contact with real folk-songs, meeting national songs only
later, when he went up to Edinburgh University. He called them
'a kind of sacrilege':

the airs of most Scotish tunes, which are still chaunted in the pastoral
districts of Scotland, are much more simple than the sets which are
found in collections, and which have passed under the hand of a
composer.[1]

National songs had reached a crisis, and there was no obvious
solution to it; the situation facing aspiring editors in 1780 was
far more complex than that which Ramsay had faced in 1720. On
the one hand were the antiquarians, wanting to excavate the layers
of genteel deposit and unearth genuine oral folk-song, which was
still widely current in Scotland; on the other hand there were
undoubted opportunities for developing the national song repertory
as it stood: hundreds of new reels and strathspeys had just been
written which were crying out for words, and an affluent public
was ready to buy new song books. A compromise between the
two approaches was needed. Between 1780 and 1830 many new
collections were published in Edinburgh, all nationalistic in spirit,
many experimental in method; but none of them managed to
blend scholarship, taste, and popular appeal in quite the right
proportions.

George Thomson's *Select Collection* (6 volumes, 1793 on) was in
many ways a spiritual descendant of Ramsay. Thomson's method
was to select already popular songs, and then commission new
words to them from prominent living Scottish poets, coupling
them with new musical settings by prominent living European
composers. Between 1792 and 1804 he enlisted as his musicians,
successively, Pleyel, Kozeluch, Haydn, and Beethoven. In theory
this looks a good method, but in practice it did not work; Thomson's foreign composers did not understand the modes of Scots
folk-tunes (Kozeluch sent Thomson's first batch back from Vienna
under the impression they were full of copyists' errors),[2] and his
poets' new words mostly turned out inferior to those they were
intended to replace. Burns's contributions to the collection were

[1] Leyden, *Preliminary dissertation*, p. 275.   [2] Hadden, p. 298.

an exception. Thomson was an amateur publisher with little feel for public demand. By the end of his life he had spent a lot of his own money and produced, not the standard classic he was aiming at, but a monstrous white elephant.

Walter Scott's *Minstrelsy of the Scottish Border*, published in 1802, was a collection of oral songs, mostly taken down from folk-singers in the Borders by himself and John Leyden. In many ways it is an unsatisfactory publication also, though it had great influence in literary circles. Scott was unmusical and printed no tunes, so his collection was no use to concert-performers. He also believed that Scotland became more 'Scottish' the further back one went into the past (this is a more subtle form of the same nostalgia that had already attacked the national song tradition), and his book tends to be biased in favour of old songs; he liked ballads which referred to ancient genealogies and customs, and passed over the more recent oral songs of which the national song repertory could really have benefited from an injection. He also indulged in rewriting the songs he collected, without recording the original versions properly, so that his work is of less value than it could have been, even as a piece of scholarship.

Then there were the frankly commercial collections of the professional singers: Domenico Corri and Peter Urbani. Urbani's *Select Collection* (6 volumes, 1792–1804) is innovatory in including about twenty new 'Scots tunes' composed by himself; but they did not catch on with the public. There were also the charlatans: James Hogg did a special line in so-called 'Jacobite' songs, describing the events of the 1715 and 1745 rebellions, but mostly written long afterwards, if not actually by Hogg himself. Hogg wrote to George Thomson on the subject on 14 February 1822:

If you therefore adopt the songs, please publish them simply as *Jacobite* songs, leaving the world to find out whether they are old or new. This has a far better effect than saying '*A Jacobite song by such and such an author*'. The very idea that perhaps they may be of a former day and written by some sennachie of the clan gives them double interest.[1]

Rules for faking up a tradition!

[1] Hadden, p. 182.

Among this confusion of aims and ideals only one man reached anything like a centre-of-the-road position, and that was Robert Burns. Burns's achievement was no easy matter; it involved intimate acquaintance with all the different forms of 'Scots song' current at the time, coupled with immense powers of digestion and assimilation. Burns was able to recombine organically the various strands of the tradition, which were fast breaking off from each other and drifting away in separate directions. But this was a heroic task for which Burns was uniquely qualified, and it is not surprising that he had no successors: David Daiches says of his achievement that it was

a highly precarious balancing between a number of conflicting forces; it was a *personal* achievement, and was not available for fruitful imitation.[1]

Burns was born at Alloway, Ayrshire, in 1759, of working-class parents. The first kind of national song he got to know must have been oral folk-song, probably including traditional medieval ballads; later he read broadsides and polite English lyrics and Ramsay; on his first visit to Edinburgh in 1786 he met educated bawdy (a sort of forerunner of the modern rugby song) at the Crochallan Fencibles club, and was caught up in the antiquarian movement. His ideas on what national song consisted of embraced all these genres.

In April 1787 he met the music-publisher James Johnson, who was then on the point of publishing the first volume of *The Scots Musical Museum*. The meeting was portentous; Burns was invited to help with the editing:

When Johnson originally asked Burns for assistance he did not presumably realise what a congenial task he was offering the poet. As the months went by, Burns took over more and more of the editorial duties, until by the middle of 1787 he was in fact though not in title the real editor of the collection. His letters to Johnson give some indication of the assiduity and enthusiasm with which he tracked down Scottish songs and threw himself into the business of

---

[1] Daiches, *Paradox*, p. 88.

collecting, editing, restoring, rewriting, and creating. The great body of Burns' poetic output between early 1787 and late in 1792 went into the *Museum*.[1]

It is not generally realized how important the antiquarian side of Burns's work on Scots songs was: even if Burns's own lyrics had subsequently proved ephemeral he would still have ranked as the outstanding folk-song collector of his generation. The tunes of 'Ca' the yowes' and 'Up wi' the carles of Dysart' were his discoveries, as were the words and tune of the ballad 'Tam Lin', which were printed for the first time in volume five of the *Museum*.

Burns's rewriting of song lyrics is too vast a subject to be tackled here; it has already been discussed in detail by Daiches and Hecht.[2] I shall only select here a few points from their excellent accounts. Volume one of the *Museum*, prepared by Johnson before Burns appeared on the scene, was a standard collection based largely on Allan Ramsay's work, and containing a hundred songs. The Ramsay repertory, stretched to its limits, might just about have provided a further hundred songs for a second volume; so the fact that the *Museum*, in the actual event, ran to six volumes and six hundred songs shows how large Burns's contribution to the book was. Burns pressed several hundred new song-tunes into circulation, both by printing tunes which had previously only existed in oral currency, and by setting words to reels and strathspeys which had up till then only been instrumental pieces. In addition to the songs in the *Museum*, he also contributed about a hundred items to George Thomson's *Select Collection*.

The *Museum* had its drawbacks as a collection, too. Its print was cheap and nasty to look at. Its musical settings, done by the organist Stephen Clarke, were often extremely dull and uninteresting; in his eagerness to avoid the excessive decoration of Corri and Urbani, Clarke tended to err in the opposite direction. Furthermore, Clarke and Johnson decided to notate the settings in figured-bass, and not to provide opening and closing 'symphonies' (instrumental leads), presumably in order to save paper. This was an unfortunate decision for 1787, for by 1800 figured-bass had gone

---

[1] Daiches, *Burns*, p. 233.   [2] Ibid., pp. 268 f.; Hecht, *Burns*, pp. 178 f.

completely out of fashion, and instrumental leads had definitely come in; when rival editors of the time speak complacently of their own collections having 'the proper symphonies and accompaniments' they are usually referring, back-handedly, to Johnson's *Museum*. The collection was not particularly successful financially, and Johnson died destitute in 1811. Reprints of the work were called for, in the interests of scholarship, in 1839, 1853, and 1962, and it is nowadays regarded as a standard classic; but it cannot have appeared so at the time.

Burns's songs proved to be more lasting than either *The Scots Musical Museum* or Thomson's *Select Collection*. Their reintegration of oral and literary tradition atoned, in a sense, for Ramsay's mistakes earlier in the century; and national songs in Scotland have been identified with Burns, and no one else, ever since.

8

THE HARMONIZATION OF FOLK-TUNES

T HE problem recurred all through the eighteenth century: every time a new book of national songs was produced it was necessary to try to fit the tunes up with classical harmony. Scottish folk-tunes of the period give a preliminary, but misleading, appearance of being amenable to classical harmonization; when the crucial moment comes, however, they have a way of slipping out of the arranger's grasp and running away, chuckling to themselves. Most Scottish folk-tunes are in recognizable keys, and many have quite a strong sense of classical tonality: frequently a tune will open by stating the notes of the tonic triad. 'My love she's but a lassie yet' is a typical example, and such tunes increased in number as the eighteenth century progressed. Yet nearly all of them also include melodic procedures which defeat harmonization altogether.

As I said earlier, the folk tradition in Scotland was essentially monodic. There were no harmonic folk-instruments in Scotland until the concertina arrived in about 1880; and eighteenth-century folk-tunes, though influenced by classical tonality, yet retained gapped-scale melodic shapes, double-tonic sequences, and a habit of ending the melody on a note other than the stated tonic. I should like to examine each of these phenomena in turn, and see how they stood up to attempts at harmonization.

GAPPED SCALES

'Peggy I must love thee'

'Peggy I must love thee' was first recorded in the 1680s as a London 'Scotch song', but it is certainly older than that, and may have been used as a dance tune at the sixteenth-century Scottish court. Allan Ramsay furnished it with new words in the *Tea-table Miscellany*, thus ensuring its survival in Scotland up to 1800. It is a typical gapped-scale Scots melody. I want to make a comparison using the following eight texts:

A. 'A new Scotch Tune' arranged by Henry Purcell in *Musick's Handmaid Part 2*, 1689;

B. 'Scot[c]h Tune' in 'Princess Anne's lute-book', *c.* 1690;

C. 'Meggie I must love the' in 'John Leÿden's lyra-viol manuscript', *c.* 1695;

D1. 'pege I most Love the' in George Bowie's music book, 1705;

D2. 'Pegy I mosst Love thee' in ditto;

E. 'Peggie I must love thee' in Adam Craig's *Collection of the Choicest of the Scots Tunes, c.* 1725;

F1. 'Peggy I must love thee' in William Thomson's *Orpheus Caledonius*, first edition, 1725; and

F2. 'Peggy I must love thee' in ditto, second edition, 1733.

As sung in Scotland in about 1700 the tune probably went like this:[1]

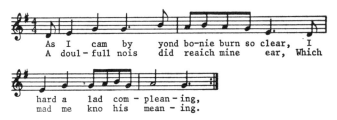

As I cam by yond bo-nie burn so clear, I
A doul-full nois did reaich mine ear, Which

hard a lad com-plean-ing,
mad me kno his mean-ing.

So far the tune is completely pentatonic. At the same time it has a definite feel of G major—partly because the notes of the G major triad account for three-fifths of this particular pentatonic scale. The tune seems to want to establish a G major tonality, yet its first strong beat is an E which is not harmonizable by a G major

---

[1] The tune is an editorial conflation of texts *A* and *D1*. The words are supplied from a manuscript book 'Boght at Inverary 1714' now in the North Ayrshire Museum, Saltcoats, with a few editorial emendations. That these words were common currency in Scotland at the time is shown by an entry, *c.* 1710, in James Gairdyn's music book (NLS MS. 3298), where the tune is headed 'As I went down yon burn so clear'.

chord. It also uses an E as a functional 'dominant' at the half-close (bar 2 note 5^2); this is perfectly satisfactory so long as the tune remains unharmonized—any note of the pentatonic scale apart from G would serve here as a 'dominant'—but classical harmony would normally require a D major chord at this point, which the note E will not fit. The most important functional aspect of this part of the tune is that it is all set low down in the voice.

The second strain begins by repeating the opening in a higher position:

It is tempting to interpret the F naturals in bar 8 (the first notes to occur outside the pentatonic scale) as part of a classical modulation to the subdominant; but the temptation should be resisted. I think the notes are intended as non-directional flattened sevenths, as is certainly bar 10 note 2. But there is some confusion here, which is reflected in later texts: *C* and *D2* give F sharps in bar 8, while *C*, *D1*, *D2*, *E*, *F1*, and *F2* alter bar 10 note 2 to G, the tendency being to reduce the harmonic uncertainty by replacing the F naturals with something else.

Purcell set the tune for solo keyboard as follows (text *A*):

A New Scotch Tune

¹ Not numbering the quaver upbeat.

Purcell has had to open with a subdominant chord in order to accommodate the stressed E at the beginning of the tune; and bar 2 note 4 has been altered from G to F sharp to allow a D major harmonization. But what are we to make of the chord under bar 2 note 5? Is it supposed to be A minor first inversion with the bass suspended, or D major with the tune pretending that [music] is equivalent to [music]? The listener's mind tends to flit ambiguously between the two possibilities. At bar 8 note 1 the flattened seventh is dealt with in a characteristically Purcellian manner; but as a result, the melodic phrase is extended so that it cadences at bar 9 note 1 instead of at bar 8 note 5, and no longer fits the metrical scheme of the original lyric. The over-all coherence of the arrangement is greatly helped by the imitative quaver-figures which Purcell introduces in the player's left hand.

Text *B* is an arrangement for lute in 'Princess Anne's lute-book':[1]

Scot[c]h Tune

[1] The present whereabouts of this manuscript are unknown. I have worked from a facsimile given in Shield, p. 57. The example is transposed to facilitate comparison. Bar 9 note 1 lower note was originally a fourth lower.

This is strongly dependent on text *A*—it has the same alteration
of bar 2 note 4, and the same modulation in the middle of the second
strain. But it is more successful than Purcell in many ways: the
sketchiness of lute-style allows the arranger to leave great melodic
arcs unsupported in mid air, and harmonic ambiguities are not
forced upon the listener's attention but remain dormant. The
awkward E at the beginning of the tune is dealt with imaginatively:
it is displaced an octave, Stravinsky-like, so that the opening suggests, without actually stating, a chord of E minor, and the whole
tune is cross-barred so as to throw the stress off the note on to the
next-but-one-following G, so reinforcing a sense of G major tonality.

The setting for lyra-viol in 'John Leyden's lyra-viol manuscript'[1]
(text *C*) is disappointing by comparison. The accompaniment is no
more than a drone on any available open strings:

The same may largely be said of the keyboard arrangement by
Adam Craig, published in Edinburgh *c.* 1725. The accompaniment
is an uneasy compromise between drone-bass and harmonic bass,
and the main value of the arrangement lies in its melodic
decorations (text *E*):[2]

---

[1] In Newcastle University Library. This transcript was very kindly supplied to
me by Miss Heather Wilson.

[2] The example is transposed down a tone to facilitate comparison.

Peggie I must love thee

The decorations are strongly violinistic, which is not surprising since Craig was a fiddle player, 'second violin to McGibbon, in the Gentlemen's Concert' in Edinburgh, according to Tytler.[1] In fact McGibbon later used Craig's arrangement as the basis for his own *fiddle* variations on the same tune.

In text *F1*, William Thomson's setting for voice and continuo in *Orpheus Caledonius*, first edition (London, 1725), all the problems which we have so far encountered recur in more acute forms. Voice and continuo is an uncompromising medium; the bass of the harmony is brought out on the cello, and the logic, or lack of logic, between it and the voice part is immediately apparent:

Peggy I must love thee

Thomson has tried here, though not very successfully, to disguise the initial E with an appoggiatura; he has altered bar 2 notes 1–4 and bar 3 notes 3–6 from circuitous pentatonic shapes into straightforward scales which are easier to handle; he has had to use a C major chord for his half-close, though this is a weak gesture and

[1] Tytler, p. 510 n.; and see EMS minute-books (MS.), accounts, 1727, where McGibbon and Craig are listed as professional players to the society.

overloads the tonality with subdominant; his first-inversion-dominant-7th chord under bar 2 note 1 seems out of place, and his D major chord under a stressed G at bar 3 note 3 is clumsy in the extreme. Thomson seems to have been aware of these defects himself, as he had another shot at harmonizing the tune in 1733, for the second edition of his book (text *F2*):

Peggy I must Love thee

'As from a Rock past all_ re-lief, the Ship-wrackt *Co-lin_*

spy - ing, his Na - tive Soil, o'er - come_with_Grief, half

sunk_in waves,__ and dy - ing: With the next Morn - ing

Sun_ he_ spys, a Ship which gives un - hop'd_ sur-prise, new

Life springs up, he lifts his Eyes with Joy, and waits_her mo-tion.

(It will be noted that Allan Ramsay's lyric has by this time supplanted the earlier one.)

Thomson's 1733 setting is a distinct improvement on his 1725 one. He introduces new scalic figures into the bass-line, imitating those in the tune, and varies the harmony in the repeat of the first strain. He also cheats by leaving rests under bar 1 note 1. But several parts still sound rather odd, particularly the quaver up-beats to bars 14 and 15, which he has not managed to absorb into the classical harmonic system.

Indeed, there is no reason why the problem should be soluble at all, except by fluke in individual cases: a tune developed in a monodic tradition will not necessarily fit into a harmonic one.

DOUBLE-TONIC SEQUENCES

'Where will our goodman lie?'
'Bonny Ann'
'The collier's bonny lassie'

Double-tonic sequences are characteristic of many Scots tunes of the period. They occur in a melody when a strongly triadic phrase is stated, and then immediately repeated transposed down a tone. The sea-shanty 'What shall we do with a drunken sailor?' contains a familiar example. They are normally accompanied (if at all) by a drone-bass which alternates between the tonic and the note immediately below. Double-tonic sequences with the first phrase in the minor, the second in the major, can be found in the dance music of England and Ireland in the seventeenth century, as well as in that of Scotland. Sequences with both phrases in major keys are, however, more common in later Scottish music; they are a striking example of Scots folk music absorbing elements of classical tonality but making something totally unclassical out of them; they reached their peak as a technical device in the work of the Gows at the end of the eighteenth century.

The following is an example of a major-key sequence, from George Bowie's music book, written in Edinburgh in 1705:[1]

wher will our Good man ly   5

---

[1] In private possession of Dr. Francis Collinson.

If accompaniment were needed it would be supplied by a drone-bass which would play G in bars 1–2, F in bars 3–4, G in bars 5–6, F in bar 7, G in bar 8, and the same again for the second strain.

The whole strength of double-tonic sequence lies in its lack of chromatic inflection. This can be demonstrated empirically by sharpening the Fs in bars 9, 13, and 14 of the tune above, and flattening the B in bar 12; one could also try sharpening the F in bar 15 and putting a dominant 7th chord under it. The debilitating effect which this has on the tune should be sufficiently convincing. The piece's virility results from the fact that it uses a row of nine fixed notes, from which the player can extract, in turn, a scale of G major with a flattened seventh, and a scale of F major with a sharpened fourth. Now George Bowie's manuscript, from which this piece is quoted, is a fiddle book; and the fiddle would have no technical difficulty in playing the F sharps and B flats needed to establish classical G and F major. Why did a new modal melodic device come into existence at a time when classical harmonic influence was so strong?

I believe a probable answer is: because of the technical limitations of folk wind instruments. The folk wind instruments in use at the time were the Border bagpipe, the stock-and-horn, the home-made whistle, and the recorder; they all had a thumb-hole at the back of the pipe, and seven, perhaps fewer but certainly not more, finger-holes in front. (It will be remembered from Chapter 5 that Burns described the stock-and-horn as having 'six, or seven, ventiges on the upper side, & one back-ventige'.) Allowing that the techniques of cross-fingering, half-covering, and overblowing were almost unknown in folk circles,[1] this would give the folk wind-player an

---

[1] Overblowing in the Border bagpipe, at any rate, was a rare art. See Campbell (MS.): 'Donald Maclean . . . was the only one who could play on the pipe the old popular tune of "Sour plumbs of Gallashiels"—it required a peculiar art of pinching the back hole of the chanter with the thumb in order to produce the higher notes of the melody in question.'

outside range of nine notes, with no possibility of chromatic alteration to any of them. That would be exactly what was needed for playing this type of 'double-tonic' tune.

(On a home-made wind instrument the nine notes would, in any case, probably not be in tune with each other, because of the tendency to bore finger-holes in positions comfortable to the fingers, irrespective of the resulting intonation. The degree to which fourths and sevenths were sharpened or flattened would probably vary considerably from one pipe to the next. Some of this ambiguous intonation has nowadays been standardized in the traditional mistuning of the modern Scottish bagpipe.)

Needless to say, double-tonic sequences were misunderstood once they reached the classical arranger. Here, as an example of what happened, is the opening of a set of piano variations on 'Bonny Ann' by Donald Ross, published in Edinburgh *c.* 1800. Ross's bass-line is passable, but he inflects the tune chromatically so that bar 1 is in classical A major and bar 2 in classical G major; and he perpetrates a hideous dominant 7th chord in bar 4:

Rock bottom is reached when composers start introducing *explanatory modulations* between the phrase 'in one key' and that 'in the other'. An early example of this may be found in Alexander Munro's flute sonata on 'Bony Christy' in *A Collection of the best Scots Tunes*, published in 1732. A particularly funny example is Kozeluch's setting of 'O saw ye bonny Lesley' (i.e. 'The collier's bonny lassie', renamed) in volume one of George Thomson's

Select Collection. Kozeluch lived in Vienna and had never heard a note of real Scottish folk music. Here he is wrestling with the unfamiliar melodic construction, and getting all hot under the collar —the sforzando mark is a sign of irritation:

NON-TONAL ENDINGS

'*The birks of Aberfeldy*'
'*The broom of Cowdenknowes*'
'*Ay wakin O*'

Many Scots tunes have a habit of ending up on a note other than the stated tonic. This must not be confused with the idea of a tune's 'being in a mode': 'The birks of Aberfeldy' makes a good illustration of the distinction between the two. It appears as follows in the *Scots Musical Museum*, volume two, 1788:

The tune has a key-signature of two sharps and it ends on a B, but it is not in the Aeolian Mode nor even in B minor; it is definitely in D major, and simply ends on the wrong note from a sort of personal preference. There are many eighteenth-century tunes of this kind; it is probable that they sprang from an earlier corpus of modal tunes and were partly, but not wholly, converted to the tonal system by the influence of classical music; and that the endings stuck out against absorption into classical tonality. Certainly an earlier version of the same tune, 'The Birks of abbergaldie', set for recorder in James Thomson's music book of 1702,[1] is, if not completely modal, at least far less tonally orientated than the version above; it seems to go half-way back to a modal original:

The Birks of abbergaldie

The usual final notes of such tunes are the second, third, fifth, and sixth degrees of the scale; this is significant since these are the four notes which, together with the tonic, make up the pentatonic scale. Such tunes therefore hark back to an earlier pentatonic melodic system where all five notes of the scale were interchangeable in function, and a tune could close equally well on any of them.

The eighteenth-century harmonizer was often puzzled as to how to treat this type of tune. 'The broom of Cowdenknowes' was a recurrent problem; it closed on the second degree of the scale:[2]

The Broom of Cowdenknows

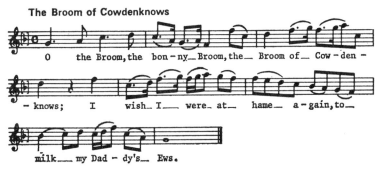

O   the Broom, the bon-ny Broom, the Broom of Cow-den-knows; I   wish I   were at   hame   a-gain, to   milk my Dad-dy's Ews.

Was one supposed to harmonize the last note by a dominant chord (C major), or a supertonic one (G minor)? Or just possibly, as an English composer in the 1920s might have done, by a supertonic major (G major)? The point is that there were no theoretically correct answers, as the whole idea of harmonization was wrong, anyhow. William Thomson tried different solutions in each edition

---

[1] NLS MS. 2833.
[2] Example from Thomson's *Orpheus Caledonius*, 2nd edn. (London, 1733).

of *Orpheus Caledonius*; Domenico Corri in *New and complete collection of the most favourite Scots songs* (Edinburgh, *c.* 1783) tacked an instrumental 'symphony' on to the end of it to bring it round to F major again.

Around 1800 'The broom of Cowdenknowes' suffered drastic new treatment: the phrase

was added on to the end of the tune: educated singers apparently could not bear the 'unfinished' sound of the traditional version any longer. The new ending appears in George Thomson's *Select Collection* volume three, 1802, surrounded by hideous melodic decoration.[1] Curiously enough, this was not a unique occurrence, for an exactly parallel addition was made to the tune 'Ay wakin O' at the same period; 'Ay wakin O' originally ended on the fifth degree of the scale. Its new ending also appears in volume three of Thomson's *Select Collection*,[2] so if Thomson was not personally responsible for both additions it at least looks suspiciously like it. I can only agree with William Stenhouse, who wrote in 1820:

In Mr George Thomson's Collection of Scottish Songs, the air of 'Ay wakin, oh!' is enlarged so as to finish on the key-note, and the time is changed from treple to common. The tune, however, is far better in its native wildness and simplicity . . .[3]

Thus in the small tussle with individual notes and chords we catch glimpses of a much larger evolutionary process. The gulf between the folk and classical traditions widened during the seventeenth century; classical music explored deeper and deeper into the possibilities of tonal harmony, and folk music was left behind in the monodic Middle Ages. But during the eighteenth century folk music began to catch up again. It absorbed many of the

[1] Also in Corri's *Select Collection of the most favourite Scots songs* (Edinburgh, 1802), Schetky's *Collection of Scottish music . . . arranged for military band* (London, *c.* 1805), and doubtless elsewhere.
[2] Also in Urbani's *Select Collection*, vol. 6 (Edinburgh, 1804), under the title 'Jess MacFarlane'.
[3] Stenhouse, no. 213.

elements of tonality in a very short time, and it says much for its integrity and vigour that it did so without losing its identity in the process. The retained identity expressed itself, however, in odd melodic corners which did not conform to the classical system; and when the next cross-influence occurred between the two traditions, and attempts were made to harmonize folk-tunes, it was these odd corners that caught the classical arrangers out.

9

CHURCH MUSIC

So far we have considered only forms of music which were either 'folk' or 'classical', or a fairly straightforward mixture of the two. Church music is a different matter; in eighteenth-century Scotland it had its own tradition, and was not obviously connected with any other forms of music current in the country. To understand church music fully we must go back beyond 1700, and trace its development from 1560, the year in which the Reformation in Scotland came into power.

The church's attitude towards music has varied at different times in its history. In some periods it has decided that God should be worshipped in music embodying man's highest imagination and skill, and so patronized classical music; in others it has decreed that God should be worshipped in music so simple that everyone can join in, and so utilized folk music. The Protestant churches have found the second approach by far the more congenial; they incline towards folk music, and at times even manifest deep-seated hatred of classical music as representative of the rat-racing, high-living kind of society which seems to be their natural enemy.

The personal musical tastes of the early Scottish reformers are not known; it is quite possible that John Knox and his colleagues enjoyed classical music as a secular relaxation. What is clear, however, is that they did not want it in church. Soon after 1560 cathedral and collegiate choir schools were allowed to run down, and the funds supporting them were diverted elsewhere; church organs were neglected, and congregations were set to work learning to sing plain metrical psalms. From then on metrical psalms became the centre of the church's artistic life; to begin with they were sung to English and Genevan psalm tunes, but Scottish tunes in a similar style were soon being written and added to the repertory. More complex and imaginative music than this was, however, not wanted, and Scottish composers were discouraged from writing it. Accordingly, Scottish church music took on a character of uninspiring drabness, which had a dampening effect on creative musical talent for many generations to come.

Musical patronage, however, was not wholly lacking. In 1579 Parliament passed an act encouraging local authorities to reopen the decayed choir schools as civic establishments. These became, under the new dispensation, burgh music schools with special responsibilities for providing music in the main church of the town where they were situated. By 1600 a network of them had been formed, covering the greater part of the Lowlands, and acting as a means by which the new Reformed church psalmody could be disseminated. The master of a burgh music school was always also precentor at the church, and the schoolchildren acted as the church choir. In Stirling in 1621, for example, the furnishings in the church were altered to give the master and children of the music school reserved seats under the pulpit; the Kirk Session decided that 'the pulpet and Reederis letrun sal be taine doune and reedefeit again' and the joiners were told to

mak commodious seattis about the fit thairof for the maister of the sang schuil and his bairnis to sit on, for singing the psalmes in the tyme of the holie serveice of the Kirk.[1]

All this time the repertory of the Reformed church grew, until by 1635—the year that the great Scottish Psalter was published—it comprised something over two hundred pieces. These were principally metrical psalm tunes set in simple four-part harmony, about fifty of the tunes being original Scottish ones. The repertory also included psalm tunes set 'in reports', that is, with the tune accompanied by three, four, or five parts in imitative counterpoint, like a simple, somewhat primitive chorale prelude; and five anthems, pieces stylistically similar to the 'psalms in reports', only not based on a pre-existing melody.[2] There was no instrumental music in the Reformed church at all: nearly all church organs had been

---

[1] Stirling Kirk Session minute-books, quoted from Patrick, *Four centuries*, p. 135.
[2] Elliott; and see Elliott's *Fourteen psalm-settings of the early Reformed church in Scotland* (London, 1960), preface.

abandoned or destroyed, and brass instruments never came into use. Unaccompanied choir was the staple diet.

Charles I's Scottish coronation, which took place in Holyrood Abbey, near Edinburgh, on 18 June 1633, should have been a great stimulus to Scottish church music. It was assumed that Holyrood would be asked to provide the music for the ceremony, and Edward Kellie, master of the Scottish Chapel Royal, went to London in 1631 on that assumption. He discovered what music had been used for Charles's earlier coronation at Westminster Abbey in 1626, and spent five months having it copied out. Meanwhile he had scouted round Edinburgh and engaged sackbut and cornett players and an organist, and had reinforced the Chapel Royal choir. He probably even started rehearsals. But at that point he was told that the king was bringing his own musicians up from London for the ceremony, and that his services were not required after all. After that the Chapel Royal presumably went back to singing four-part metrical psalms.[1]

So perhaps the mundane level of Reformed church music was not all John Knox's fault. Nevertheless it must be said that Scotland produced no church music at this time even remotely comparable to the anthems of Gibbons, Weelkes, and Tomkins in England, or to the organ preludes of Sweelinck or Scheidt on the Continent. The Scottish 'psalms in reports' are desperately unexciting as works of art: they have the academic faults without the academic virtues, and are emotionally desiccated without being particularly technically competent. Scotland's only real success lay in her original psalm tunes, some of which are very fine considered simply as tunes.

But after 1635 the position, even such as it was, deteriorated. In 1650 a revised psalter was issued which contained no music at all; and by the time the next psalter with music came out—which was John Forbes's 'Aberdeen psalter' in 1666—the repertory had shrunk drastically; for Forbes's psalter contained only twelve common-metre metrical-psalm tunes in simple harmony, plus a tune for Psalm 25 and one solitary relic of choral polyphony, 'Bon Accord in reports'. The twelve common-metre tunes were 'Common Tune',

[1] Willsher.

'King's Tune, 'Duke's Tune', 'English Tune', 'French', 'London', 'Stilt' (or 'York'), 'Dunfermline', 'Dundee', 'Abbey', 'Martyrs', and 'Elgin', and they quickly became established as a new sanctioned, limited repertory. The second edition of the Aberdeen psalter, dated 1671, was entitled *The Twelve Tunes, for the Church of Scotland*, and such manuscript books of this period as include psalm tunes also restrict themselves to selections from these twelve.[1]

Several explanations of this shrinkage have been put forward: that church services suffered in the confusion that overtook Scotland during the Civil War; that the 1650 psalter gave all the psalms in standardized, common-metre versions and so a wide variety of tunes was no longer necessary. But for whatever reason, the fact remains that the repertory dwindled because the church did not care enough about music to look after it properly. By 1700 there are signs that many of the music schools had closed down, and that the Aberdeen one was pre-eminent among the survivors. Church music in Aberdeen at this time deserves a detailed study.

The main church in Aberdeen was the St. Nicholas, and the Aberdeen music school was situated next door to it. St. Nicholas Church was an ancient building which had been reconstructed and added to several times over the seven centuries preceding 1700. In the late seventeenth century it was divided in two internally by a stone wall (as indeed it still is), and thus catered for two distinct congregations. There does not seem, however, to have been rivalry between them: in 1688 the church had three ministers, Dr. Andrew Burnet in the west, Dr. George Garden in the east, and Dr. William Blair who officiated in both.

It seems likely that, at this stage, the music school supplied choirs to both ends of the church; it is also likely that both congregations used the same music, just as they shared the church's third minister. I suggest that their repertory was identical with the contents of the printed Aberdeen psalter.

For the Aberdeen psalter gives every impression of having been printed primarily for local consumption. It went through five

---

[1] Louis de France's music book, EUL La.III.491, *c.* 1680; Agnes Hume's music book, NLS Adv. MS. 5.2.17, 1704.

editions, dated 1666, 1671, 1706, 1714, and 1720, and (with one unimportant exception) was the only psalter with music published in Scotland at all between 1635 and 1723.[1] Its apparently slow, steady sale is consistent with the idea of its being used as a textbook by successive generations of Aberdeen music-school pupils. Furthermore, the 'Bon Accord in reports' at the end of the book was a local speciality—*Bon Accord* is Aberdeen's town motto— and may not have been in use in other parts of the country. It seems to me that we can take the Aberdeen psalter as exact evidence of what was being sung in the St. Nicholas Church at the end of the seventeenth century.

'Bon Accord in reports' was thus Scotland's most advanced piece of church music at the time, and as such, deserves quotation in full:[2]

Its old-fashionedness is almost incredible for a 'modern' piece in 1700. The contrapuntal style recalls English composers' efforts at anthem-writing in the 1560s, while the notation assumes that singers are still *au fait* with sixteenth-century rules of *musica ficta*. Music-school pupils must have got heartily sick of the piece; with a repertory of only fourteen tunes it would come round in rotation remarkably often, and would have to be sung perhaps eight or ten times on each occasion, to accommodate all the verses of whatever psalm was chosen to go with it. In fact the whole business of singing regular services with such a small repertory must have been tedious in the extreme; music pupils must have been glad that secular music was more modern and varied.

But in 1695, after a series of upheavals due to Episcopal clergy refusing to swear oaths of allegiance to William and Mary, Dr. Burnet was summoned to Edinburgh and thrown into prison, and the Episcopally-minded members of his congregation were ejected from St. Nicholas. Aberdeen town council were sympathetic towards Episcopacy, even though Presbyterianism was, after 1690, the state religion. They arranged for the Episcopalians to have the use of the vacant Trinity Church down by the river Dee, and services continued until, in the aftermath of the 1715 Rebellion, all Episcopal activities were clamped down upon, and the clergy bound over to keep the peace under threat of imprisonment.

In this situation the Episcopal congregation decided to found a completely new church. It would be registered as an outpost of the Church of England, and so would not be subject to Presbyterian interference; and it would employ an Anglican-trained minister from outside Aberdeen, since none of the local Episcopal clergy available could conduct a service without being immediately clapped into gaol for six months. The St. Paul's Episcopal Chapel was founded at the north end of Aberdeen in 1720, and opened in 1722.[1]

It is hard to guess what the Episcopalians did for music after they were expelled from St. Nicholas. Did the music school send a choir down the hill to Trinity Church on Sunday mornings? James Nicoll's preface to the 1714 edition of the Aberdeen psalter has some interesting, if confusing, evidence. He writes:

this CITY has been Fam'd . . . for MUSICK, for which it's inferiour to none in the Nation; so that Strangers upon their hearing that pleasant Harmony, that is to be found in our *Churches* in singing the Psalms, have been oblidged to acknowledge, that they never observed that Heavenly Exercise, more pleasantly performed any where than in this CITY; which certainly is owing to . . . having always skilfull *Musicians* as Masters of our Musick School.

'Churches' in the plural begs the question, since Nicoll has no hesitation in giving the music school credit for all the beautiful

[1] Smith, introduction.

singing that was going on in the town. In fact only the St. Nicholas and Trinity churches were in use at the time, though Aberdeen was full of ecclesiastical remains of one kind and another: this was in the city itself. Other nearby churches which Nicoll might have had in mind were St. Clement's in Fitty, a fishing village immediately south-east of Aberdeen, and St. Machar's Cathedral in Old Aberdeen to the north. The last is unlikely, however, since Old Aberdeen was a town in its own right, separated from Aberdeen by a clear half-mile of open fields, and in any case had a music school of its own.[1] Another possibility is that Nicoll was referring only to the St. Nicholas Church, but that it was known locally as 'the churches', plural, because it housed two congregations. But all things considered, I think it probable that the music school did farm out a choir to the Episcopalian congregation during the 1710s.[2]

After St. Paul's Chapel was opened in 1722, Episcopal music became strongly Anglican in tone, matching the congregation's imported minister. An organ was installed,[3] the first one in a public Scottish church since the Reformation, and the choir was set to work learning Anglican chants. Edward Burt, an Englishman, who visited St. Paul's in 1726, wrote that it had 'an organ, the only one I know of, and the service is chanted as in our cathedrals'.[4] They probably also added English psalm tunes to their repertory. St. Paul's may have started its own musical establishment at this time, independent of the music school and the St. Nicholas Church; certainly the two had separate musical directors in 1737, when Andrew Tait was organist at St. Paul's[5] while Charles McLean was master of the music school and precentor at St. Nicholas. But the following year McLean abandoned his post and went south to Edinburgh,[6] and the new St. Nicholas precentor, James Chalmers,

---

[1] See Gordon, who gives maps and an illustration of the Aberdeen town skyline in 1661.

[2] A continental analogy is suggestive. The Leipzig music school, where Johann Sebastian Bach was cantor from 1723 to 1750, sent out choirs every Sunday to four different churches in the town. But the churches were, of course, all of the same denomination.   [3] Lawrence, p. 6.   [4] Burt, vol. 1, p. 205.

[5] '*Mr* Andrew Tait *Organist of* St. Paul's *Chapel in* Aberdeen' appears in the subscription list of Charles McLean's *Twelve Solo's or Sonata's op. 1* (Edinburgh, 1737).

[6] See Chapter 2 above, 'Music schools'.

felt incompetent to continue the music school part of the job and had Tait appointed instead.[1] Later, in 1749, Chalmers and Tait collaborated over *A new and correct set of Church Tunes*, which was printed by Chalmers, edited by Tait, and included a new psalm tune, 'Aberdeen or St. Paul's', of Tait's composition. So it is clear that Presbyterian and Episcopal musicians worked together in Aberdeen all through the political upheavals of 1688, 1715, and 1745.

If church music in Aberdeen was nothing to get excited about, outside Aberdeen it was far, far worse. Music schools in small burghs found it increasingly difficult to get properly qualified staff as the seventeenth century progressed, and the schools were shut down or converted into ordinary parish schools. Gradually, all over the country, church choirs broke up and congregations were reduced to singing psalms in unison, unharmonized. The music books wore out and were thrown away, and replacements could not be obtained. The precentor's job became less musically specialized, and began to be combined with other parish jobs like being secretary to the Kirk Session, ringing the church bell, digging graves, and reading portions of scripture to the congregation before the minister arrived to take the service. William Chrystie, for example, who was master of the Old Aberdeen music school in 1725, was also session-clerk and reader at St. Machar's Cathedral—and this was a church which still preserved a reasonable musical tradition.[2]

Once the principle of combined jobs was accepted, precentors began to be appointed whose musical abilities were minimal. The idea that a psalm tune was written *in a specific key* was forgotten; precentors would start psalms on a random note, often wildly too high or too low. Sometimes when this happened the precentor would apologize and begin again; using a pitch-pipe, however, was taboo.[3] Congregations slipped back into nasal, reedy, folk-song voice production; with no choir to keep them in order their singing lost

[1] Farmer, *Music making*, p. 20.   [2] Orem, p. 128.
[3] Patrick, *Four centuries*, p. 129; An encouragement to the cultivation of church music (MS.), pp. 47 f.

its regular pulse and their rhythm disintegrated into uncoordinated rubato. Some precentors found even twelve tunes too many to cope with and the parish's repertory was reduced to a mere two or three. A method of performance called 'lining' became universal, in which the precentor chanted each line of the psalm on a mono-tone (usually the fifth degree of the scale)[1] before the congregation sang it—a kind of dictation process which saved the congregation the trouble of reading the words out of the psalter for themselves. Finally congregations began to embroider the tunes with com-plicated melodic decorations.

These decorations were known as 'quavers', and they soon reached such complexity that it became difficult to pick out the original tune among the mass of notes. The following example gives some idea what these decorations sounded like; it is the tune 'French', recorded by Dr. Mainzer as sung in a Highland church in 1844, to Psalm 121:[2]

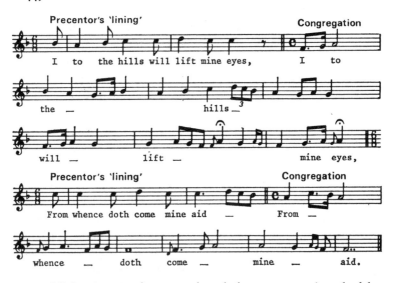

In addition it must be remembered that congregations had by this stage lost the art of singing in time with one another: it was

---

[1] 'An encouragement to the cultivation of church music' (MS.), p. 56.

[2] From Patrick, *Public worship*, p. 44. An undecorated version of the tune, for comparison, may be found on p. 182 below.

normal for time-lags to occur between one part of a congregation and another, so that every line of the psalm was sung in a kind of multiple canon. This way of singing may, after a while, have been deliberately cultivated; it certainly became established in most places as the 'church' style, and acquired religious associations for the people who took part in it. Standard practices of decoration began to evolve: Robert Bremner records how an old man, precentor in a rural church in about 1740, told him firmly that 'there ought to be eight Quavers in the first Note of the *Elgin* tune'.[1]

A modern folk-lorist would describe this kind of singing as 'heterophony'. It is important to realize its significance: that church music had changed from being, in 1635, a minor and uninteresting branch of *classical* music to being, by 1700, a weird and complex type of *folk* music. A glance back at our folk-classical-characteristics table in Chapter 1 will confirm this. Church music had become, during the seventeenth century, monodic, orally transmitted, static in repertory, and without definitive texts.[2] Its singers no longer required formal education—Bremner wrote: 'When a Precentor was wanted, the principal Qualifications requisite were Poverty and a loud Voice for reading the Line . . .'[3] Performances worked on a 'prompt' system of a familiar folk type, with a leader who remembered the words and a crowd who followed him passively: from the point of view of performance conventions, psalms were very similar to sea-shanties on board ship, 'precentor' and 'congregation' corresponding to 'shantyman' and 'crew'. Indirect similarities exist, too, between psalms and traditional oral ballads. The twelve sanctioned tunes were all in common metre, which is identical to ballad metre; and a somewhat horrifying story is told[4] of a precentor at Greenock, John McQuisten, who one Sunday during the service accidentally jumped from the middle of Psalm 107 into the ballad 'Sir Patrick Spens', without noticing the difference. The whole congregation followed him blindly; perhaps they had some excuse—both texts are stories about shipwrecks.

[1] Bremner, *Rudiments*, 2nd edn., p. xii n.
[2] The tunes had been embroidered haphazardly and had lost standard pitch, itself, of course, a feature of a definitive text.
[3] *Rudiments*, 2nd edn., p. xii.
[4] Patrick, *Four centuries*, pp. 167 f. No earlier source for this story is given.

This kind of mistake was apparently quite common in ballad singing, for Scott wrote in 1802:

The reciter, making it a uniform principle to proceed at all hazards, is very often, when his memory fails him, apt to substitute large portions from some other tale, altogether distinct from that which he has commenced.[1]

This incident therefore shows how similar, in a number of ways, the two traditions were at the time.

Many educated members of congregations seem to have disliked heterophonic psalm-singing; but one writer, Lady Anne Barnard, described it sympathetically in these terms:

. . . the horrid discords with which a Presbyterian congregation assails the ears—a discord to me now more pious in its sounds of willing praise than all the organs or hired choir-singers in the world, and exceeded by nothing in the sensations it awakens but by a congregation of converted Hottentots joining in one hymn.[2]

'Hottentots' strikes the right note here: it underlines the singing's strange aesthetic effect, totally alien to the classical music culture. Twentieth-century listeners would probably share Lady Barnard's fascination. But most eighteenth-century classical musicians regarded it with dislike and contempt; a favourite word to describe it was 'confusion':

The tenor part[3] . . . ingrossed any little regard which was shown to church music, and people imagining they might perform it according to their various humours, the greatest confusion was soon introduced, and the melody too entirely lost in many places.[4]

While Bremner wrote:

The Tenor, which was the only Part attempted, and which was conveyed only by the Ear from one Generation to another, was now so corrupted by Graces and Quavers, as they called them, that the Tune was entirely defaced, and the original Note . . . had no more

---

[1] Scott, introduction.
[2] Diary entry, *c.* 1805, quoted from Patrick, *Four centuries*, p. 143.
[3] In seventeenth-century psalters the tune is always placed in the tenor part.
[4] *Aberdeen Intelligencer*, 17 December 1754, letter.

Share of the Performance than the Nonsense they thought proper to add to it.

Had these nonsensical Graces been the same every where, it would have been the less Matter; but, on the contrary, every Congregation, nay, every Individual, had different Graces to the same Note [some parishes may well have standardized their decorations: I think Bremner is overstating his case here] which were dragged by many to such an immoderate Length, that one Corner of the Church, or the People in one Seat, had sung out the Line before another had half done; and from the whole there arose such a Mass of Confusion and Discord as quite debased this the noblest part of Worship. This they called the old Way of singing, for which there were many Advocates, though in fact it was the new, or rather no Way at all.[1]

This kind of attitude towards heterophonic singing gained ground between 1720 and 1750, particularly in social circles where classical music flourished: that is to say, among young, upper-class people in the vicinity of Edinburgh and Aberdeen. By the mid century a substantial section of the public was ready to see heterophonic psalm-singing stamped out and a more classical form of church music put in its place; and when that in fact happened, it did so quickly and decisively, showing that the time had been ripe. Between January 1755 and December 1756 heterophonic singing went out of use in all the churches in both Edinburgh and Aberdeen, and parish-church choirs were formed to sing the psalms in regular four-part harmony instead.

The *Scots Magazine* covered the various stages of the reform in some detail. This is significant evidence in itself, since it suggests that it was exactly the educated classes that read the *Scots Magazine* who wanted church music improved, and were interested to read what was going on. The impetus for reform came from Aberdeenshire.

Presbyterian music declined in the north-east of Scotland after 1720, and even the St. Nicholas Church in Aberdeen lost its choir, and was reduced to unharmonized singing, some time before

---

[1] *Rudiments*, 2nd edn., pp. xii f.

1754. A letter to the *Aberdeen Intelligencer* on 17 December that year noted that:

Harmony, or concord of different parts . . . continued in some measure till of late, as appears by a set [of music] published at Aberdeen in the year 1714 [i.e. the fourth edition of the Aberdeen psalter]. Yet through inattention it declined by degrees, till the harmony is now so entirely lost, that very few have any idea of this great effect in music, which is so proper to give it the grandeur and solemnity requisite in churches.

Episcopalian music in the north-east, however, improved. The organ in St. Paul's, Aberdeen, installed in 1722, was only the first of several: St. Andrew's Chapel, Banff, had one by 1737.[1] The first Edinburgh church organ was installed in December 1747.[2] But what really set things moving was a piece of private enterprise by a landowner, Sir Archibald Grant, laird of Monymusk in Aberdeenshire. He was a keen amateur classical musician[3] and took great interest in the singing at the church on his estate. During the 1740s he planned a local reform of church music, as these extracts from his daybook show: the village schoolmaster was to start a church choir, and the 'folk' style of singing was to be eradicated:

Septr 1746. Take measures for Church Choir & y^t all can join properly in praise, & give books & premiums to encourage hopeful children; to read the line of psalms plain & not drone ye reading or singing; elders to tell this in respective quarters.

Aprile 1748. Scool Master teach singing & all young people & good voices when taught sit together in Church to lead rest, and sing the new psalms etc. allowed by Assembly—& none but choise psalms at all times.[4]

Choir practices were apparently held in Sir Archibald's library, accompanied by a chamber organ which he had installed, while on

---

[1] '*Mr* Ferdinand Shoneman, *Organist of* St. Andrew's *Chapel in* Banff' appears in the subscription list of McLean's *Twelve Solo's* of 1737.

[2] *Scots Magazine*, December 1747.

[3] Sir Archibald became a member of the Aberdeen Musical Society in about 1750. His private collection of music books is listed by Farmer in *Music making*, p. 118.

[4] *Selections from the Monymusk papers*, p. 171. Millar Patrick suggests that the 'new psalms etc.' were the first edition of the Paraphrases, issued experimentally in 1745. See *Four centuries*, p. 151.

Sundays the laird himself sat with the choir in church. But the schoolmaster evidently proved unsatisfactory as a choir-trainer, for in 1753 Sir Archibald acquired a better one—Thomas Channon, an English private soldier stationed at Aberdeen:

When Gen. Wolf's regiment was lying at Aberdeen in 1753, some of the soldiers were heard practising church-music in the reformed way; and one *Thomas Channon*, being found both capable and willing to teach, was employed, first of all, in the parish of Monymusk, in the presbytery of Garrioch. The success of the attempt there . . . induced a number of ministers of the synod [of Aberdeen] to apply to Lt-Gen. Bland for a discharge to him from the army; which his Excellency granted accordingly.[1]

Soon Channon was running several choirs in the neighbourhood of Monymusk. Rumour reached Aberdeen as to the novelty and success of his teaching, and in a mixture of anger, curiosity, and trepidation the authorities invited him to come to Aberdeen to give a demonstration of what he was doing.

The demonstration took place in the St. Nicholas Church on 2 January 1755, as part of the Sunday service. Channon brought a select choir of 70 persons with him, divided into 18 basses, 30 tenors (five of whom doubled as altos), and 22 sopranos. They sang psalms in three and four-part harmony; well-known tunes during the service, and recommended new tunes afterwards. St. Nicholas was packed for the occasion, and after the demonstration 'several hundred' people 'both in Old and New Aberdeen' signed on as Channon's pupils, among them

several gentlemen in the magistracy in both towns, masters of both colleges, members of the session, many of the most respectable inhabitants, their ladies and daughters, numbers of tradesmen, servants, and common people, besides students at both colleges.[2]

Channon's aims were as follows: he had proposed reintroducing harmonized singing as it had been done 'about the time of the reformation of religion', and 'as to the melody',

The reformation consists in these articles.
1. Chusing the best tunes of those which were formerly used in

[1] *Scots Magazine*, August 1755.   [2] Ibid., July 1755.

the churches in Scotland, composing some new tunes, and collecting others from the best authors . . .

    2. Teaching the tune or sounds truly and plain, without quavering, or any kind of affectation.

    3. Teaching them to the proper time, without which all must run into confusion.[1]

There were, of course, many people whom Channon's demonstration displeased. Aberdeen Kirk Session held a protest meeting about it on 20 January 1755, and argued whether the reforms should be accepted by the Aberdeen churches; the Synod also discussed the matter when it met in May. Eventually it was decided to approve harmonized singing and the formation of choirs, but not to allow additions to the repertory beyond the statutory twelve tunes. And so the new movement in 'classical' church music was officially recognized.

It is symbolic that the Aberdeen music school finally closed down for ever in the mid 1750s, at exactly this time; its days of usefulness were over.

The movement spread to Edinburgh almost instantaneously. 'Improvements in a neighbouring County', wrote Bremner, meaning Aberdeenshire,

opened the eyes of those in Power here [Edinburgh]; upon which there was a Committee appointed, consisting of a Number of the Ministers, Lords of Session, Barons of Exchequer, Musical Society, and the whole Town-council. The first Step this Honourable Committee took, was to appoint a proper Number of Church-tunes; and after they were carefully examined by the best Masters, I was appointed to print them . . .[2]

and that became the collection *The Rudiments of Music*, published by Bremner in Edinburgh in 1756. The contents of this collection are quite revolutionary. It begins, cautiously, with eight of the standard twelve tunes, but then proceeds to twenty-two tunes not part of

---

    [1] *Aberdeen Intelligencer*, 17 December 1754, letter. This plan of reform may well have been drafted by Sir Archibald Grant; its substance is very similar to the entries in his daybook.

    [2] *Rudiments*, 2nd edn., p. xiii.

the accepted repertory, some of them in triple-time with dotted rhythms in the new English 'devotional' manner; then to a selection of anthems, sacred canons (e.g. Byrd's 'Non nobis domine'), and canticle chants. The last section shows strong English influence, as though Bremner had raked through English publications in search of easy choir pieces, irrespective of their un-Presbyterian tendencies. The publication is notable as the first official expansion of the repertory beyond the 'twelve'; it is also a practical comment on the Aberdeen Synod's restrictive decision of the previous May. It is interesting that the committee appointed to advise on church music should have included a contingent from the Edinburgh Musical Society: it shows once again how closely classical musicians were bound up with the reform.

The need was felt for a choir-trainer to do for Edinburgh what Channon was already doing for Aberdeen, and on 26 November 1755, Edinburgh town council resolved 'that a master well skilled in the theory and practice of church music shall be immediately employed to teach in the city.'[1] On 7 April 1756 they appointed Cornforth Gilson, a member of the cathedral choir at Durham.[2] As in Aberdeen, public response to the new music was enormous, and Gilson soon had more pupils than he knew what to do with:

An universal Spirit diffused through all Ranks. Men of seventy and Boys of seven Years old were at School together, and equally keen of Instruction. Their Diligence enabled the Teachers to produce very fine Concerts in a few Weeks . . . so that in a few Months the former erroneous Manner of singing was entirely forgot.[3]

The movement also spread to Glasgow and Dundee, and made some headway into country areas; in 1762 Bremner published *A plan for teaching a Croud*, an instruction manual describing how to start parish choirs from scratch in country towns.

By 1800 heterophonic psalm-singing had disappeared from Lowland churches almost entirely. It continued, however, in the Highlands, and there are indications that it also continued, in the Lowlands, as part of family evening prayers in private houses. Burns's

[1] *Scots Magazine*, November 1755.   [2] Ibid., March 1756.
[3] Bremner, *Rudiments*, 2nd edn., p. xiii.

poem 'The Cotter's Saturday Night' gives a picture of family prayers in a farm labourer's cottage in Ayrshire, in about 1780:

> 'Let us worship God!' he says, with solemn air.
>
> They chant their artless notes in simple guise;
> They tune their hearts, by far the noblest aim:
> Perhaps 'Dundee's' wild warbling measures rise,
> Or plaintive 'Martyrs', worthy of the name;
> Or noble 'Elgin' beats the heavenward flame,
> The sweetest far of Scotia's holy lays.
> Compared with these, Italian tricks are tame . . .

'Wild warbling measures' would be a nonsensical way to talk about the tune 'Dundee' as it appears in printed books; but it makes an excellent description of heterophonic singing. This would tie up with the family's evidently old-fashioned repertory, which probably consisted just of the three tunes mentioned. By 'Scotia's holy lays' Burns means the 'twelve'. One can well imagine this kind of family worship having no truck with innovations like Methodist hymn tunes and Dr. Watts's lyrics, and resisting them long after they had been admitted into services at the parish church.

The parish-choir movement may thus be seen as a victory for classical music over folk music. There are other aspects to it, though; from another angle it appears as a victory for English music over Scottish. Around 1755 there was a sudden demand in Scotland for large numbers of educated church musicians, just at a moment when the native tradition had sunk to such a low ebb that none were being produced. The result was that Scotland had to import from the nearest available source—England. Channon and Gilson, whom we have just met, were English; so were Thomas Moore, employed to teach church music in Glasgow in 1755, and Musgrave Heighington, organist at the Episcopal church in Dundee in 1760. Stephen Clarke, organist at the new Episcopal chapel in Edinburgh from 1771, came from Durham. St. Paul's Chapel, Aberdeen, had a native Scot, Andrew Tait, as organist; but when he retired in the mid 1770s his two next successors were Robert Barber and John Ross, both from Newcastle. Even R. A. Smith, who was precentor at Paisley Abbey from 1807 to 1823, and at St.

George's, Edinburgh, from 1823 to 1827, and reckoned the greatest Scottish choir-trainer since the Reformation, was educated south of the border and 'retained the English style of speech all his life'.[1] Such musicians introduced Anglified psalm tunes and anthems to their newly formed choirs, and for a time Scotland became, as far as church music was concerned, a satellite of England.

But in compensation perhaps, a new local church 'folk' tradition emerged: the parody practice-verse.

Some preliminary explanation is needed about practice-verses. It must be understood that in Scotland the metrical psalter was regarded as a sacred book, second only to the Bible, and its use was restricted to worship and religious study. Using it for singing practice would have been sacrilege—degrading it to a mere piece of equipment for exercising the vocal chords. Therefore special non-scriptural verses were made up to practise psalm tunes on, and the psalms themselves were kept for Sundays.

In the early eighteenth century the general public never came in contact with practice-verses, as they didn't *rehearse* psalms at all. Indeed many of them were probably unaware of their existence; they were used only by solitary precentors and by boys at music schools. But during the 1750s large numbers of people joined choirs for the first time, and were suddenly introduced to them. Singing familiar psalm tunes to strange words was a novelty, and furthermore a novelty with humorous possibilities. And there were plenty of people around to share the joke with.

For it must be borne in mind that parish-church choirs were as much a social innovation as a musical one. They contained people of both sexes (unlike music-school choirs, which had only boys and men), and their members were mostly young and unmarried; they cost nothing to join; their members met regularly for practice on weekday evenings; on Sundays they sat together in church in reserved pews, or in a special choir gallery. In many places the choir must have become the social focus for the neighbourhood's young people, and practice-night developed into the big night out of the week, comparable to the quarterly dance and the twice-yearly

[1] Patrick, *Four centuries*, p. 193.

fair. It was in this setting that parody practice-verses flourished, and began to be invented in large numbers.

Some of them may perhaps have been written by choir-masters with a sense of humour, and used officially at practices; since they do convey useful information about the tunes they are set to, as well as having a slight mickey-taking element. For example:

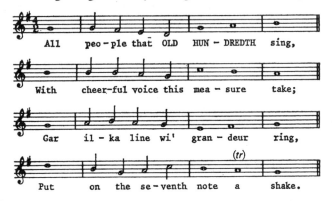

All peo-ple that OLD HUN-DREDTH sing,

With cheer-ful voice this mea-sure take;

Gar il-ka line wi' gran-deur ring,

Put on the se-venth note a shake.

Or:

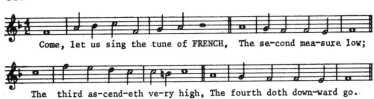

Come, let us sing the tune of FRENCH, The se-cond mea-sure low;

The third as-cend-eth ve-ry high, The fourth doth down-ward go.

But most of them are clearly unofficial. There was a traditional practice-verse which ran:

> O mother dear, Jerusalem,
> When shall I come to thee?
> When shall my sorrows have an end,
> Thy joys when shall I see?

which was parodied as:

> O mither dear, Tod Lowrie's lum,
> Whan sweepit will it be?
> For a' the soot's come tummlin' doon,
> An' spilet ma grannie's tea.[1]

[1] *Lum*: chimney / *spilet*: spoiled.

Two verses were invented for the tune 'Bangor' which were intended to be sung by boys to annoy girls:

> O B. NGOR's notes are unco high,
> An' try the lassies sair;
> They pech an' grane an' skirl an' skreich,
> Till they can sing nae mair.

> The high high notes o' BANGOR's tune
> Are unco sair to raise;
> An' trying hard to reach them gars
> The lassies burst their stays.[1]

One verse was borrowed from a well-known folk-song:

> I wish my love was a red rose,
> Grown in my garden wall,
> And I to be a drope o' dew;
> Upon her I would fall.

Another was a parody of Psalm 84, addressed, appropriately, to Sir Archibald Grant of Monymusk:

> How lovely is thy dwelling-place,
> Sir Archie Grant, to me;
> The home-park and the policies,
> How pleasant, sir, they be.

and many more examples of the genre are known.[2] Millar Patrick suggests that they were sung by giggling groups of teenagers walking home arm-in-arm through the fields after choir-practices; probably they were also muttered semi-audibly during services by the boys in the back row. Certainly they were a very successful genre; examples were transmitted orally from one end of the country to the other, and many of them survived for generations.

This, then, was Scottish church music during the eighteenth century. From a literary point of view it is a magnificently coherent whole, with the metrical psalter running right through it as a solid backbone. But from a musical point of view it is incoherent

---

[1] *Unco*: extremely / *gars*: causes to.
[2] These examples are all taken from Patrick, *Four centuries*, pp. 151, 171 f.

and fragmented, veering uncertainly between classical and folk genres, making contradictory gestures, taking pride in its pure Presbyterianism and importing musicians from England, encouraging the formation of choirs and then clamping down on their repertories. The church was not sure how it stood about music; it was not sure how much it wanted, or what sort.

But it was not alone in its confusion, for as we shall see in our last chapter, this kind of muddle was common in Scottish dealings with music.

Attitudes

10

NATIONALISM AND XENOPHOBIA

W E are now, finally, in a position to look back over eighteenth-century Scottish music and to comment on the attitudes of people towards it. We have seen that Scotland possessed two distinct musical cultures, which interacted to some extent, but by no means totally; and that many people were equally at home in both. Since neither culture absorbed or dominated the other, there must have been a barrier between them which restricted their influence on each other. This barrier was not social, but psychological: people reacted to the two kinds of music in psychologically different ways, and so kept them apart in their minds.

There is evidence that many Scots noticed this phenomenon, and were puzzled by it, at the time. Dr. Gregory's account of the difference between 'learned' and 'vulgar' music has already been noted in Chapter 1. Andrew Erskine had noticed the same thing, for he wrote to James Boswell on 1 May 1762,

I am fond of the country to a degree; things there are not so artificially disguised as in towns . . . as for example, it was only in the country, I could have found out Lady J—'s particular attachment, to the tune of *Appie MacNab*; in the town, no doubt, she would have pretended a great liking for Voi Amante.[1]

This was an amusing incongruity: 'Eppie McNab' was a current and extremely obscene folk-song.[2] The subject reappears in another of Erskine's letters, where he satirizes the jew's harp by writing about it as though it were a classical music instrument:

I have often wondered, Boswell, that a man of your taste in music, cannot play upon the Jews harp; there are some of us here that touch

---

[1] Erskine, letter of 1 May 1762.
[2] The words were recorded by David Herd *c.* 1765; see Hecht, *Songs*.

it very melodiously, I can tell you. Corelli's solo of *Maggie Lauder*, and Pergolesi's sonata of *The Carle he came o'er the Craft*, are excellently adapted to that instrument; let me advise you to learn it. The first cost is but three halfpence, and they last a long time.[1]

Even a musician like Stephen Clarke, who was deeply sympathetic to both kinds of music, could not resist jokes of this type:

Mr James Miller . . . was in company with our friend Clarke; and talking of Scotch music, Mr Miller expressed an ardent ambition to be able to compose a Scots air. Mr Clarke, partly by way of joke, told him to keep to the black keys of the harpsichord, and preserve some kind of rhythm, and he would infallably compose a Scots air.[2]

These passages were funny because of the disparity between the two traditions; because people's reactions to folk and classical music were so dissimilar that they normally never made this kind of connection between them at all. Folk music flourished when its repertory remained the same, classical music flourished when its repertory developed; folk music was peculiar to Scotland, classical music was common to Europe; folk music required no formal education for its appreciation and propagation, classical music required a great deal of it. Upper-class Scots in the eighteenth century used each kind of music in ways corresponding to, and symbolized by, these functional features. In folk music they found an expression of conservatism, of national identity, and of community with all social classes of fellow Scots; in classical music they found an expression of progress, of participation in Europe, and of community with the educated classes of England, Holland, France, Germany, and Italy.

These might seem to be complementary aspects of the same object; it would seem, on the face of it, logically possible to regard Scotland as a country with both a 'national past' and a 'European future', and to find a use for two associated types of music accordingly. But Scottish history did not work out that way; more and

---

[1] Erskine, letter of 23 November 1761.

[2] Burns, *Letters*, letter to George Thomson, November 1794. Clarke may have been recalling a note in Sir John Hawkins's *History of Music*, vol. 4, p. 4 n., 1776: 'It may be observed that the front row of a Harpsichord will give a melody nearly resembling that of the Scots tunes.'

more, as the eighteenth century progressed, Scots found that they were being forced into an either-or choice between these two attitudes towards their native land. This came about, briefly, as follows.

At the end of the seventeenth century Scotland was a wretchedly poor country. It had a medieval agricultural system which was so inefficient that people were liable to die of starvation during the winter following a bad harvest; this happened several years running in the 1690s. Foreign trade was also at a low ebb; there were trade restrictions even between England and Scotland up till 1707. But despite her poverty, Scotland was a constant political threat to England. The crowns of the two countries had been united in 1603, but there was no guarantee that they would stay that way, as the laws of succession were not identical in each country; and the two parliaments were separate. England feared invasion, via Scotland, by France. So in 1707 a deal went through by which Scotland gave up her independent parliament and laws of monarchical succession in exchange for entry into England's trade areas. The Act of Union of 1707 was therefore, for Scotland, an economic gain at the expense of national pride. The Scottish people were by no means whole-heartedly in favour of it. The economic gain took thirty years to make itself felt. Meanwhile, in the Highlands, a violent political reaction took place, in the Rebellions of 1715 and 1745.

By about 1770 many Scots people had become somewhat muddled in their attitude towards their country: social and economic progress seemed possible only by a kind of denial of Scotland's past. And by Walter Scott's time the defeated Bonnie Prince Charlie had become a symbol of Scotland's lost glory, a kind of folk-hero, even in the minds of loyal Hanoverians. Scotland had caught a type of schizophrenia in which its politics and economics looked forwards, while its culture looked backwards.

The Act of Union of 1707 had landed Scots people with, among other things, a language problem. The country's political capital became, suddenly, London instead of Edinburgh, and the upper classes realized that they would have to learn to speak and write standard English if they were going to survive. Glossaries of

Scots dialect and English words were published; classes were held in southern pronunciation; aristocrats sent their sons to English public schools so that they would acquire the right accent and the right friends. Then there was a reaction; during the 1770s there was a widespread scare that dialect speech was about to die out altogether.[1] The upshot of this was that Scottish literature in the last third of the eighteenth century was split down the middle: half the poetry of the period was written in classical Augustan forms, in imitation of those practised in England, and the other half was written in colloquial dialect forms, and neither part had much connection with, or enriching effect upon, the other. Here too, 'progress' and 'nationalism' were twisted so that they became opposing, rather than complementary, ideals.[2]

Sadly, but perhaps inevitably, moves were made to split up folk and classical music and to draft them, similarly, into opposite camps. Unifying forces existed, like the fiddle dance music which partook of both traditions, but they were not strong enough wholly to prevent the growth of schism. There was a tendency in classical music circles to regard folk music as primitive and beneath serious consideration—Robert Bremner took this attitude[3]—and in folk music circles to regard classical music as a foreign upstart and a parasite. The second of these attitudes became widespread in the later part of the century.

The people in eighteenth-century Scotland who voiced dislike of classical music were remarkably unanimous in their opinions; they disapproved of it, not because it was expensive or socially exclusive, but simply because it was 'Italian': it was a symbol of foreign interference with Scottish life. This is an attitude of mind commonly called 'xenophobia'. Paradoxically, many of them actually enjoyed classical music personally, while objecting to it on nationalistic grounds; enjoyment and disapproval coexisted in their minds; they were objecting purely on principle. Two important spokesmen of this kind were the poets Allan Ramsay and Robert Fergusson.

---

[1] See McDiarmid's introduction to Fergusson, vol. 1, p. 140.

[2] Eighteenth-century Scottish literature has been brilliantly discussed from this angle by Daiches in *Paradox*.

[3] Witness the tone of his *Rudiments*, 2nd edn., pp. 50–4.

Allan Ramsay may be seen in the 1720s identifying himself with
the classical music tradition. I have already suggested that Ramsay
was strongly motivated by emulation of the London poet and playwright Thomas D'Urfey; and among D'Urfey's activities was the
writing of lyrics for cantatas with titles like 'OCEAN'S GLORY . . .
A Royal ODE or CANTATA; made in Honour of King GEORGE's
Coronation. Set to Musick by Dr. PEPUSCH, after the Italian manner'.[1] Ramsay decided to create a Scottish version of this genre;
he looked round Edinburgh for a suitable composer to collaborate
with. By good fortune one Bocchi, an Italian cellist, had arrived in
Edinburgh in July 1720,[2] and he agreed to take part in Ramsay's
scheme. Accordingly there appeared in the *Tea-table Miscellany*
in 1723 'A Scots Cantata. The Tune after an Italian Manner.
Compos'd by Signior Lorenzo Bocchi'. It is a solo cantata, scored
for soprano, obbligato violins, and continuo, with dialect words;
it opens with a recitative:

RECITATIVE

Blate Jonny faintly teld fair Jean his mind;
Jeany took Pleasure to deny him lang.
He thought her Scorn came frae a Heart unkind,
Which gart him in Despair tune up this Sang:

proceeding to an aria with instrumental ritornelli and a da capo
section:

AIR

O bonny lassie, since 'tis sae,
That I'm despis'd by thee,
I hate to live; but O I'm wae,
And unko sweer to die.

Dear Jeany, think what dowy Hours
I thole by your Disdain;
Ah! should a Breast sae saft as yours
Contain a Heart of Stane.[3]

---

[1] *Pills to Purge Melancholy* (London, 1718), vol. 1.

[2] *Edinburgh Evening Courant*, 11–12 July 1720.

[3] The music was published in Bocchi's *Musicall Entertainment for a Chamber op. 1*
(Dublin [1726]). *Blate*: shy / *gart*: caused to / *wae*: unhappy / *unko sweer*: extremely
reluctant / *dowy*: doleful / *thole*: suffer.

Yet simultaneously Ramsay wrote a poem which delivers a scurrilous attack on classical music, jokes about castrati and all, from the point of view of a nationalist-minded folk-fiddler:

> [He] bann'd wi' birr the corky cowp,
> That to the papists' country scowp,
>   To lear ha, ha's,

(*Ramsay's glossary*: Curs'd strongly the light-headed fellows who run to Italy to learn soft music)

> Frae chiels that sing hap, stap, and lowp,
>   Wantin the B[a']s.

Classical music is dismissed as utterly effeminate compared with 'virile' Scots folk music:

> That beardless capons are na men,
> We by their fozie springs might ken;
> But ours, he said, cou'd vigour len'
>   To men o' weir,
> And gar them stout to battle sten'
>   Withoutten fear.[1]

Allan Ramsay's position was undecided, to say the least.

Robert Fergusson, also, had claims to being a classical music sympathizer. He had an excellent singing voice, and as an undergraduate regularly led services in the university chapel at St. Andrews. In 1769, when he was nineteen, he was engaged to write additional lyrics for the Edinburgh production of Arne's *Artaxerxes* at the Theatre Royal, and during the course of the production he met and was befriended by the great castrato Tenducci, who was singing in it. Years later Tenducci wept upon recalling the tragic circumstances of Fergusson's death.[2] Fergusson was also friendly with the composer John Collet, who set his 'Ode on the Rivers of Scotland' to music;[3] and the description of opera performances in his poem 'The Canongate Play-house in Ruins', which I have already quoted in Chapter 2, shows that he had a

---

[1] Ramsay, *Poems*, vol. 1, 'Elegy on Patie Birnie'. *Fozie*: lethargic / *springs*: instrumental tunes / *stend*: march hastily.

[2] Grosart, p. 87; Campbell, p. 298.

[3] Fergusson, *Poems* (Edinburgh, 1773). The music is not extant.

most exact knowledge of what an opera orchestra sounded like. Fergusson was certainly a person who knew his way round the classical music culture.

But early in the 1770s Fergusson changed tack and joined the anti-classical faction; in 1772 he published an 'Elegy on the Death of Scots Music' which attacked classical music for having choked folk music to death:

> Now foreign sonnets bear the gree
> And crabbit queer variety
> Of sound fresh sprung frae *Italy*
>   A bastard breed!
> Unlike that saft-tongu'd melody
>   Which now lies dead.[1]

He singled out the Edinburgh violinist William McGibbon (d. 1756) as the last true folk-music champion:

> *Macgibbon's* gane: Ah! waes my heart!
> The man in music maist expert
> Wha cou'd sweet melody impart,
>   And tune the reed
> Wi' sic a slee and pawky art;
>   But now he's dead.

Significantly, the arguments in this poem are without factual basis. Scottish folk music in 1772 was, of course, not dying at all, but in an exceptionally healthy condition; a huge corpus of traditional ballads was still going strong, new reels and strathspeys were being written daily, and the great Gow family were about to emerge into national prominence. McGibbon, also, was a strange figurehead to choose in this context, for as we have seen he was primarily a classical musician and far from opposed to Italian trends; indeed, McGibbon expressly headed one of his trio-sonatas—the fifth of the 1734 set—'in Imitation of Corelli'. One might also get the impression from this that Fergusson knew McGibbon personally; seeing, however, that McGibbon died when Fergusson was aged six, it is in fact unlikely. The poem must therefore be

---

[1] *Weekly Magazine*, 5 March 1772. *Gree*: prize. *Dead* is pronounced 'deid'.

regarded as an expression, merely, of a certain state of mind about classical music.[1]

A further attack on classical music may be found in another Fergusson poem, 'The Daft-Days':

> *Fidlers*, your pins in temper fix,
> And roset weel your fiddle-sticks,
> And banish vile Italian tricks
>   From out your quorum,
> Nor *fortes* wi' *pianos* mix,
>   Gie's *Tulloch Gorum*.[2]

'Tullochgorum', the strathspey-tune referred to here, had a lyric which itself contained a strongly worded anti-classical music manifesto. It was first published in 1776:

> What needs there be sae great a fraise
> Wi' dringing dull Italian lays,
> I wadna gie our ain Strathspeys
>   For half a hunder score o' them;
> They're dowf and dowie at the best,
>   Dowf and dowie, dowf and dowie,
>   Dowf and dowie at the best,
>   Wi' a' their variorum;
> They're dowf and dowie at the best,
> Their *allegros* and a' the rest,
> They canna please a Scottish taste,
>   Compar'd wi' Tullochgorum.[3]

This lyric was well known all over late eighteenth-century Scotland.

[1] It is just possible that the 'Macgibbon' referred to was not William, but a lesser known relation; for example, a piece entitled 'Duncan McGibbon's Scotch measure' occurs in NLS MS. 2085 (Edinburgh, *c.* 1742). Also the line 'And tune the reed'—if it is not there merely for the rhyme—would indicate that the musician intended was a bagpiper or oboist, whereas William McGibbon was a fiddler. But the obvious explanation seems the most likely.

[2] *Weekly Magazine*, 2 January 1772. Note that the line 'Nor *fortes* wi' *pianos* mix' gives away that Fergusson had actually listened attentively to galante orchestral music.

[3] *Weekly Magazine*, 2 May 1776. *Dowf*: insipid. The passage was a *locus classicus* of how to use Italian musical terminology satirically in dialect verse. Note how the word '*allegros*' is deliberately mis-stressed and made to conform to strathspey rhythm, suggesting classical music being trampled under foot by folk music.

A more thoughtful and, at first sight, rational criticism of classical music was put forward by Topham in his account of Edinburgh in 1775:

> The modern Music of this Country . . . is not of the same excellence, or breathes that natural spirit and agreeable sweetness which distinguishes that of former times. At present they rather endeavour to imitate other nations, than to have a style peculiar to themselves; and their pieces are made up of such variety of tastes, that they may be said to be harmonic Oglios. Such is the case of my Lord Kelly, whose admirable talents and genius in this science have been corrupted and restrained by his poorly copying the compositions of other masters . . . too close an observance of the Italian manner has corrupted him, and many other composers of this Country.[1]

But on closer examination this too turns out to be a specious argument, combining misguided theory with poor observation of the facts. Classical music in Edinburgh in 1775 was extremely flourishing; all that Topham was objecting to was its lack of distinctive national characteristics. The 'Music . . . of former times' with which he was comparing it was, of course, earlier *folk* music not earlier classical music, so the comparison was hardly a useful one. Elsewhere[2] Topham states that music was 'the constant topic of every conversation' in Edinburgh at the time, so it is likely that he picked these ideas up second-hand from people he met at social gatherings, rather than thinking them out for himself. In that case we may regard this passage as a record of current Edinburgh opinion on the subject.

Classical music was not unaware of the nationalistic feelings that were building up against it, even among its own supporters, and to combat them it tried to develop some local peculiarities which people could identify as Scottish. It was customary, for example, at the Edinburgh and Aberdeen Musical Societies all through the eighteenth century, to include national songs in the concerts; this was one way in which people tried to give the classical music tradition a national flavour. During the 1770s, also, attempts

[1] Topham, pp. 373 f.   [2] Ibid., p. 378.

were made to identify the Earl of Kelly's un-Italian, Mannheim-based composition style as a Scottish characteristic, as though Kelly were a sort of Grieg or Mussorgsky ahead of his time. Topham wrote (again, I suspect, echoing current opinion) how Kelly's 'imagination . . . in his wilder compositions . . . has indulged itself in all its native freedom',[1] while Robertson said that in Kelly's music 'the *fervidum ingenium* of his country bursts forth'.[2] But to everyone's disappointment Kelly's style became more Italianate and less 'Scottish' as he grew older.

It was not till about 1780, however, that the most drastic nationalist development began: this was the introduction of national song tunes, in large numbers, into sonatas and concertos. J. C. Bach seems to have started the trend off by publishing, in London in 1777, a piano concerto whose slow movement consisted of a set of variations on 'The yellow-hair'd laddie'. He can hardly have foreseen the consequences: soon every composer in Edinburgh and Aberdeen was writing piano sonatas with folk-tune rondo finales, folk-tune slow movements, even folk-tune second subjects in the principal movements, until the introduction of pre-existing popular material was almost an obligatory feature of the style. At an immediate level this was beneficial, as it helped composers' work to sell; but as far as the European development of the sonata was concerned, it was a complete blind alley. Scots tunes were not particularly suitable for use in dramatic sonata-form works; they mostly progressed in stiff 8- and 16-bar phrases, and Scottish composers showed none of Beethoven's skill in breaking folk-tunes down into smaller, more workable units. And as well as imposing four-square rigidity on their phrasing, the tunes also obstructed composers' own thematic inventiveness. The consequences were disastrous and final. Scottish classical music found itself disqualified from the European mainstream and unable to rejoin it. By 1800 the hundred best national songs had all been incorporated into sonatas and no further development was possible—the idea had been used up; and after that, in the face of generally adverse economic conditions, Scottish classical composition ground to a halt.

[1] Topham, p. 374.   [2] Robertson, p. 436.

It seems especially surprising that this should have happened when we remember that all the important Scottish composers between 1780 and 1800 were immigrants: Schetky, Stabilini, the Corris, Butler, and Ross. Such composers must have used Scots tunes in their works purely as a conciliatory gesture towards the native folk-tradition of the country they had adopted. Sad to say, it was not an unqualified success, even as such; for as immigrants, the composers tended to decorate the tunes according to classical music conventions, and that upset nationalist feelings yet again. In 1801 John Leyden even used the word 'composer' as a term of abuse:

The peasant may change a tune, from the inaptitude of his ear; but he is no musical composer, to alter or mangle the airs with which he is acquainted . . .[1]

Classical music ran off the rails by taking too much notice of folk music at the same time, ironically, as folk music ceased to be a living force in upper-class life. During the eighteenth century the social gap between the upper and lower classes had widened; agriculture had been modernized and began to pay off, so that land-owners were far wealthier than they had been; the upper classes found new kinds of social amusement in the urban night-life of Edinburgh and London; they cultivated English accents; they turned into a different sort of person from what they had been in 1700. They were still, of course, nationalists at heart, but their nationalism expressed itself more and more only through the fashionable folk-song modes—the fiddle dance music and national songs. Gradually the tide of traditional oral folk-song ebbed away, leaving them high and dry.

(Even at this stage, upper-class children had lower-class domestic servants to teach them songs; upper-class children were brought up on folk culture for some generations further though they did not share it with their own parents. The children of the advocate Charles Sharpe, for example, were told folk-tales at Hoddam Castle, Dumfriesshire, in the 1780s by a character called 'Nurse

[1] Leyden, *Preliminary dissertation*, p. 275.

Jenny'; the fourth child of the family, Charles Kirkpatrick Sharpe, left an interesting record of her stories many years afterwards.)[1]

As this class-stratification proceeded it was compensated for, somewhat surprisingly, by the rise of the antiquarian movement and by a new, selfconscious, interest in folk music. Denied direct access to the oral tradition, the upper classes tried instead to hang on to it through print. Many antiquarians were active between 1780 and 1830, travelling round country areas taking down oral songs from the lower classes and then selling them, in printed collections, to the upper classes. Large numbers of folk-song collections were published in Scotland around this time, many of them lavishly produced, so that it is clear that there was a general market for them. The upper classes also lapped up didactic writings on folk-song such as William Tytler's inventive *Dissertation on the origins of Scots music*, which was reprinted several times, and Walter Scott's interminable genealogical notes to the *Minstrelsy of the Scottish Border*. Some members of the upper classes even did a little collecting themselves. There is an interesting manuscript in the National Library of Scotland[2] which was made by a teenage girl, seventeen-year-old Alicia Anne Spottiswoode of Spottiswoode House, Berwickshire, in 1827. It contains items headed 'Old Song which I learned from Mary Blythe a Yetholm gipsy', 'An old song which I learned from Thomas Waldie's playing on the fiddle', and ' "The gallant shoemaker" which I learned from Thomas Waldie who learned it from hearing Mrs Kennedy of Green Knowe's sister play it on the fiddle. *Very old indeed*';[3] not to mention a piano piece rather suspiciously entitled 'Yᵉ Spotyswoode's Coronach'. It is probably significant that this young lady lived only twelve miles from Abbotsford, the residence of Sir Walter Scott; she retained an interest in folk-song collecting all her life.[4]

Publications of folk-songs increased in number up till 1828. It seems finally to have struck the upper classes, however, that the whole idea was futile, and that they were trying to glue dead

¹ In Chambers, *Popular rhymes*, pp. 70 f., 87 f.

² NLS MS. 842.

³ 'The gallant shoemaker' was in fact one of the tunes which Ramsay had used in the *Tea-table Miscellany* a hundred years earlier.

⁴ She married Lord John Scott of Dalkeith in 1836.

leaves back on to a tree: and after Sir Walter Scott's death in 1832 the antiquarian folk-song movement abruptly fizzled out.

CONCLUSION

Edinburgh in 1700 had been musically a provincial backwater, maintaining no local composition whatsoever, and supporting only about a dozen professional musicians,[1] most of whom were downtrodden, underpaid, and obliged to spend a large part of their lives teaching untalented upper-class children. Edinburgh by 1775 had turned into a European musical centre, with three excellent resident composers and several virtuoso, highly paid, Italian and German resident singers and players. And at this point people began to get frightened. They had forgotten what it felt like to belong to a successful international musical centre: nothing remotely like it had happened in Scotland since the last cultural flowering of the Court in the 1590s, more than six generations before. Certainly they had wanted classical music to succeed, but not that well. They felt it had gone too far; they tried to retreat from the expense, the newness, the foreign-ness of it all. Reasons were invented why classical music was a bad thing; and instead of making further progress, classical music was allowed, even encouraged, to surrender the advanced position it had achieved, and waste its energies attempting unnatural liaisons with folk music. There was perhaps a danger all through the eighteenth century that this might eventually happen, since so many Scottish composers dabbled in folk music in their spare time. By the time composers realized they had made a mistake, society had moved on, and the damage was done: by 1800 it was impossible for Scottish classical music to regain the position it had held in 1775.

Then the upper classes outgrew the oral song tradition. This was bound to have happened sooner or later, as a part of the social evolution which was going on all over Europe; but it meant that, by 1830 or so, the upper classes were left remarkably empty-handed. Their classical music had silted up and their folk music

[1] Tytler, p. 508 n., suggests that the concert in Edinburgh on St. Cecilia's Day 1695 employed eleven professional musicians; this was probably the full number of those residing in the town at the time.

dwindled away. Their fiddle dance music and the national songs lasted them till at least 1914, but mainly because of the hard-wearing qualities of both traditions; in both the creative peaks had, in fact, largely been passed by 1800.

   This, then, is the study of a life-cycle in a country's musical culture. It is a study of how classical music grew up at an opportune moment in a kingdom remote from the centre of Europe, how it flourished briefly and then, meeting adverse conditions, died out again; and how it had a stimulating effect, even in this short time, upon the country's native folk music. It is not perhaps a book for Scottish nationalists, nor for those who, in the words of Samuel Johnson, 'love Scotland better than truth'. Eighteenth-century Scottish classical music was, even at its best, only a minor tributary of the European mainstream. It is nowadays completely forgotten as far as the general public is concerned, even in Scotland, just as sixteenth-century Scottish music was forgotten in the eighteenth century. It produced no outstanding native masterpieces, with the possible exception of Kelly's overtures, and even they have since mostly been thrown away or lost. Nor is Scotland likely to do any better next time; another classical music renaissance is in progress in Scotland at present, and it seems to me quite probable that the same mistakes, or twentieth-century versions of the same mistakes, will be made all over again. Scotland's real music remains her folk music.

   I hope nevertheless that the reader has found this study profitable. If we are no nearer to resolving the paradox of Scottish culture, we have at least enlarged our understanding of the European classical music tradition by viewing it from a strange and unfamiliar angle.

General bibliography excluding music

I. PRINTED

ARNOT, HUGO. *History of Edinburgh*. Edinburgh, 1779.

BAILLIE, LADY GRISELL. *The household book of Lady Grisell Baillie, 1692–1733*. Edinburgh, Scottish History Society, 1911.

BAPTIE, DAVID. *Musical Scotland past and present*. Paisley, 1894.

BEATTIE, JAMES. *James Beattie's day-book*, ed. Ralph Walker. Aberdeen, Third Spalding Club, 1948.

BOSWELL, JAMES. The Yale edition of the private papers of James Boswell, ed. Frederick A. Pottle. Vol. 1 *Boswell's London Journal, 1762–3*. London, 1950. Vol. 4 *Boswell on the Grand Tour: Germany and Switzerland, 1764*. London, 1953.

BREMNER, ROBERT. *The rudiments of music*. 1st edn., Edinburgh, 1756. 2nd edn., Edinburgh, 1762.

—— 'Some thoughts on the performance of concert music', in SCHETKY, J. G. C. *Six Quartettos . . . op. 6*. London, 1777.

BRONSON, BERTRAND H. *The traditional tunes of the Child ballads*. 4 vols. Princeton, New Jersey, 1959– .

BROWN, JAMES D., and STRATTON, STEPHEN. *British musical biography*. Birmingham, 1897.

BUCHAN, PETER. *Ancient ballads and songs of the north of Scotland*. 2 vols. Edinburgh, 1828.

BURNEY, CHARLES. *A general history of music, from the earliest ages to the present period*. 4 vols. London, 1776–89.

BURNS, ROBERT. *The complete poetical works*. London, n.d.

—— *Letters*, ed. J. de Lancey Ferguson. 2 vols. Oxford, 1931.

—— *The merry muses of Caledonia*. London, 1966.

BURT, EDWARD. *Letters from a gentleman in the north of Scotland, 1726*. New edn. 2 vols. London, 1815.

CAMPBELL, ALEXANDER. *An introduction to the history of poetry in Scotland*. Edinburgh, 1798.

CHAMBERS, Robert. *Domestic annals of Scotland.* 3rd edn. 3 vols. Edinburgh, 1874.

—— *Popular rhymes of Scotland.* Edinburgh, 1870.

—— *The songs of Scotland prior to Burns.* Edinburgh, [1862].

—— *Traditions of Edinburgh.* Edinburgh, 1868.

CHAPPELL, WILLIAM. *Popular music of the olden time.* 2 vols. London, 1859.

CHILD, FRANCIS J. *English and Scottish popular ballads.* 5 vols. London, [1882–98].

CLERK OF PENICUIK, SIR JOHN. *Memoirs of the life of Sir John Clerk of Penicuik, 1676–1755.* Edinburgh, Scottish History Society, 1892.

COCKBURN, ALISON. *Letters and memoir of her own life by Mrs. Alison Rutherford or Cockburn,* ed. T. Craig-Brown. Edinburgh, 1899.

COLLINSON, FRANCIS. 'The oyster dredging songs of the Firth of Forth', in *Scottish Studies.* Vol. 5. Edinburgh, 1961.

—— *The traditional and national music of Scotland.* London, 1966.

The Complaynt of Scotland, ed. J. A. H. Murray. London, Early English Text Society, 1872.

CORRI, DOMENICO. 'Life', in *The singer's preceptor.* London, 1810.

CUDWORTH, CHARLES. 'The English symphonists of the eighteenth century', in *Proceedings of the Royal Musical Association.* Vol. 78. London, 1952.

DAICHES, DAVID. 'Eighteenth century vernacular poetry', in KINSLEY, JAMES. *Scottish poetry: a critical survey.* London, 1955.

—— *The paradox of Scottish culture: the eighteenth century experience.* London, 1964.

—— *Robert Burns.* London, 1966.

DALRYMPLE, SIR DAVID, LORD HAILES. *The correspondence between Thomas Percy and David Dalrymple,* vol. 4 of *The Percy Letters,* ed. A. F. Falconer. Louisiana, 1954.

DALYELL, SIR JOHN G. *Musical memoirs of Scotland.* Edinburgh, 1849.

DAUNEY, WILLIAM. *Ancient Scottish melodies from a manuscript of the reign of King James VI.* Edinburgh, Bannatyne Club, 1838.

DAY, CYRUS L., and MURRIE, ELEANORE B. *English song-books 1651–1702.* London, 1940.

DIBDIN, JAMES C. *The annals of the Edinburgh stage.* Edinburgh, 1888.

DICK, JAMES C. *The songs of Robert Burns.* London, 1903.

DUNBAR, EDWARD D. *Social life in former days in Morayshire.* 2 vols. Edinburgh, 1865–6.

ELLIOTT, KENNETH. 'Scottish music of the early reformed church', in *Transactions of the Scottish Ecclesiological Society*. Vol. 11. Aberdeen, 1961.

ERSKINE, ANDREW. *Letters between the Hon. Andrew Erskine and James Boswell, Esq.* London, 1763.

Extracts from the records of the burgh of Edinburgh, 1689 to 1701, ed. Helen Armet. Edinburgh, 1962.

FARMER, HENRY G. 'Concerts in eighteenth century Scotland', in *Proceedings of the Royal Philosophical Society of Glasgow*. Vol. 69. Glasgow, 1945.

—— *A history of music in Scotland.* London, 1947.

—— 'Kellie', in *Die Musik in Geschichte und Gegenwart*. 14 vols. Kassel, 1949–68.

—— *Music making in the olden days.* London, 1950.

—— 'An old Scottish violin tutor', in *Proceedings of the Society of Antiquaries of Glasgow*. Vol. 65. Glasgow, 1931.

—— 'The Royal Artillery concerts', in *Music Review*. Vol. 6. Cambridge, 1945.

FERGUSSON, ROBERT. *Poems*, ed. Matthew McDiarmid. 2 vols. Edinburgh, Scottish Text Society, 1954–6.

FLETT, J. F. and T. M. 'The Scottish country dance. Its origins and development', in *Scottish Studies*. Vol. 11, pts. 1 and 2. Edinburgh, 1967.

—— —— 'Social dancing in Scotland 1700–1914', in *Scottish Studies*. Vol. 2. Edinburgh, 1958.

—— —— *Traditional dancing in Scotland.* London, 1964.

GLEIG, GEORGE. 'Memoir of Archibald, Earl of Kellie', in *Scots Magazine*. Edinburgh, October 1802.

GLEN, JOHN. *Early Scottish melodies.* Edinburgh, 1900.

GORDON, JAMES. *Abredoniae utriusque descriptio, 1661.* Edinburgh, Spalding Club, 1842.

GRAHAM, HENRY GRAY. *Social life in Scotland in the eighteenth century.* 2 vols. London, 1899.

GRANT, JAMES. *History of the burgh schools of Scotland.* London, 1876.

GRAY, W. FORBES. 'The musical society of Edinburgh and St. Cecilia's Hall', in *The Book of the Old Edinburgh Club*. Vol. 19. Edinburgh, 1933.

GREGORY, JOHN. *A comparative view of the state and faculties of man with those of the animal world.* Edinburgh, 1765.

GREIG, GAVIN, and KEITH, ALEXANDER. *Last leaves of traditional ballads and ballad airs.* Aberdeen, 1925.

GROSART, ALEXANDER B. *Life of Robert Fergusson.* Edinburgh, 1898.

HADDEN, JAMES C. *George Thomson the friend of Burns.* London, 1898.

HAMILTON, HENRY. *An economic history of Scotland in the eighteenth century.* London, 1963.

HARRIS, DAVID FRASER. *St. Cecilia's Hall in the Niddry Wynd.* Edinburgh, 1899.

HAWKINS, SIR JOHN. *A general history of the science and practice of music.* 5 vols. London, 1776.

HECHT, HANS. *Robert Burns.* London, 1950.

—— *Songs from David Herd's manuscripts.* Edinburgh, 1904.

HERD, DAVID. *Ancient and modern Scots songs.* 2 vols. Edinburgh, 1769–76.

HOGG, JAMES. *The domestic manners and private life of Sir Walter Scott.* Glasgow, 1834.

—— *Jacobite Reliques.* 2 vols. Edinburgh, 1819–21.

HONEYMAN, WILLIAM C. *Scottish violin makers, past and present.* Newport-on-Tay, 1898.

H[OWIE], W. H. 'Scotland's musical Earl', in *The Scotsman.* Edinburgh, 31 August 1957.

INNES, COSMO NELSON. *Sketches of early Scotch history and social progress.* Edinburgh, 1861.

INNES-SMITH, R. W. *English-speaking students of medicine at the University of Leyden.* Edinburgh, 1932.

JACKSON, JOHN. *The history of the Scottish stage.* Edinburgh, 1793.

JAMIESON, JAMES H. 'Social assemblies of the eighteenth century', in *The Book of the Old Edinburgh Club.* Vol. 19. Edinburgh, 1933.

KENNEDY, WILLIAM. *Annals of Aberdeen.* 2 vols. London, 1818.

KIDSON, FRANK. *British music publishers, printers, and engravers.* London, [1900].

—— 'James Oswald and the Temple of Apollo', in *Musical Antiquary.* Vol. 2. London, 1911.

KINCAID, ALEXANDER. *History of Edinburgh.* Edinburgh, 1787.

KINLOCH, GEORGE R. *Ancient Scottish ballads.* London, 1827.

KROHN, ERNST C. 'Reinagle Alexander', in *Die Musik in Geschichte und Gegenwart.* 14 vols. Kassel, 1949–68.

LAING, DAVID. 'Introduction', to JOHNSON, JAMES. *The Scots Musical Museum.* Edinburgh, 1839.

LANGWILL, LYNDESAY G. 'The piper, drummer and bellman of Lanark in olden times', in *The Hamilton Advertiser.* Hamilton, 21 January 1939.

LAUDER, SIR JOHN, LORD FOUNTAINHALL. *The decisions of the Lords of Council and Session, from June 6th 1678 to July 30th 1712.* Vol. I. Edinburgh, 1759.

LAW, ALEXANDER. *Education in Edinburgh in the eighteenth century.* London, 1965.

LAWRANCE, ROBERT MURDOCH. *John Ross, composer, Aberdeen, his circle and work.* Aberdeen, 1927.

LEYDEN, JOHN. *Poems and ballads, with a memoir of the author by Sir Walter Scott.* Kelso, 1858.

—— *The poetical remains of the late Dr. John Leyden, with memoirs of his life by the Rev. James Morton.* London, 1819.

—— *Preliminary dissertation to the Complaynt of Scotland.* Edinburgh, 1801.

LOCKHART, JOHN G. *Memoirs of the life of Sir Walter Scott.* 7 vols. Edinburgh, 1837.

MACKENZIE, HENRY. *The anecdotes and egotisms of Henry Mackenzie, 1745–1831,* ed. Harold W. Thompson. London, 1927.

MAIDMENT, JAMES. *Analecta Scotica.* 2 vols. Edinburgh, 1834–7.

MAITLAND, WILLIAM. *History of Edinburgh.* Edinburgh, 1753.

MARR, ROBERT. *Music for the people.* Edinburgh, 1889.

MARTIN, BURNS. *Allan Ramsay: a study of his life and works.* Cambridge, Mass., 1931.

MOTHERWELL, WILLIAM. *Minstrelsy ancient and modern.* Glasgow, 1827.

MUIR, WILLA. *Living with ballads.* London, 1965.

NEVILLE, SYLAS. *The diary of Sylas Neville, 1767–88,* ed. B. Cozens-Hardy. London, 1950.

NICOLL, J. R. ALLARDYCE. *A history of English drama 1660–1900.* 6 vols. Cambridge, 1952–9.

Notes from the records of the Assembly Rooms of Edinburgh. Edinburgh, 1842.

Old Scotch ballads, broadsides, etc. 1679–1730. NLS: Ry.III.a.10.

OREM, WILLIAM. *A description of . . . Old Aberdeen, in the years 1724 and 1725.* Aberdeen, 1791.

PASQUALI, NICOLO. *The art of fingering the harpsichord.* Edinburgh, [1758].

—— *Thoroughbass made easy.* Edinburgh, [1757].

PATRICK, J. MILLAR. *Four centuries of Scottish psalmody.* London, 1949.

—— 'Public worship in Scotland from the Reformation to the present day', in *Manual of Church Praise.* Edinburgh, 1932.

PERCY, THOMAS. *Reliques of ancient English poetry.* 3 vols. London, 1765.

PLANT, MARJORIE. *The domestic life of Scotland in the eighteenth century.* Edinburgh, 1952.

PRICE, FRANK PERCIVAL. *The carillon.* London, 1933.

RAMSAY, ALLAN. *The ever green. Being a collection of Scots poems wrote by the ingenious before 1600.* 2 vols. Edinburgh, 1724.

—— *Poems.* 2 vols. Edinburgh, 1721–8.

—— *The Tea-table Miscellany.* 4 vols. Edinburgh, 1723–c. 1737.

REES, ABRAHAM. *The new cyclopedia.* London, 1819.

RITSON, JOSEPH. *Scottish songs.* 2 vols. London, 1794.

ROBERTSON, THOMAS. *An inquiry into the fine arts.* London, 1784.

ROGERS, CHARLES. *Life and songs of the Baroness Nairne.* London, 1869.

SAINSBURY, JOHN. *Dictionary of musicians.* 2 vols. London, 1827.

SCHETKY, J. G. C. 'Some observations and rules for violoncello playing', in *Twelve duetts for two violoncellos, op. 7.* London, c. 1780.

SCHETKY, LAURENCE OLIPHANT. *The Schetky family, a compilation of letters.* Portland, Oregon, 1942.

S[CHETKY], S. F. L. *Ninety years of work and play.* Edinburgh, 1877.

SCOTT, WALTER. *Minstrelsy of the Scottish border.* 3 vols. Kelso, 1802.

Selections from the Monymusk papers, 1713–55, ed. Henry Hamilton. Edinburgh, Scottish History Society, 1945.

SHARP, CECIL. *English folk song: some conclusions.* With a preface by Maud Karpeles. 14th edn. London, 1965.

SHARPE, CHARLES KIRKPATRICK. *Minuets &c. composed by the Right Honourable Thomas Earl of Kelly.* Edinburgh, 1836.

SHIELD, WILLIAM. *Rudiments of thorough bass for young harmonists.* London, c. 1815.

SHIRE, HELENA M. 'Court song in Scotland after 1603: Aberdeenshire', in *Transactions of the Edinburgh Bibliographical Society.* Vol. 3. Edinburgh, 1957.

—— *Song, Dance and Poetry of the court of Scotland under King James VI.* Cambridge, 1969.

SIMPSON, CLAUDE M. *The British broadside ballad and its music.* New Brunswick, 1966.

SIMPSON, IAN J. *Education in Aberdeenshire before 1872.* London, 1947.

SMITH, ALEXANDER E. 'The register of St. Paul's Episcopal Chapel, Aberdeen', in *Miscellany volume 2.* Aberdeen, New Spalding Club, 1906.

SMITHERS, DON. 'Seventeenth-century English trumpet music', in *Music and Letters.* London, October 1967.

SMOLLET, TOBIAS. *The expedition of Humphry Clinker.* 3 vols. London, 1771.

SMOUT, T. C. *A history of the Scottish people, 1560–1830.* London, 1969.

STARK, JOHN. *Picture of Edinburgh*. Edinburgh, 1820.

STENHOUSE, WILLIAM. 'Illustrations', in JOHNSON, JAMES. *The Scots Musical Museum*. Edinburgh, 1839.

SYMON, J. A. *Scottish farming past and present*. Edinburgh, 1959.

TERRY, C. S. 'John Forbes's "Songs and Fancies" ', in *Musical Quarterly*. London, October 1936.

—— and WILLSHER, HARRY M. 'The music school of Old Machar', in *Miscellany volume 2*. Aberdeen, Third Spalding Club, 1940.

THOM, WALTER. *The history of Aberdeen*. Aberdeen, 1811.

[TOPHAM, EDWARD]. *Letters from Edinburgh written in the years 1774 and 1775*. London, 1776.

TREVELYAN, GEORGE MACAULAY. *Illustrated English social history*. 4 vols. London, 1949–52.

TROW-SMITH, ROBERT. *A history of British livestock husbandry*. 2 vols. London, 1957–9.

TULLIBARDINE, MARCHIONESS OF. *A military history of Perthshire, 1660–1902*. Perth, 1908.

TYTLER, WILLIAM. 'On the fashionable amusements and entertainments in Edinburgh in the last century', in *Transactions of the Society of Antiquarians of Scotland*. Vol. I. Edinburgh, 1792.

WALKER, WILLIAM. *The bards of Bon-Accord, 1375–1860*. Aberdeen, 1887.

—— *Extracts from the commonplace-book of Andrew Melville*. Aberdeen, 1899.

WATSON, JAMES. *A choice collection of comic and serious Scots poems*. 3 vols. Edinburgh, 1706–11.

WILLSHER, HARRY M. 'Scottish coronation of Charles I', in *The Scotsman*. Edinburgh, 2 August 1952.

WOOD, WALTER. *The east neuk of Fife*. Edinburgh, 1887.

WOODFILL, WALTER W. *Musicians in English society from Elizabeth to Charles I*. Princeton, New Jersey, 1953.

WORDSWORTH, DOROTHY. *Recollections of a tour made in Scotland A.D. 1803*, in vol. I of *Journals*, ed. E. de Selincourt, London, 1941.

II. MANUSCRIPT

Aberdeen Musical Society minute-books. 2 vols. 1748–95. APL.

ARMSTRONG, NORMA. The Edinburgh Stage, 1715–1820. Unpubl. Library Association thesis, 1968. EPL.

CAMPBELL, ALEXANDER. Travels in the border country in search of folk music. 1816. EUL La.II.378/2.

Edinburgh Musical Society library catalogue. 1765. EUL La.III.761.

Edinburgh Musical Society library catalogue. 1782. EPL.

Edinburgh Musical Society minute-books. 4 vols. 1728–98. EPL.

Edinburgh Musical Society plan-books. 3 vols. 1768–71 and 1778–86. EUL La.III.562–4.

EMS. *See* Edinburgh Musical Society.

An encouragement to the cultivation of church music, by a preacher in the Church of Scotland. *c.* 1802. EUL Dc.8.16.

LAING, DAVID. Various notes on old Scots music. EUL La.IV.20.

ROSS, JOHN. A catalogue of the Aberdeen holdings in King's College Library and the Public Library of the works of John Ross. Compiled by J. Murdoch Henderson, 1962. APL.

Royal College of Physicians of Edinburgh minute-books. Royal College of Physicians Library, Edinburgh.

SADIE, STANLEY J. British chamber music, 1720–90. Unpubl. Cambridge Ph.D. thesis, 1958. CUL.

SAINSBURY, JOHN. Autobiographical letters sent to J. Sainsbury from musicians as material for his *Dictionary of Musicians* of 1827. 1823–4. GUL R.d.84–9.

SLEIGH, GORDON. David Mallet. Unpubl. Oxford B.Litt. thesis, 1951. Bodleian Library, Oxford.

TERRY, C. S. Notes on music-schools in Scotland. *c.* 1930–6. AUL MS. 699.

WILLSHER, HARRY M. Music in Scotland during three centuries. Unpubl. St. Andrews D.Litt. thesis, 1945. St. Andrews University Library.

YOUNG, DAVID. A collection of the newest countrey dances perform'd in Scotland. Edinburgh, 1740. Bodleian Library, Oxford MS. Don.d.54.

Bibliography of Scottish manuscripts containing folk-tunes, 1680–1840

Date	Instrument or voice	Title or name of original owner	Provenance	Present location and remarks
c. 1680	Violin	'Lessones for ye violin'	Newbattle Abbey, Midlothian	NLS MS. 5778.
c. 1680	Violin	..	Panmure Ho., Angus	NLS MS. 9454.
c. 1680	Violin	'James Guthrie manuscript'	Scottish	EUL MS. La.III.111.
c. 1680	? Cittern	W. Kerr	Newbattle Abbey, Midlothian	Lost. Contents-list (mid 19th c.) by David Laing in EUL MS. La.IV.20.
c. 1690	Keyboard	'an old virginal book'	Scottish	Lost. Partial contents-list among Stenhouse's *Illustrations*.
1692	Lyra-viol	'The Blaikie manuscript'	Scottish	Dundee Public Library.
c. 1695	Lyra-viol/ violin	'John Leyden's lyra-viol manuscript'	Scottish	Newcastle University Library.
1700– c. 1750	Violin, etc.	James Gairdyn	Scottish	NLS MS. 3298.
c. 1700	Keyboard	..	Panmure Ho., Angus	NLS MS. 9458.
1702– c. 1720	Recorder/ violin	James Thomson	? Edinburgh	NLS MS. 2833.
1704	Keyboard/ vocal/violin	Agnes Hume	Scottish	NLS Adv. MS. 5.2.17.
1705	Violin	George Bowie	Edinburgh	In private possession of Dr. F. Collinson, The Ley, Inner- leithen, Peeblesshire.
1709	? Keyboard	'Mrs Crockat's music book'	Scottish	Lost. Partial contents-list among Stenhouse's *Illustrations*.

Date	Instrument or voice	Title or name of original owner	Provenance	Present location and remarks
1710	Keyboard/ violin	Margaret Sinkler	Glasgow	NLS MS. 3296.
1714	Keyboard, etc.	Martha Brown	Inverary	North Ayrshire Museum, Saltcoats.
1717	Violin	George Skene	Aberdeen	NLS Adv. MS. 5.2.21.
1723	Violin	Patrick Cuming	Edinburgh	NLS MS. 1667.
c. 1738– c. 1742	Violin	Walter M'farlan	Edinburgh	3 vols. NLS MSS. 2084–5. Vol. 1 was lost c. 1800, see Laing, *Scots Musical Museum*, p. li.
1739	Keyboard	Elizabeth Young	Scottish	NLS Adv. MS. 5.2.23.
1740	Violin	'A collection of the newest countrey dances perform'd in Scotland'	Edinburgh	Bodleian Library, Oxford, MS. Don.d.54.
c. 1740	? Recorder/ flute	..	Scottish	NLS Adv. MS. 5.2.22.
c. 1740	Flute	..	? Aberdeen	APL 23775.
c. 1740– 1777	Violin	..	? Edinburgh	NLS Adv. MS. 5.2.25.
c. 1750	Violin	..	Scottish	NLS MS. 2086.
c. 1750	Violin/ keyboard	..	Scottish	NLS Adv. MS. 5.2.24.
1752	Flute	F. Coloquhon	Scottish (or Irish)	GML M18106.
c. 1760	Flute	..	Scottish	NLS Adv. MS. 5.2.20.
c. 1760	Violin	James Christie	Banff	AUL MS. 2422.
1761	Violin	John Niven	Aberdeen	AUL MS. 2232.
c. 1765	Cittern/ keyboard	..	Nisbet Ho., Berwickshire	NLS MS. 5449.
c. 1765	Flute	..	Scottish	NLS MS. 3327.
c. 1765– c. 1790	Violin, etc.	..	? Edinburgh	NLS MS. 3346.
1768	Violin	James Gillespie	Perth	NLS MS. 808.
c. 1770	Violin	..	Scottish	NLS MS. 3378.
1777	Violin	James Massie	Aberdeen	AUL MS. 795².
1780	Violin	William Trotter	Whitsome, Berwickshire	EPL Sp.C. M43S.
c. 1780	Keyboard	..	Scottish	NLS MS. 3340.

Date	Instrument or voice	Title or name of original owner	Provenance	Present location and remarks
c. 1780	Flute	John Doig	probably Scottish	GML M17371.
c. 1780– *c.* 1800	Violin	John Anderson	Inverness	SSS uncatalogued accession in December 1969.
c. 1780– *c.* 1800	Bagpipe/ violin/vocal	John Sutherland	N. of Scotland	GML M7212.
c. 1795	Tenor voice and string quartet	Peter Urbani	Edinburgh	EPL WM 1746 U72.
1797	Violin	..	Scottish	SSS MS. 2.
c. 1805	Violin	Peter Macewen	Scottish	EPL WM 43.
1819	? Theatre-orchestra	..	? Edinburgh	Set of 7 part-books. NLS MS. 3328–34.
1820-1	Violin	Thomas Sheils	Crieff	In private possession of Mrs. W. J. Macaulay, 7 Merchiston Avenue, Edinburgh 10.
c. 1820	Violin	..	probably Scottish	GML M17365.
c. 1820	Keyboard	..	Scottish	GML M17364.
1822	Violin	James Steuart	? Aberdeen	NLS MS. 782.
1823	Violin/ vocal	Francis Craigmile	? Aberdeen	AUL uncatalogued accession in January 1968. 3 vols.
1824	Vocal	Andrew Blaikie	Borders	NLS MS. 1578.
1824	Violin	Thomas Macindoe	Falkirk	GML M17361.
1827	Vocal/ keyboard	Alicia Anne Spottiswoode	Spottiswoode Ho., Berwickshire	NLS MS. 842.
1830-5	Violin	Colin McRae	Scottish	EUL Dk. 5.13.
c. 1830	Violin	Alexander McLaren	Pitlochry	AUL MS. 2424.
c. 1830	Guitar	Georgina Gregory	Edinburgh	AUL Forbes-Leith collection 24.
1835	Violin	James Virtue	Polwarth, Berwickshire	EPL Sp.C. M43S.
1839	Violin	James Webster	New Deer, Aberdeenshire	AUL MS. 2421.
c. 1840	Violin	..	Scottish	SSS MS. 1.
c. 1840	Violin	..	Aberdeenshire	SSS uncatalogued accession in December 1969.

Bibliography of sources of compositions of the Earl of Kelly

(Compositions of Kelly's are shown in italics.)

I. PRINTED

1761   *Six overtures in eight parts op. 1* (Edinburgh).

1762   The same reprinted (London).

[1763]   The harpsichord or spinnet miscellany vol. 2 (London) includes: *keyboard transcription of the overture op. 1 no. 2, first movement.*

[1765]   The Maid of the Mill, vocal score (London) includes: *keyboard transcription of the overture 'The Maid of the Mill'.*

c. 1765   Six simphonies in four parts ... by J. Stamitz, his pupil the Earl of Kelly, and others (London) includes the following probably by Kelly: *no. 4 of the set.*

[1766–70] The periodical overture in 8 parts (London) includes the following by Kelly: *nos. 13, 17, 25, and 28 in the series.*

1769   *Six sonatas for two violins and a bass* (London).

c. 1775   A collection of favourite airs in score sung ... by Tenducci (London) includes: *aria 'Death is now my only Treasure'.*

c. 1780   *The favourite minuets perform'd at the Fête Champêtre given by Lord Stanley at the Oaks* (London) contains: *Lady Betty Stanley's minuet; Lord Stanley's minuet; Dutchess of Gordon's minuet; Miss Hamilton's minuet; General Burgoine's minuet; Miss Nesbit's minuet; The Fête Champêtre minuet; Mrs Ker's minuet.*

c. 1785   The overture ... adapted for the harpsichord or piano forte (Edinburgh) is a *keyboard transcription of the overture op. 1 no. 3.*

1797   The Vocal Magazine vol. 1 (Edinburgh) includes: *song 'Ye little loves that hourly wait'.*

c. 1800   A complete collection of much admired tunes ... arranged ... by John Clarkson (Edinburgh) includes: *Mrs Kerr's minuet; the Dutchess of Gordon's minuet; the Fête Champêtre minuet;* and the following probably by Kelly: *Miss McLeod's minuet; Miss Montgomery's minuet.*

1836   *Minuets, &c. composed by the Right Honourable Thomas Earl of Kelly* ed. C. K. Sharpe (Edinburgh) contains: *Capillaire minuet; the*

Duchess of Gordon's minuet; the Duchess of Buccleuch's minuet; the Countess of Errol's minuet; Lady Anne Barnard's minuet; Lady Margaret Fordyce's minuet; Lady Murray of Clermont's minuet; Lady Maxwell of Monreith's minuet; Lady Cunynghame of Livingstone's minuet; Lady Wallace of Craigie's minuet; Mrs. Fordyce of Ayton's minuet; Mrs. Campbell of Shawfield's minuet; Mrs. Houston of Johnstone's minuet; Mrs. Hamilton of Bangour's minuet; Miss General Morris's minuet; Mrs. Cumming's minuet; Mrs. Nicholson's minuet; minuet; minuet; minuet from no. 4 of 'Six simphonies in four parts'; Imitation of a Scottish Tune; song 'Ye little loves that hourly wait'; aria 'Death is now my only Treasure'.

1839   The same reprinted (Edinburgh).

II. MANUSCRIPT

c. 1765   NLS MS. 633 (Scottish) includes: *The Dutchess of Gordon's minuet; Miss Murray's minuet; Miss Blair's minuet; minuet by the Earl of Kelly; Miss Myrton's minuet.*

c. 1765–90   NLS MS. 3346 (? Edinburgh) includes: *A minuet by Th. Hon^l Th. Earl of Kelly; a minuet by the Honble the Earl of Kelly.*

c. 1770   NLS MS. 3378 (Scottish) includes: *Mrs. Grant of Arndilly's minuet; the Caplear minuet; the Dutches of Gordon's minuet; Miss Eglington Maxwell's minuet; Miss Jessy Chalmers' minuet.*

1780   William Trotter's Musick Book, EPL (Whitsome, Berwickshire) includes: *Lady Errol's minuet; Lady Mary Lindsay's minuet; the Dutches of Buccleugh's min^t—by Lord Kelly; Miss Eglington Maxwell's minuet; Miss Blair's minuet; Miss Chambers' min^t now call'd Mrs. Comings; Lady Cunningham's minuet; the Dutches of Gordon's minuet; minuet by Lord Kelly.*

c. 1780   NLS MS. 3340 (Scottish) includes: *Minuet, in the Maid of the Mill*—Lord Kelly; i.e. *keyboard transcription of the third movement of the overture.*

1782   Fitzwilliam Museum, Cambridge, 149/32 F 14 (English) includes: *Overture in E flat—Kelly*; i.e. *keyboard transcription of the overture op. 1 no. 4.*

c. 1810   GML M18077 (English) includes: *Lord Stanley's minuet.*

III. A NOTE ON WORKS OF DOUBTFUL AUTHORSHIP

'Lord Kelly's reel' for solo violin is included in AUL MS. 2232 (Aberdeen, 1761) and in NLS MS. 808 (Perth, 1768).

'Lord Kelly's strathspey' for solo violin is included in AUL MS. 2424 (Pitlochry, *c.* 1830).

'Largo' for violin and continuo, based on the folk-tune 'The Lowlands of Holland', is included in NLS MS. 1782 (Scottish, *c.* 1790).

A manuscript in the library of Christ Church College, Oxford, listed by Robert Eitner in *Biographisch-Bibliographisches Quellen-Lexikon* (Graz, 1959) under 'Kelly' as containing 'Airs for violin by Kelly', is of late seventeenth-century date, and has no connection with the sixth earl.

Music books belonging to the Aberdeen Musical Society, c. 1755

THE following is a transcription from Aberdeen Musical Society minute-books:[1]

Handel's Overtures
Corelli's Concertos
Stanley's Concertos
Gluck's Sonatas
Corelli's Sonatas
Handel's Oratorios 1st Collectn
Gemeniani's Corelli
Church Musick in Manuscript
The fire Musick unbound
6 New Overtures
Scarlatti's and Avison's Concertos
Corelie's Posthumous Works
Mr Handel's Select Airs
Mr Handell's Sonatas
Martini's Sonatas
Barba's Sonatas
A Concerto by Jomelli
A Concerto by Sig^r Hasse
Humphries Sonatas
Barsantis Concertos in ten part
Barsantis Overture in five part
Geminiani's Concertos
Arn's Overtures, And Hebdens Concertos
Hasses 18 Flute Concertos
Rameau's Organ Concertos
The Songs in Comus and the Dragon of Wantley
Geminiani's Scots Tunes in Score
Triemer's & Morigi's Solos

[1] In APL. This catalogue is discussed in my article 'An eighteenth-century Scottish music library', *R.M.A. Research Chronicle*, no. 9 (1971).

Ruges Concertos
Six Books of Manuscript Musick
Hasses and Vinci's Overtures
Martini's 8th Overtures and Six Grand Concertos Op: 7 & 8th
Martini's 8th Overtures and Six Concertos Op: 10th & 11th
Handels 12 Grand Concertos
Martini's Concertos Op: 5th
Geminiani's Concertos Op: 5th
Defesch's Concertos
the Instrumental parts of Felton's Organ Concertos
the Instrumental parts of Handel's Organ Concertos

(Margin note against the last two entries: 'N:B: the Organ parts are Mr Tait's Own property'.)

Sigr Bozzi's Sonatas for two Violins and A Bass
Gem: Solos made concertos
Avison's Eight concertos
Hass's French horn Concertos

The following items were probably added to the list later than 1755:

Marcello's Psalm Tunes bound
Geminiani's Violin Instructions
Ciampia's Concertos
Festings Concertos
A 2d Set of Geminiani's Con:
A 2d Set of Festings Do /
Pasqualis Overtures
Oswalds Seasons
Avison's Concertos Op: 4th
Avison's 12 Concertos
Wiedimans Concertos
Pasquali's Through Bass
Brebners Scots Tunes

Music books belonging to Sir John Clerk of Penicuik, *c.* 1750

THE following is a transcription from a list in the Clerk Papers, Scottish Record Office, Edinburgh.[1] It commences in ink:

Corelli Opera Quinta
Corelli Opera Sesta

Divertimento

Lampugnani Opera prima
Bat: Martini Opera prima
Franc: Geminiani Opera seconda
Francesco Geminiani Opera terza
Franc: Barsanti Opera terza
Six Solo's by Will: McGibbon
Songs in the Opera Called Clotilda
Sei Concerti da Gius: Tartini Oper prima Lib: 2do
Concerti da Tomaso Albinoni Oper Nona Lib: 1mo ed 2do
Concerti da Carlo Tessarini Oper: prima Lib: 1mo ed 2do
Concerti di Pietro Locatelli Oper: Quarta Parte 1ma ed 2da
Concerti di Hasse Opera prima
Concerti di Schiassi Opera 1ma Lib 1mo ed 2do
Cimento del'Armonia de Ant: Vivaldi Opera Ottava Lib 1mo e 2do
Concerto ed Simphonie d Ant Brescianillo Oper: prima Lib: 1mo e 2do
Concerti di Giusep: Tartini Oper Seconda
Sei Concerti di Giusep: Tartini Oper: prima Lib: 1mo
Sei Concerti d'Alcuni Famosi Maestri Lib: 1mo
Concerti da Anton: Bonporti Oper: 11ma
Concerti di Giusep: Valentini Opera Settima Lib: 1mo ed 2do
Concerti di Giusep: Alberti Opera prima
Suonate a tre di Giusep: Valentini Opera quinta
Fantasie a Tre di Giusep Valentini Opera terza

[1] GD 18/4553.

Concerti da Tomaso A[l]binoni Oper: 5ta
Trattimenti Musicali da Gaetano Schiassi Oper 1ma
Allettamenti di Giusep: Valentini Opera Ottava
Idee per Camera di Giusep: Valentini Oper Quarta
Sei Sonate a Viol: Solo di Giuseppe Tartini Opera 1ma
Sonate per il Flauto Traversiero da Roberto Valentini Oper: 12ma
Capricci da Girolamo Frescobaldi
Pieces de Clavessin Composee par Henry d'Anglebert

The list continues in pencil:

Carlo cavallini Opera 6ta
Solos di Tartini oper 7ma
Somis Opera 2da
Groneman Opera 1ma
Castrucci Opera 2da
Veracini Opera 1ma
Hass Opera 2da
A[l]binoni Conc Opera 10ma
Vivald[i] Opera 12ma
Sei Conc d'alcuni Maestri
Sonate a tre d Hasse Oper 2da
Locatelli a tre Oper 2da

The following note is a later addition in blunt pencil:

Memorandum buy Oper Quinta of Festing Consisting of eigh[t]
Concertos.

Index

(main entries are shown in bold type)